SOLDIERS IN REVOLT

SOLDIERS IN REVOLT

The American Military Today

DAVID CORTRIGHT

Anchor Press/Doubleday
Garden City, New York
1975

for Tricia

Excerpt from *Gedichte*, Volume 4, by Bertolt
Brecht. Copyright © 1961 by Suhrkamp Verlag,
Frankfurt am Main. All rights reserved.

Library of Congress Cataloging in Publication Data

Cortright, David.
    Soldiers in revolt.

    Includes bibliographical references and index.
    1. United States—Armed Forces—Political activity.
2. Soldiers—United States.   3. Vietnamese Conflict, 1961–
—Protest movements—United States.   I. Title.
UA23.C674   355.03′32′73
ISBN 0-385-11083-9
Library of Congress Catalog Card Number 74-15376

CONTENTS

FIGURES

PREFACE

Soldiers in Revolt is a product of the struggle within the American military against repression and the Indochina intervention. It grew directly out of my own personal involvement in that effort and has been, from beginning to end, molded by the thoughts and actions of GI organizers. The book is an attempt to document the GI movement from the perspective of those involved—to speak for and with the hundreds of thousands of low-ranking servicemen whose resistance has transformed American military and political life. Part I offers a comprehensive view of rank-and-file unrest as it developed in all the services, from the early years of Vietnam to the present. Part II discusses the consequences and implications of these developments and suggests alternatives for a more democratic military.

The idea of presenting a historical account of GI resistance first occurred to me during my Army term, in 1970 and 1971. Actual work began in January 1972, when I arrived at the Institute for Policy Studies in Washington, D.C., and occupied much of my time for nearly two and a half years. During the book's preparation, I talked to literally hundreds of active-duty organizers, Vietnam veterans, and military counselors; at one time or another over the past five years, I have spoken or corresponded with practically every major activist in the GI movement. In a very real sense, the ideas and concepts of *Soldiers in Revolt* are those of the servicemen and -women who have struggled for peace and justice.

It would be impossible for me to list here all the people and sources I have consulted for this book. A detailed description of the methodology employed is presented in Appendix A. In addition to the names listed there, the following persons have offered special help in the book's preparation: Monica Heilbrunn, my ex-wife and former activist with GIs for Peace; Ernie Thurston, of the Reservists Committee to Stop War; Dennis Oney, former member of GIs for Peace; Jerald Bachman, of the University of Michigan's Institute for Social Research; Susan Hewman, of the Lawyers Military Defense Committee; Rick Allan, former European correspondent of *Overseas Weekly*; Dr. John Ives, psychiatrist at the University of Vermont; Marilyn Elrod, assistant to Congressman Ron Dellums; and Mr. Roger Kelley, former Assistant Secretary of Defense for Manpower and Reserve Affairs. I have also received special aid from staff members of the United States Servicemen's Fund (USSF): Lenore Monsonis, Paul Lauter, Skip Delano, and Doug LaFrenier. I owe a special word of thanks to three men who read and commented on portions of the first draft and whose ideas played a major role in shaping the book's final form: David Addlestone of the Lawyers Military Defense Committee offered invaluable firsthand information on the breakdown of the Army in Vietnam and contributed substantially to Chapter 2. George Schmidt, formerly of the Chicago Area Military Project, read through sections of the manuscript and provided numerous factual corrections and interpretive suggestion; George's lucid comments influenced nearly every part of the book. Max Watts, friend of "Resisters Inside the Army" in Europe, likewise read early drafts of the book and responded with a wealth of valuable criticisms based on firsthand knowledge, as well as an inspiring historical perspective on the roots of GI resistance; Max's enthusiastic support contributed greatly to *Soldiers in Revolt*, particularly Chapter 5.

My deepest thanks must go to the Institute for Policy Studies and the Union Graduate School of Antioch College. The IPS/UGS co-operative graduate program provided a constructive and challenging forum for research and social investigation and offered important assistance throughout my work. I am especially grateful to former UGS director Roy Fairfield, to administrative assistant Betty Pool, and to faculty adviser John Pool. The greatest support for this study, without which the entire project would have been impossible, came from the Institute for Policy Studies. The stimulating environment at the Institute—marked by contact with the leading scholar/activists in the country and by association with nearly every major progressive movement in the society—guided every stage of my work. I owe special thanks to Joe

Collins, to fellows Len Rodberg and Ralph Stavins, and to the Institute's brilliant co-director Richard Barnet.

My greatest debt is to my principal adviser over the past two and a half years, Marcus Raskin. His knowledge and teaching have touched every section of this book, and his enormous personal warmth and sensitivity have profoundly influenced my life. I can only hope that *Soldiers in Revolt* in some small way contributes to the reconstructed society that is his vision.

INTRODUCTION

by Marcus Raskin

Dave Cortright is a son of the American working class. He is gifted, open, wonderfully competent, and without guile. He is also as hard as nails, and by nature cannot betray his friends or passively witness his nation's discredit. In other words, he has ideals that go to the core of him as a person. I will have more to say about this later.

Cortright is my student, and he has written a book on GI protest which grows out of his own experience in the crucial years of 1968–72 and his superb ability to analyze the events of the military forces during that period. Perhaps, in a less politically conscious era, Cortright would have written a novel, creating a mood of the time, using the stuff of it. Instead, he chose to capture the period as a reality within everyone's grasp, mediated through neither personal artistry nor the "added touch" of the novelist. He writes, instead, a history that otherwise would have remained buried by conventional historians, who would have referred to the soldier rebellions as background noise to the decisions of the "policy makers" and generals. In other words, the GI uprisings during this period would have been smothered and lost in official histories had Cortright not painstakingly assembled an activists' history of the GI struggle against the war in Indochina.

Cortright's account, however, is not a first-person history or a confessional. It is an objective account of events that caused admirals to quake and generals to think more than twice about sending soldiers into battle. In Cortright's account, we learn that the struggle was not only against the war, but also against an authoritarian military machine oiled for world imperialism but sluggish in its purpose and doubtful of its mission. We learn also that the struggle of the enlisted man and the dissident officer was against the culture of obedience and against the collective consciousness filled by the public relations and venal thoughts of the GIs' commanders. Cortright shows us collective action against the foolish military authoritarianism that has been used by all armed forces as an instrument to confound draftees and enlisted men and to make sure that they stay in line.

Cortright reveals the full scope of the GI rebellion that brewed in the armed forces. From time to time incidents were noted by the media, but for the most part these incidents were seen by the civilian society as sporadic. The widespread nature of these incidents remained hidden. We learn that the struggle against the war in Indochina was not restricted to the supposedly pampered children of the middle classes who wanted to stay in school, or on dope, or otherwise not perform their patriotic duty. Before the conventional wisdom is set in concrete, authors of this period will now have to take account of Cortright's thesis: namely, that the struggle against the war in Indochina moved from the campus and was continued within the military itself by the children of all classes—the poor, working, and middle classes. This is an important political fact which would most likely have gone unrecorded among journalists, academics, and politicians. To be aware of this fact is to be relieved of the comfortable belief that the armed forces are a quiet, apolitical group that takes no part in politics.

The Indochina war teaches quite another lesson. We have been made aware that the officer corps and the GIs have opposing political points of view. In the sixties, the dissident viewpoints among the armed forces reflected a sense of ideals that no genocidal war could fulfill. The morality of the soldiers and some of the officers was far different from that expressed in the officer manuals, which assumed the rightness of the American Cause and of the use of any tools in the service of that Cause. We learn in the Cortright account a fact that seems obvious, once stated: moral considerations are not the "stuff" of discussions in the planning and action offices of the White House and the Department of Defense. It is no wonder that the values of the GI community and the questions they were concerned with were shocking to a general staff that operated on the theory of absolute obedience and control from the top. The military brass, confused but unrelenting in their demands, expected the enlisted men to perform imperial war tasks whatever their feelings or convictions. As Cortright notes, those who did not go along found themselves paying a high price.

> It would probably be safe to assert . . . that nearly every serviceman seriously attempting to resist war and injustice has suffered some sort of privation. Whether it be the loss of a security clearance, removal from a job, transfer to some isolated post, discharge under less than honorable conditions, or outright imprisonment, GI activists have paid a stiff price for their commitment.

Cortright, of course, was one of those who suffered such privation—in his case, punitive transfer and a subsequent federal court suit.

There was a charge among enlisted men that, through the war, officers achieved status, obtained promotions, and tested their strategic doctrines. Even capitalism seemed less important than bellicosity and militarism, judging by the waste of material and energy that was so characteristic of the Indochina war. Officers who did not go along also paid a price. Some paid with much more than a lost promotion. There are thousands, but one case that continues to haunt us is that of Howard Levy.

In its 1974 spring term, the Supreme Court handed down a decision in the Levy case. Howard Levy was a captain in the Medical Corps of the Army who refused to train Green Berets. He said that the United States was wrongly involved in Vietnam. He said that he would not "go to Viet Nam" and would refuse orders to do so. He also said that "Special Forces personnel are liars and thieves and killers of peasants and murders [sic] of women and children." He disobeyed the commandant's order to set up a training program for Green Berets. This was held to be willfully disobeying "a lawful command of his superior commissioned officer," "conduct unbecoming an officer and gentleman," and prejudicial to "good order and discipline in the armed forces." In his trial, Levy introduced a Nuremberg defense. He said that he was being asked to commit crimes against humanity, that the war itself was an illegal and immoral war. This defense got nowhere. He served two and one-half years in the prison stockades. He kept appealing through the courts. On the Court of of Appeals level, Levy won his case on the grounds that the Articles of the Uniform Code of Military Justice, under which he was convicted, were unnecessarily vague. The Supreme Court, however, overturned the Court of Appeals, saying that conduct unbecoming an officer and a gentleman is not vague.

My purpose in talking about this case in introducing Cortright's book is to discuss Mr. Justice Blackmun's opinion, which asserts that there is a standard of "right" to which members of the military should be held. Alas, we learn that this standard is not the standard of personal accountability written at Nuremberg and hewn out of the blood of tens of millions of people in World War II. Instead, we learn from Justice Blackmun's opinion that the moral precepts of "right and wrong are the same now as they were under the Articles of the Earl of Essex (1642) or the British Articles of War of 1765 or the American Articles of War of 1775." Blackmun went on to say, "Relativistic notions of right and wrong, or situation ethics, as some call it, have achieved in recent times a disturbingly high level of prominence in this century, both in the guise of law reform, and as a justification of conduct that persons would normally eschew as immoral and even illegal." Blackmun's belief in natural law may be correct but his reference point, to the Articles of the Earl of Essex, is fatuous. Can he mean that flogging and serfdom were "right," that stealing is "wrong" but the systematic destruction of villages, forceful removal of populations, and massive bombings in undeclared wars are right as well? If the Supreme Court is serious about believing that ethics goes beyond a particular situation, it is going to be faced with choosing ethical principles. Which will it choose? Justice Blackmun appears to have chosen the ethical standards of Curtis LeMay, Buzz Wheeler, Mel Laird, and company. This sense of ethics assumes the use of nuclear weapons, the necessity of continuous war, the use of resources in the society for the war machine. But Blackmun could have chosen the right and wrong of Levy—and Cortright—which gives the rest of us, both our citizens here and people abroad, a chance to breathe. Cortright shows how the soldiers understood the Nuremberg obligations in their guts as part of what civilization must mean and must adhere to if we and it are to survive. And Blackmun could have concluded with Mr. Justice Jackson's view: that the people and the soldiers are positively proscribed from participating in criminality and murderous imperialism.

A point of method should be mentioned. Cortright's book departs from the way most political histories are written. Usually histories are written around major events. Thus, President Nixon "decided," the Supreme Court "decided," etc., as if such decisions do not occur in the context of continuous and co-operative struggle. By way of example, it took four years of struggle within France by an aroused resistance to place de Gaulle in a position where he both *could* and *had to* get out of Algeria. Unfortunately, conventional accounts are not written in such a way as to credit the struggles of the unnamed. As a result, it becomes possible for scholars to write and think about history believing that a few people make the great events. The history of the Indochina war is a denial of that theory. The military leaders were forced out by their armed forces and the people who said, "No more." It was not a decision taken out of free will by a President who knew right from wrong, or a Supreme Court, for that matter, declaring that the war was illegal and immoral and unconstitutional. It was the struggle of millions of people that restricted the American role in Indochina. As Cortright shows, it was a struggle of young, inexperienced, enlisted men, living in an encapsulated and alien world, who struggled together to make their hearts and voices heard. It is extraordinary how Cortright has caught this sensibility. He has done it in a cool, dispassionate way. He does not overstate his material. Where he may err, it is because he is too inclined to accept the statements of Defense Department officials on numbers as authoritative rather than, at best, approximate. But where he relies on his direct research, his direct interviews with the GIs, the work is impeccable and far-reaching.

A final word to students of military history: This field, as much as any other, is written from the top down. It is not written from the point of view of the daily struggles and fears of the GI. This was understandable where the armed forces themselves acted as robotlike extensions of commanders. However, where such conditions no longer obtain, where the enlisted men themselves developed their own purpose and point of view, the military historian must now reject "official" statements in favor of materials from the draftees and enlisted men, namely, interviews, personal letters, orders, and underground newspapers. Kutuzov knew that a soldier who ran the wrong way in the heat of battle was equal in effect to any plan of Napoleon. We should remember this lesson from Tolstoy's *War and Peace*—that the words and thoughts of the generals are not enough to understand how things work and how forces come into being to change the direction of history.

Cortright has made an important beginning, which can teach us how, in our methodology, we should study other institutions that are closed but are a caldron of the colonized. The colonized seek rights beyond those assigned to them within their closed universe, and action scholarship can help them in their attempts to achieve full personhood.

MGR

2 July 1974
Washington, D.C.

General, your tank is a mighty vehicle.
It shatters the forest and crushes a hundred men.
But it has one defect:
It needs drivers.

General, your bomber is awesome.
It flies faster than a hurricane and bears more than an elephant.
But it has one defect:
It needs a mechanic.

General, a man is quite expendable.
He can fly and he can kill.
But he has one defect:
He can think.

BERTOLT BRECHT
(*translation: Boykin Reynolds*)

PART I

CHAPTER 1

THE MACHINE BREAKS DOWN

"The morale, discipline and battle-worthiness of the U.S. armed forces are, with a few salient exceptions, lower and worse than at any time in this century and possibly in the history of the United States." With these lines, former Marine Colonel Robert Heinl opened his stunning exposé, "The Collapse of the Armed Forces," in the June 1971 issue of *Armed Forces Journal*. The article landed like a bombshell on the journal's normally complacent and self-congratulatory pages and sent shock waves throughout the services. A year later, Morris Janowitz, the dean of military sociologists and intimate of many leading Pentagon officials, offered the same gloomy assessment to the readers of the influential journal *Foreign Affairs*: "The military establishment, and especially its ground forces, are experiencing a profound crisis in legitimacy due to the impact of Vietnam, internal racial tension, corruption, extensive drug abuse, loss of command and operational effectiveness, and widespread anti-military sentiment. . . ." Even the Marine Corps, traditionally viewed as an elite and highly motivated force free of internal dissension, has admitted grave difficulties. In a September 1971 article in *Marine Corps Gazette*, Major H. L. Seay, head of the Senior NCO School of the 2nd Marine Division, lamented that there are "more problems today than ever before in the history of the Marine Corps, i.e., drug abuse, leadership imbalance, high UA [unauthorized absence] rate, lack of motivation, an unpopular war, and racial tension." At the end of 1972, Colonel Heinl, again writing in the *Armed Forces Journal*, sounded the alarm over problems in the Navy as well: ". . . in addition to mounting incidents of shipboard sabotage and other affrays and disorders short of mutiny, the Navy has undergone at least five and probably six episodes— three within the past month—which fully qualify within the legal definition of mutiny." Never before in modern history have the armed forces been so shaken by internal turmoil and disaffection; as *Fortune* magazine accurately put it, "our gravest military problem is manpower." In this and the following six chapters, we shall explore in depth the pervasive manifestations of this crisis within the ranks—from the simple inability to sustain force levels, to the development of political opposition and resistance among GIs, to the collapse of the infantry in Vietnam. Our analysis begins with a general view of the internal disintegration of the military, looking first at the problem of personnel shortages.

I

Staffing America's vast military apparatus has never been easy, but in recent years finding adequate manpower has become an almost impossible task. Beginning in the late 1960s, disdain for military service reared up within the society, halting the gallop of escalation in Vietnam and forcing the Pentagon into a "reluctant retrenchment"—an abrupt reduction in manpower levels and mission requirements. Since 1969, total active-duty military strength has declined by nearly 40 per cent, from 3.5 million to less than 2.2 million; the armed forces are now smaller than at any time in twenty-five years. Top military officers claim that these reductions are the result of Congressional manpower cuts, but the real reasons for the decline lie elsewhere, as Pentagon leaders themselves occasionally acknowledge. During a 1971 exchange with members of the House Appropriations Defense Subcommittee, Army personnel chief General Walter Kerwin admitted that lowered manpower levels were based on what "could be maintained within the expected resources . . . because we're not getting the people in." Navy manpower chief Vice-Admiral David Bagley testified a year later, "we are experiencing a shortage of enlisted personnel, largely because of recruiting shortfalls." The Pentagon's manpower crisis is the result of unprecedented opposition to military service among young people, expressed in resistance to the draft and ROTC and in critically low recruitment and retention rates.

The draft has never been popular in America, but Vietnam sparked the largest eruption of public outrage since the Civil

War, nearly crippling the Selective Service System and creating widespread social upheaval. One measure of this was a sharp jump in the number of conscientious-objector registrations, which reached a record total of over sixty-one thousand in fiscal year 1971; the last three years of conscription witnessed nearly 145,000 successful C.O. claims. In fiscal year 1972, in fact, there were actually more conscientious objectors than draftees. These figures do not include the far greater number who attempted but failed to qualify as objectors (approximately 125,000 applied during fiscal 1971). In addition, many hundred thousands more swamped the system with draft-classification appeals to state or presidential review boards (over 168,000 such appeals in fiscal 1969). And millions of others obtained phantom disabilities, flocked to exempt occupations and schools, or employed any one of a hundred other means of dodging the draft. An entire generation seemed absorbed in just one overriding concern: to escape the clutches of Uncle Sam.

The most visible and effective form of opposition to Selective Service was overt resistance. The Chicago Area Draft Resisters (Cadre) has estimated that by early 1971 total induction refusals exceeded fifteen thousand and the number of people failing to report approached one hundred thousand. By the latter years of the war, nearly every major city faced a huge backlog of induction-refusal court cases. In New York, for example, the eastern-district federal court listed 2,162 complaints of Selective Service violations in fiscal year 1970. The Oakland, California, area experienced particularly high levels of draft resistance: In a six-month period ending in March 1970, 50 per cent of those called failed to report, and 11 per cent of those that did show refused induction. In Chicago, the number of reported draft delinquencies tripled in three years, from 1,495 at the end of 1966 to 4,324 in December 1969. During fiscal year 1969, Selective Service officials listed 31,831 delinquency investigations. For the entire Vietnam War era, 206,000 persons were reported delinquent to the Justice Department by Selective Service.

In addition to encountering defiance of its orders, the draft system became the target of an increasing number of violent attacks—what amounted to a small-scale guerrilla war. By September 1969, sixty-five of the nation's four thousand local boards had been attacked or harassed, including eleven incidents of burning or mutilation of records. Draft Director Curtis Tarr's first semiannual report opened with a description of "systematic" attacks in June of 1970 that nearly destroyed all the records necessary to maintain the draft in the states of Delaware and Rhode Island. In the same report, Tarr went on to lament "a long list of attacks against Selective Service operations," including bullet holes in the Marysville, California, office and assaults so frequent in Berkeley that the windows of the local board had to be replaced with plywood. A later report stated that "a survey of disruptions at local boards showed almost 300 incidents from January through September, 1970." Selective Service headquarters in 1972 furnished the House Internal Security Committee a copy of its "events log" covering the period January 1971 through March 17, 1972. Occupying twenty pages of Congressional testimony, the remarkable document lists 196 acts of disruption directed against the draft during those months. It's no wonder that the Nixon administration moved promptly to eliminate the draft as a principal means of fulfilling its promise to pacify America—a point we will return to in Chapter 9.

Growing anti-militarism has also led to trouble in the Reserve Officers' Training Corps (ROTC) program, the main source of junior officers. Total college ROTC enrollment dropped from 218,000 in the 1968 academic year, to 87,807 in 1971–72, and 72,500 in 1972–73. As with the draft, the decline of ROTC was accompanied by a rising wave of violent attacks against system installations. In the 1968–69 academic year, Army ROTC units sustained twenty-three serious attacks, resulting in property damage totaling ten thousand dollars. In the same year, Navy ROTC units sustained fifteen thousand dollars in property damage. The 1969–70 academic year witnessed the largest number of anti-ROTC incidents in American history. Service ROTC units sustained 323 assaults, resulting in $155,000 worth of government property loss and $1.25 million damage to colleges. Thirty buildings were fire-bombed in the spring term alone, with 165 attacks occurring during the campus uprisings following the Cambodian invasion. In 1970–71, the number of incidents subsided, although there were ninety-nine acts of violence, resulting in $420,000 damage. The year 1972 witnessed a similar pattern of reduced opposition. The bombings of North Vietnam in April, however, triggered renewed protest and attacks against the ROTC system. From 1969 to 1972, thirty-eight ROTC units were expelled from college campuses, largely because of pressure from radical student activists. The latter years of the war thus produced an immense increase in student resistance to the military.

Opposition to the armed forces swelled not only among middle-class college students but among young people throughout society. Not merely the draft and ROTC, but the entire system of manpower recruitment, has entered a period of chronic difficulty. While attention has focused on draft-card burnings and similar happenings on college campuses, other, less affluent young people have created equally serious manpower problems by not enlisting as they once did. The small towns and working-class neighborhoods of America, traditionally the source of most enlisted volunteers, have displayed a growing skepticism toward the military and are no longer supplying the recruits necessary to sustain force levels. Since the late 1960s, the services have consistently failed to meet monthly recruiting objectives. The typical pattern, illustrated in Figure 1, finds shortages in the Army and particularly alarming deficits in the Navy.

	Recruiting Objective	Actual Enlistments	Percent of Goal
ARMY	112,600	103,500	92.0%
NAVY	71,200	57,700	81.2%
MARINE CORPS	37,400	36,300	97.0%
AIR FORCE	59,000	58,200	98.7%
ALL SERVICES	280,200	255,700	91.0%

Figure 1
Active-duty enlistments, July 1971 through February 1972.

Inadequate sailor enlistment has become a particularly serious dilemma. In May of 1972, for example, the *Navy Times* admitted that "quality recruiting has become our number one headache." In Congressional hearings a year later, Admiral Zumwalt listed manpower difficulties as still the Navy's number one problem. The admiral conceded that the Navy had failed to meet its recruiting objective for twelve consecutive months, September 1971 to August 1972. To reverse these shortages, enlistment standards were lowered to accept a greater percentage of recruits from lower-income families, but the effort only created new problems in critical occupational areas. In fiscal 1972, the Navy increased its quotas of non-high-school-graduate and mental-category-IV enlistees,* and as a result failed to draw enough people into skilled positions. In August of 1972, Secretary Laird warned that the Navy's six-year nuclear-propulsion enlistment program had declined to the point where it could "interfere with the manning of nuclear powered ships." The General Accounting Office, in its 1973 study of voluntary recruitment, similarly reported that the Navy was seven thousand short of its requirement for long-term technical trainees. The agency further asserted that not only the Navy but the Army and the Marine Corps would experience continuing deficits, perhaps totaling eighty-three thousand in 1974, unless quality standards were abandoned. Despite reduced force levels, the services thus seem unable to attract the people necessary to maintain capabilities.

Of all the military's enlistment woes, none is more intractable than the problem of recruitment for the reserves. The standby forces traditionally have been a haven for middle-class draft evaders, and during the late 1960s every branch was swamped with applicants anxious to avoid being sent to Vietnam. With the winding down of the war and the decline in inductions, however, the once extensive waiting lists of young people scrambling to join have been depleted. In January 1971, the Army National Guard waiting list was sixty-two thousand, but by October of that year it fell below sixteen thousand. By the end of 1971, shortages began to appear, and they have grown steadily worse since. By mid-1972, the reserves were forty-five thousand men understrength, with most of the shortage in the Army Reserve and the National Guard. Since 75–80 per cent of reserve enlistments previously have been draft-motivated, the end of conscription has greatly exacerbated these problems. Moreover, as disgruntled Vietnam-era reservists end their six-year term of service, with little prospect of re-enlistment, recruitment needs will increase,

---

* All servicemen are placed in mental categories according to their scores on written aptitude tests, with category I the highest and category IV the lowest.

making a bad situation worse. Reserve shortages surpassed fifty thousand early in 1973 and have continued to grow.

One of the most closely watched measures of service performance is re-enlistment. Pentagon officials often use retention rates as a gauge of troop morale and organizational efficiency. Not surprisingly, the internal discontent of recent years has been reflected in falling re-enlistment rates—further aggravating manpower difficulties. First-term re-enlistment rates declined steadily during the Vietnam War, plunging in 1970 to 12 per cent—the lowest yearly figure on record. Since then, over-all retention has returned to normal, but deficiencies continue to plague many critical job areas. Few servicemen in skilled positions are re-enlisting, and the resulting imbalances have created severe problems in certain occupations. The Army's generator-repair specialty, for example, posted a 1972 re-enlistment rate of only 4.7 per cent and had a shortage of 64 per cent. Overall, 238 of 463 Army job positions were understaffed at the end of fiscal year 1972. The worst problems have occurred in the Navy, where, according to Vice-Admiral Bagley, "low retention has had a major impact on personnel management and fleet readiness." In 1972, twenty-nine of the Navy's 103 job ratings, including many requiring extensive training, had first-term re-enlistment rates below 10 per cent. Among the Navy's nuclear-trained enlisted petty officers, retention dropped below 3 per cent in late 1972—a serious threat to the nuclear fleet, according to Admiral Rickover. Overall, fifty-seven of the Navy's ratings were understaffed at the end of fiscal year 1972.

The cumulative result of these failings is a manpower crisis that threatens to undermine American military strength. *Fortune* magazine warned in 1971 that "dangerous shortages of men prevail in every branch of service, seriously impairing combat capability." General Westmoreland conceded in 1972 Congressional testimony that "we are short trained people" and that maintaining force levels in one theater could be accomplished only "at the expense of reducing forces elsewhere in the world." At the time of the 1970 Jordanian crisis, for example, the 82nd Airborne Division reportedly was able to deploy only two of its three brigades, largely due to manpower shortages. Even after withdrawing from Vietnam and trimming its world-wide commitments, the Army has continued to face personnel deficiencies. In 1973 testimony before the House Armed Services Committee, General Creighton Abrams lamented "substantial readiness problems in the Army" and admitted, "we still have a number of problems with our personnel situation which impact adversely on Army-wide readiness." The gravest manpower problems exist within the Navy. Years of inadequate recruitment and low retention have left the fleet with serious shortages in many of its most important skilled positions. By the end of fiscal year 1972, the Navy's enlisted career force was 17 per cent below mandated strength, and a substantial number of experienced E-4 and E-5 slots were understaffed. In Senate hearings on the 1974 Defense Budget, Admiral Zumwalt claimed that the major combat fleets were falling below readiness requirements, primarily because of manning failures. Zumwalt characterized readiness in the Atlantic fleet as "unsatisfactory" and the situation in the Pacific as "marginal." In the same hearings, Navy Secretary Warner described Navy preparedness as dangerously deficient, with 1973 end strength expected to fall twenty-eight thousand short of authorized levels. Asserting that over-all fleet manning had already dropped below 90 per cent, the Secretary warned of the menacing implications of this steady deterioration: "We have found 96 per cent manning to be the threshold below which we begin to encounter serious operational, maintenance, personnel management and training difficulties."

II

A sure sign of the malaise within the ranks is the staggering level of desertions in recent years. During the five peak years of Vietnam involvement, the Army desertion rate increased nearly 400 per cent, from 14.9 incidents per thousand in 1966 to 73.5 per thousand in 1971. During the same period, the desertion rate for the armed forces as a whole jumped threefold, from 8.4 to 33.9 per thousand. While desertions have typically increased at the end of major wars, the massive levels of recent years are truly unprecedented. The Army's 1971 rate was three times as great as the highest Korean War levels and even surpassed the World War II maximum of 63 per thousand during 1944. (In making such comparisons, it is important to keep in mind that, unlike those of World War II, most Vietnam-era desertions did not take place under fire, indicating that servicemen took off not because of danger but because of disgust.) Army desertion and AWOL rates in 1971 were the highest in modern history: seventeen AWOLs and seven desertions for every one hundred soldiers. The significance of such figures can be seen by trying to assess their cumulative impact. The Pentagon reports that a sizable portion of AWOL incidents involve recidivists, and it thus would be misleading simply to add AWOLs and desertions to find the total number of absentees. However, even assuming that half the AWOLs were repeat incidents, the total number of runaways exceeded fifteen per hundred, meaning that at least one out of every seven soldiers went over the hill during 1971. These facts are summarized in Figure 2.

The post-1970 trends in absenteeism deserve special comment. The most obvious development is the drop in Army desertion and AWOL rates. To a certain degree, of course, this is a result of the end of the Vietnam War and the extensive internal reforms implemented during 1971. A good deal of the explanation, however, has less to do with changed attitudes among soldiers than with altered personnel procedures. The Army's 1971 decision to allow early discharges to Vietnam veterans and other short-timers obviously reduced the likely AWOL rate. Similarly, a general disciplinary crackdown on troublemakers, reflected in greatly increased use of punitive discharges, likewise lowered absences. The fact that AWOL and desertion rates have remained at near-record levels despite the end of the war, though, strongly suggests that the ground forces continue to face serious internal unrest. Indeed, absenteeism in the Marine Corps is higher now than during the war. Perhaps the most important trend in these figures is the rise in absentee rates within the Air Force. As the Vietnam War shifted from a ground invasion to an air war, the Air Force began to experience internal disruption, indicating that unrest within the various services evolved in direct relation to their role in the Indochina war. The AWOL rate increased by 34 per cent in 1970, by 59 per cent in 1971, and by 83 per cent in 1972, the peak year of the air war; the desertion rate jumped almost 300 per cent from 1968 to 1971 and continued at record levels during the bombing of North Vietnam and Cambodia. The Navy also has wit-

AWOL RATE

Fiscal Year	1966	1967	1968	1969	1970	1971	1972	1973
ARMY	57.2	78.0	89.7	112.3	132.5	176.9	166.4	159.0
NAVY	29.2	22.4	14.4	13.5	17.5	19.0	18.3	21.7
MARINE CORPS	N/A	N/A	N/A	N/A	174.3	166.6	170.0	234.3
AIR FORCE	3.3	3.6	3.6	4.4	5.9	9.4	17.2	16.1
TOTAL, ALL SERVICES	N/A	43.3	38.2	46.9	69.4	84.0	74.9	77.0

N/A = Not available

Unauthorized absence incidents, per thousand enlisted strength

DESERTION RATE

Fiscal Year	1966	1967	1968	1969	1970	1971	1972	1973
ARMY	14.9	21.4	29.1	42.4	52.3	73.5	62.0	52.0
NAVY	9.1	9.7	8.5	7.3	9.9	11.1	8.8	13.6
MARINE CORPS	16.1	26.8	30.7	40.2	59.6	56.2	65.3	63.2
AIR FORCE	0.4	0.4	0.4	0.6	0.8	1.5	2.8	2.2
TOTAL, ALL SERVICES	8.43	12.2	15.6	21.1	27.0	33.9	27.5	24.3

Unauthorized absences over thirty days, per thousand enlisted strength

Figure 2

nessed increased turmoil. During fiscal year 1973, as nearly half the fleet was pressed into action in the South China Sea, desertions reached an all-time high.

To understand the motivations of deserters, we should examine their social backgrounds. In general, most enlisted people are from working-class, lower-income families and have an average education level slightly below that of a high school graduate. The meager evidence available on deserters indicates that their social status and educational level fall below this standard. During Senate Armed Services Committee hearings on desertion in 1968, then Manpower Assistant Secretary Fitt provided figures on the social characteristics of deserters, obtained from a "random sampling" of all deserters. The information supplied to the Committee showed that 80 per cent of deserters were in grades E-1 and E-2 and that three fourths had less than two years of service completed. Eighty-three per cent were in "lower mental groups" (presumably categories three and four); 41 per cent had less than nine years of education. It is difficult to assess the accuracy of such Defense Department statistics, but a few other reports from newspaper journalists generally corroborate these findings. An early-1969 survey of 116 deserters living in Sweden gave the average educational level as 11.2 years; 79 per cent of those questioned had volunteered. A study done later in the year by New York *Times* reporter John Kifner, based on interviews with a number of deserters and civilian anti-war workers, found that deserters were usually younger, less educated, and more likely to come from rural regions than the average GI.

These findings were confirmed in a study conducted by the Human Resources Research Organization (HumRRO) in 1972, which concluded that unauthorized absence occurred most frequently among those from disadvantaged social backgrounds and with the least amount of education. This same HumRRO report made the important point that volunteer soldiers were more prone to go AWOL than draftees. In most cases, deserters and AWOLs are lower-class people who have joined the military believing the job-benefit claims of recruiters, only to discover through rude experience the far different realities of military life and imperial war. Reflecting their lower-class backgrounds, they have expressed their bitterness at being deceived by the recruitment racket through unsophisticated but effective means; as Bob Musil has aptly remarked: "'Like so many refugees, they have voted with their feet.'"

This information is important in clearing up widely held but distorted notions concerning the motivations of deserters and to clarify certain aspects of the debate over amnesty. Many of those who otherwise sympathize with draft resisters refuse to admit that the motivations of deserters may be just as genuine. Deserters are often portrayed as malingerers and criminals who are simply running away from their responsibilities, but even the Pentagon admits, in an officially distributed fact sheet on "Reasons/Circumstances for Desertion by Those Who Went to Foreign Countries," that only 4.5 per cent of deserters leave because of family, financial, or personal reasons. Military deserters have done the same as draft resisters in refusing to participate in the military, except that they have had to learn the truth more slowly, through actual experience, and have expressed their opposition through more drastic, less articulate methods. It is shortsighted and class-biased for middle-class spokesmen to support amnesty for draft resisters but not for deserters.

III

As the only legitimate, duly recognized means of expressing anti-war dissent, conscientious objection might be expected to have reached massive proportions during the Vietnam period. While pacifist objection in fact increased substantially, the labyrinthic procedures and formidable educational requirements of the process have severely limited its use. The potential applicant must complete an elaborate application form, write a lengthy personal history describing the development of his beliefs, collect numerous letters of personal support, and undergo three formal interviews with military officers. The process can take months and often requires the assistance of an attorney or of legal counselors. The military frequently fails to inform its people of the available procedures and in many cases actually obstructs the efforts of those who make the attempt to apply. Every applicant must submit a prenotification letter to his commanding officer stating his intent to file for conscientious objection, a re-

quirement that invites abuse. Commanders often use this occasion to intimidate the would-be objector into abandoning
his plans (and thus saving the officer from a "black eye"). I
personally witnessed such instances while at Fort Bliss. In one
case, GIs for Peace member Tom Holden encountered intense
harassment after delivering his letter of intent and was able
to gain relief only by writing to his congressman. Many potential conscientious objectors, with less perseverance than Tom
and without legal counseling, undoubtedly have been deterred by such practices.

Calendar Year	1967	1968	1969	1970	1971	1972	1973
ARMY	594	1062	1981	2198	2827	1306	1088
NAVY	105	151	271	577	861	789	449
MARINE CORPS	56	55	147	135	157	72	84
AIR FORCE	74	119	157	286	536	506	435
TOTAL, ALL SERVICES	829	1387	2556	3196	4381	2673	2056

Figure 3
In-service applications for conscientious objection.

Despite these obstacles, official Pentagon statistics, summarized in Figure 3, indicate a sharp rise in the number of
conscientious-objector applications. While objection within
the ground forces declined quickly after reaching a peak during 1971, conscientious-objector rates within the Air Force
and the Navy remained relatively high into 1972. From 1967
to mid-1971, the time of maximum ground-force involvement
in Vietnam, C.O. rates jumped almost 400 per cent in the
Army and nearly 200 per cent in the Marine Corps; objection
increased even more sharply within the Air Force and the
Navy, and, reflecting the shifting nature of the Indochina intervention, continued at high rates for a longer period of
time. Here again the figures suggest that the pattern of dissent within the services was directly related to their role in
the war effort. It should be noted also that even in the postwar, all-volunteer military, conscientious objection has remained at relatively high rates. The 1972 level, while less
than half that of peak years, was much higher than that of
prewar periods and, despite an armed force 38 per cent
smaller, was significantly greater than in 1968.

While closely related to the patterns of military involvement, conscientious objection is also dependent on political
activity and the level of counseling made available to GIs.
Veteran GI-movement activists have observed that when
legal-rights counseling and soldier organizing increase at a particular installation, so do conscientious-objector applications.
A good example of this occurred at Oakland Army Base in
early 1970. Oakland was the primary embarkation point for
Vietnam in the United States and at the time was shipping
more than a thousand soldiers a day to Indochina. In January,
activists from the Pacific Counseling Service began an extensive schedule of day and night leafleting of incoming soldiers
at area airports, informing GIs of their right to file for conscientious-objector discharge and thus delay overseas orders.
The results were startling. By March 1, twelve hundred men
had successfully delayed their orders by seeking C.O. status.
To avert a potential crisis, the Pentagon telegrammed a special regulation change to West Coast bases on March 6 stating
that GIs could no longer apply for C.O. status while transient
but would have to wait until arriving in Vietnam to apply.

Another important aspect of conscientious objection is the
rise in percentage of applications approved by the Pentagon.
In 1967 the services granted only 28 per cent of the claims
submitted, but since 1969 the rate of approval has climbed
steadily, in 1972 reaching 77.3 per cent. This dramatic reversal comes not from a sudden Defense Department warm-
ing toward pacifism in the ranks but from the pressure of
increased civilian court review. Vietnam-era conscientious objectors, blocked by the military's grudging refusal to honor
their claims, entered federal court with increasing frequency
to seek habeas-corpus relief. In the process, enlisted objectors
have been able to extract federal court decisions restricting
the Pentagon's discretion in processing in-service objection.
The legal weight of the opinions that came out of these struggles has forced the military to alter regulations a number of
times and has greatly improved the serviceman's chances of
obtaining discharge for anti-war beliefs.

IV

Another illustration of pervasive disquiet within the ranks
comes from statistics on administrative discharge. Under De-

partment of Defense Directive 1332.14 (issued in 1965), early separations for failure to meet performance standards were authorized under the categories of unsuitability, unfitness, and misconduct. Although the directive was intended to standardize procedures, in fact each service retained its own system of classification, making it difficult to state precisely the reasons for each kind of discharge. Generally, however, the following definitions apply: Unsuitability discharges are usually given to recruits and others new to the service for chronic inaptitude or repeated short-term AWOL; unfitness releases result from frequent disciplinary problems or drug abuse; and misconduct separations are issued to those facing criminal charges. For example, the Marine Corps explains its reasons for discharge in this way: Unsuitability comes from "inaptitude, defective attitude and apathy"; unfitness is "primarily attributable to drug abuse"; and misconduct is the result of a request "to escape trial by court-martial." Given these definitions, the recent jump in administrative discharges reveals a startling rise in morale problems. The Navy Department explains these increases as due to "adverse attitudes towards military service, increased disciplinary cases and expanded incidents of drug abuse." General Edwin Wheeler of the Marine Corps told the Senate Appropriations Committee in 1972 that such problems "must be viewed against the background of this country's commitment in the Republic of Vietnam and recent sociological changes within the U.S."

Fiscal Year	1967	1968	1969	1970	1971	1972	1973
ARMY	10.8	10.6	11.1	16.5	23.8	36.3	27.4
NAVY	16.8	16.6	19.9	28.5	36.5	38.2	30.0
MARINE CORPS	13.7	15.6	20.0	68.7	112.4	63.7	49.0
AIR FORCE	8.4	7.8	7.5	8.2	10.7	17.8	19.5
TOTAL, ALL SERVICES	11.6	12.4	13.0	22.7	31.4	33.7	27.9

Figure 4

Rates of discharge, per thousand enlisted strength, for misconduct, unfitness, and unsuitability.

Figure 4 examines the varying rates of punitive discharge within each service. Perhaps the most significant finding is the persistence of turbulence during 1972 and 1973. In part,

this trend reflects the military's 1972 attempt to shore up
sagging morale by purging Vietnam veterans and other unde-
sirables from the ranks before they caused difficulties, as evidenced in the Navy's late-1972 crackdown on resisters in the
Seventh Fleet (described in Chapter 6). These high discharge
rates also result from the decline in recruit quality accompanying the manpower crisis and the all-volunteer force. The surge
in enlistees from the poorer classes—traditionally those with
the greatest difficulty in adapting to military life—undoubtedly has contributed to punitive-discharge rates. In an increasing number of cases, the weeding out of potentially troublesome recruits has been accomplished through honorable or
general discharge in the first six months of service. In the
Navy, the so-called recruit attrition rate soared from 2.5 per
cent in fiscal 1968 to nearly 10 per cent in 1972; in the Marine Corps, it skyrocketed from 4.2 per cent in 1968 to an
astounding 22 per cent in fiscal 1971. Trainee discharges have
increased steadily in the Army as well, in late 1973 reaching
approximately 7 per cent. These policies help explain why
current discharge rates, while slightly lower than during the
years of peak unrest, remain disturbingly high. One final aspect of these figures is the jump in Air Force discharges during 1972 and 1973. Since attrition of airman recruits has not
changed substantially in recent years, the rise in discharges
seems directly related to morale difficulties resulting from
bombing operations in Vietnam and Cambodia.

V

Of all the aspects of the morale crisis, none has been more
thoroughly investigated than drug abuse. After sifting through
voluminous reports on the subject, one gets the impression, in
fact, that interest in the problem of drugs is far out of proportion to the real seriousness of the issue. The thousands of
pages of drug studies issued in recent years seem a diversion
from far more difficult challenges facing the military. Drug
use is not a cause but a symptom of the general disintegration
of the armed forces and deserves attention only as one of the
many manifestations of this decline.

Among the mounds of statistical analyses and official reports, the most thorough and comprehensive recent study is

	Total, All Services	Army	Navy	Marine Corps	Air Force
Marijuana	29.9% (9.1%)	42.7% (19.7%)	21.8% (8.2%)	38.0% (11.9%)	16.0% (4.5%)
Psychedelics (including hashish)	18.8% (4.9%)	29.4% (9.8%)	12.1% (1.9%)	22.9% (3.3%)	8.3% (1.1%)
Narcotics	12.2% (5.1%)	20.4% (10.0%)	6.7% (1.9%)	14.8% (3.5%)	4.6% (0.9%)

Figure 5

Use of drugs among enlisted people during previous 12 months, September 1971 (percentages in parentheses are those reporting *frequent* use, i.e., "every day," or "several times a week").

the 1971 *Department of Defense Survey of Drug Use,* conducted by HumRRO in the fall of 1971. The first scientific attempt to determine drug-use levels throughout the services, the 1971 survey involved a 73-item questionnaire administered to a sample of 36,500 enlisted men around the world. The report, summarized in Figure 5, provides the most accurate assessment available on the level of drug use within the enlisted ranks.

Thirty per cent seems to be the best over-all estimate of GI drug use. The Louis Harris organization found a similar result in a poll of 1,985 veterans conducted in early 1972: 32 per cent of the interviewees admitted having used drugs while in the military. Marijuana is, of course, the drug of choice, with 20 per cent of the Army, 12 per cent of the Marine Corps, and 8 per cent of the Navy smoking on a regular basis. Of far greater seriousness is the use of hard drugs, primarily opium and heroin. An astonishing 10 per cent of Army enlisted men report using narcotics regularly, a tragic but cogent commentary on the intolerable conditions of military life.

While the HumRRO report provides an excellent gauge of the drug problem during 1971, it does not give a comparison with previous years and thus fails to show the sharp rate of increase in drug use as the Vietnam War progressed. One indication of this can be found in Pentagon statistics of criminal investigations for possible drug violations. In calendar year 1967, 3,626 soldiers were investigated for drug use; by 1970, the number of inquiries had jumped to 22,791. In the armed forces as a whole, the rate of investigation for marijuana use more than doubled from 1968 to 1970. Similarly, administrative discharges for reasons of drug abuse climbed from 3,766 in 1969 to 8,818 in 1971. Further evidence of increasing drug use appears in studies conducted among men arriving in Vietnam. (We shall examine the special problem of drugs in Vietnam more thoroughly in Chapter 2.) One group entering the country through the 90th Replacement Battalion in late 1967 showed a 20 per cent level of marijuana use; in a similar group studied in late 1970, however, 50 per cent of the men had used drugs before entering Vietnam—an increase of 150 per cent. Drug abuse thus rose sharply during the course of the war, not just in Vietnam but throughout the services.

Despite disengagement from Vietnam and institution of the all-volunteer force, drug abuse remains widespread within the military. The rate of drug-related discharges, for example, was higher in 1972 than in 1971. The most severe drug problems today seem to be centered in West Germany. The *Armed Forces Journal* reported in December 1972 that in some units near Giessen at least 75 per cent of the soldiers had experimented with cannabis, with up to 45 per cent using it regularly. Narcotics have become particularly troublesome in Europe since 1971. In January 1973, Representatives Morgan Murphy (D-Ill.) and Robert Steele (R-Conn.), authors of a previous study on heroin in Vietnam for the House Foreign Affairs Committee, announced their findings of a "distinct increase in heroin use among U.S. soldiers in West Germany." The two congressmen released figures showing that positive detection of heroin users by urinalysis had jumped from 1.3 per cent in December 1971 to over 4.2 per cent at the end of 1972. While drug problems are particularly acute in West Germany, the Army faces a continuing drug crisis wherever it is stationed. General Creighton Abrams admitted before the Senate Armed Services Committee in 1973 that "drug abuse remains a significant problem throughout the Army."

The meaning of such widespread drug use is unclear. To a certain extent, it reflects the general rise in drug use throughout the society and has little bearing on the nature of the military. It may be, however, that for many GIs, smoking pot or hashish in the military is an act of escape or liberation, however illusory, from the "straight" world of military authority. Such countercultural rebellion has little political significance, though, for the pacifying effects of cannibis often induce docility and apathy toward social problems. Smoking pot can dull the motivation for military service, but it can also extinguish the spirit to resist. The use of narcotics, on the other hand, seems a more certain symptom of deep-seated frustration and alienation within the ranks. Servicemen who have taken to hard drugs in the military are desperately and painfully escaping from unbearable pressures. Their immersion in the squalor of drug addiction suggests a bitter rejection of self and the military environment. Moreover, while users of some narcotics can still carry on certain duties, soldiers strung out on heroin are certainly incapable of contributing their full share in extreme situations and generally constitute a serious burden on the military organization.

VI

The crisis in the ranks is also evident in other institutional measures. One of these is a rise in serviceman complaints to Congress. According to remarks before a House Armed Services subcommittee, such complaints "have increased steadily each year," with the total number of inquiries in 1971 near 250,000. Congressman Dan Daniel (D-Va.) lamented the obvious dissatisfaction indicated by these figures and criticized the military's apparent inability to deal with GI problems on a local level. Further proof of swelling unrest during the Vietnam period comes from statistics submitted to the House Internal Security Committee during 1971 on courts-martial involving serious resistance. Department of the Army figures for "certain acts of insubordination, mutiny and willful disobedience" show a steady increase in the number of such cases, from 252 in 1968 to 382 in 1970. New York *Times* reporter R. Drummond Ayers estimated that the total for such courts-martial in 1971 would exceed 450. Another sign of extensive turmoil is the growing number of non-judicial punishments administered to enlisted people. Article 15 of the Uniform Code of Military Justice (UCMJ) allows commanders to summarily impose penalties without resorting to court-martial. The rate of these punishments has increased in recent years from 137 per thousand in fiscal 1968 to 183 per thousand in 1972. Significantly, the largest percentage gain in Article 15's during 1972 occurred within the Air Force, again confirming our thesis that disaffection among airmen grew as a result of the Indochina air war.

Perhaps the most tragic symptom of disorder within the armed forces is the level of serious crime. While no comprehensive statistics are readily available, numerous reports confirm the assessment of a top Army law-enforcement official in Germany: ". . . crimes of violence are at an all-time high and climbing." Retired General Bruce Clark testified before the House Armed Services Committee that crime among soldiers in Germany had "increased generally since May 1970, reaching unprecedented levels during July 1971"; the general reported that the September 1971 level of crime represented

a 61 per cent increase over year-earlier figures. The over-all
crime rate during the summer of 1971 for the more than two
hundred thousand enlisted men stationed in Germany was an
incredible 5,100 violent crimes per month. Serious crime problems also have surfaced at Army posts in the United States. In
his investigation of the state of the Army in 1971, Ayers received reports of rising crime at several major bases: In the
197th Brigade, at Fort Benning, the 1971 crime rate was
nearly double that of 1970; in the 4th Mechanized Division,
at Fort Carson, there had been 173 thefts in just one month,
amounting to a loss of twenty-two thousand dollars in cash
and goods; and at Fort Ord the situation had deteriorated to
the point where units were forced to set up special anti-crime
guards to patrol barracks areas after dark. In a June 1973 article in *Armed Forces Journal,* Colonel Heinl also decried "the
pandemic of barracks and shipboard theft that has been
sweeping the armed forces for the past several years." The outspoken colonel echoed the view of a division commander that
barracks crime was the most serious of all the morale problems
facing the military. In large part, this increase in crime is the
result of other internal problems, particularly drug abuse and
racial tensions. Certainly it is a powerful sign of the degree of
distrust and conflict within the ranks, of just how hopelessly
far the services have drifted from the mutual trust and confidence essential to the operation and survival of an effective fighting force.

Recounting this seemingly endless tale of woes, we tend to
lose sight of what was actually happening within the ranks.
Underlying the various statistics and measures of unrest was
an Army on the verge of collapse, crippled by a virtual "general strike" among a sizable minority of enlisted people. For
example, if we look at the Army during fiscal 1971, its worst
year of decline, we find seven acts of desertion, seventeen incidents of unauthorized absence, two disciplinary discharges,
twelve complaints to congressmen, and eighteen non-judicial
punishments for every one hundred soldiers; at the same
time, 20 per cent of the men smoked marijuana frequently,
while 10 per cent used narcotics on a regular basis. The same
kind of problems existed within the other services, but with
declining severity in the Marine Corps, the Navy, and the Air
Force. Such figures suggest that as many as one fourth of all

Army enlisted men engaged in some form of rebellion against military authority. In an organizational environment requiring intense interpersonal loyalty and a high degree of co-operation, defiance of this magnitude necessarily exerted a profound influence on operational effectiveness. No armed force can function properly when faced with such internal disruption and resistance.

VII

The division within the enlisted ranks is perhaps most evident in what, for lack of a better term, may be called a GI counterculture—a community of shared values and expressions antithetical to military standards. As within civilian society, a new consciousness emerged within the services, expressed in cultural idioms and an anarchic indifference to authority. Black and white GIs, searching for an identity apart from their role in the military, formed buddy groups of "brothers" and "freaks." In the totalitarian environment of the military, solidarity was expressed symbolically through long hair and afros, rock and soul music, beads and black bracelets, peace signs and clenched fists. The consequences of open defiance could be extremely harsh, and most GIs thus normally expressed their loathing for the military through more subtle means. Vast numbers of Vietnam-era servicemen participated in countless minor acts of sabotage and obstruction designed to clog the gears of the "Green Machine." Every unit had its examples of intentionally bungled repair or paperwork, of unexplained minor damage to equipment, of constant squabbling between certain GIs and the "lifers," of mysteriously appearing peace signs, etc. The cumulative effect of thousands of such acts constituted the reality of the morale crisis.

In my own Army experience, I saw many examples of this covert resistance. My favorite involved a band performance at the Federal Building, in the heart of Manhattan's financial district, before a huge crowd of businessmen and military dignitaries. During a rendition of Sousa's *The Klaxon* march, our first clarinetist played the melody an octave and one half-step higher than written. The effect was both embarrassing to the military and extremely hilarious, as a shrill, oriental-sounding dissonance echoed through the canyons of Wall Street. Afterward, our enraged first sergeant attempted to find the culprit but unfortunately was not a capable enough musician to identify where the eerie sounds had originated; and of course none of us were about to give him any aid.

Another, more serious example involved the antics of my friends Paul Fuhs and Dennis Oney at the Defense Language Institute in Fort Bliss. When Sp/4 Fuhs was assigned to Fort Bliss, he was tapped by the command for important positions of authority. He was named section leader of his class at the Vietnamese language training center and was assigned as military intelligence agent to spy on the area GI political group, GIs for Peace. Paul and his roommate, Dennis, soon experienced a change of heart, however, and instead of aiding the Army, worked together to wreak havoc on the military. While supposedly an Army agent, Paul became a leading organizer of GIs for Peace, consistently sending the Army false reports and using government money to bolster the group's treasury. Meanwhile, back on post, the fabulous furry freak brothers (as they were sometimes known) exhorted fellow classmates, all Army security trainees with top-secret clearances, to resist orders to Vietnam. By the time Fuhs was removed as class leader (the Army finally realized something was wrong when he submitted an application as a conscientious objector), twelve out of the twenty-one original members of the class had deserted, obtained discharges, or filed for conscientious-objector status. Paul and Dennis themselves were later discharged, fourteen and twenty-six months early respectively, Paul by federal court order and Dennis through what must have been one of the most bizarre medical discharges in Army history. When the government refused to approve his C.O. application, Oney concocted the following wildly incredulous tale (excerpted from his official discharge papers):

Chief Complaint: "Someone injected LSD in my brain."
History of Present Illness: ". . . he became increasingly convinced that war was evil, the Army was run by psychotics and that he would be unable to live with his conscience if he stayed in the Army. . . . His friend advised him to take LSD and then the Army wouldn't matter. On the following day patient was told that LSD would be injected into his brain. . . . Patient since has felt he has

THE MACHINE BREAKS DOWN 27

been on a continual trip. . . . Patient describes specifically that whenever he sees something that is evil he can close his eyes and he will hear such things as voices sounding like the multitude of the heavenly hosts. He can also see and hear such things as nursery rhymes."

Perhaps the most dramatic example of this underground struggle within the ranks occurred among clerks at Fort Devens, Massachusetts. It is often said, with some justification, that the ordinary clerk, not the general, really runs the military bureaucracy, an irony immortalized in Joseph Heller's World War II character ex-Pfc Wintergreen. In 1970, an elaborate network of some seventy personnel workers at Fort Devens and other East Coast bases sprung up for the purpose of keeping GIs out of Vietnam. Four men in the proper offices at Fort Devens reportedly could delete the name of any soldier wanting to escape a levy to Vietnam. Individual orders were a bit more difficult, requiring the fixing of four men at Fort Devens and two at the Pentagon. According to reports in the Boston *Phoenix* and the *GI Press Service,* the operation was able to successfully prevent dozens of GIs from being sent to Vietnam.

The Army's most serious morale problem at home was the impact of veterans returning from the combat zone. After a twelve-month tour of Vietnam, dehumanized by the senselessness and indiscriminate destructiveness of American policy and increasingly drug-ridden and defiant of authority, veterans assigned to garrison bases were often unwilling or unable to comply with normal military standards of discipline. Having risked death, many combat veterans were simply incapable of being moved by the petty awards and punishments of military justice. Moreover, as Robert Jay Lifton has argued in *Home from the War,* many soldiers returned from Vietnam with a bitterness and rage at the deception to which they had been subjected and were in some cases motivated to resist military authority. At many bases, combat veterans sparked the development of overt resistance and political organizing. The Vietnam War and the veterans who fought it were like a cancer gnawing at the U.S. military apparatus.

CHAPTER 2

THE QUASI-MUTINY

In July of 1970 at the pre-Vietnam jungle-operations training center in Fort Sherman, Canal Zone, forty combat officers sent a remarkable letter to their Commander-in-Chief. The soon-to-be combat leaders were not seeking to degrade the service or join the growing peace movement. Their letter did not directly criticize the war, and no copies were sent to the press. Rather, they wished to inform the President of "the extent of disaffection among the American troops" and the grave threat this posed to the military. The young commanders relayed the perception that "the military, the leadership of this country—are perceived by many soldiers to be almost as much our enemy as the VC and the NVA" and cautioned that if the war continued, "young Americans in the military will simply refuse en masse to cooperate." The warning came too late, though, for by the time it was sent, the Army was already in an advanced state of decay, with many grunts in virtually open rebellion. The currents of unrest and dissension undermining American forces throughout the world surged together and were magnified in the crucible of Vietnam combat, effectively crippling U.S. military operations. Without resorting to outright insurrection, much of the American army in Vietnam refused to fight and staged a "quasi-mutiny."

Fred Gardner described the GI revolt in Vietnam as "survival-politics." Subtly and without heroics, soldiers improvised means of shirking a despised mission and engaged in their own unofficial troop withdrawal. The grunts' rebellion seldom reached the stage of formal mutiny, assuming instead less-visible forms: "search and avoid" missions, with patrols intentionally skirting potential enemy clashes or halting a few yards beyond the defense perimeter for a three-day pot party; threats against commanders, often forcing officers and NCOs to worry more about their own men than the Vietnamese; defiance of authority, with GIs blatantly disregarding dress and hair regulations and military custom; and covert obstruction, ranging from intentional inefficiency on the job to major acts of sabotage. The full story of the breakdown of the infantry has never been told, partly because its diffuse and anonymous nature defies precise definition and partly because reliable documentation is so difficult to obtain. We shall not present a detailed description here but, rather, will attempt an over-all assessment of the crisis, probing its manifestations in drug abuse, political protest, combat refusals, black militance, and fraggings. Our examination will portray the world's mightiest military force paralyzed by internal resistance.

I

On the evening of November 10, 1970, CBS-TV news shocked the nation with a six-minute broadcast of soldiers of the 1st Air Cavalry Division engaged in a marijuana smoke-in at Fire Base Aires. Americans stared in dazed bewilderment as freakishly garbed GIs gathered around the "old swimming hole" and smoked pot through the barrel of a shotgun. Bizarre as it may have been, the incident was not uncommon, for by 1970 the U. S. Army in Vietnam was overwhelmed by pervasive drug use and, more importantly, by a grave heroin epidemic. Numerous hysterical claims have been made on the extent of heroin and marijuana use in Indochina. We may gain a fairly precise and scientific view of the problem, though, by turning once again to the HumRRO 1971 Department of Defense Survey for an analysis of Army drug-use rates according to service location.

	Marijuana		Narcotics	
	Any Time in Previous Year	Daily	Any Time in Previous Year	Daily
CON. U.S.	41.3%	6.6%	20.1%	5.4%
EUROPE	40.2%	7.9%	13.3%	1.6%
VIETNAM	50.9%	13.8%	28.5%	9.2%
TOTAL ARMY	42.7%	8.1%	20.1%	5.2%

Figure 6

Drug use by service location, Army, September 1971.

UNIT, TIME OF SURVEY, NUMBER RESPONDENTS	173rd Airborne Brigade April 1970 N=1076	25th Infantry Division November 1970 N=1205	4th Infantry Division November 1970 N=1849	Engineers Battalion, Can Tho November 1970 N=482
HAD EVER USED	68%	48%	59%	43%
BEGAN USE IN U.S.	46%	38%	41%	27%
BEGAN USE IN VIETNAM	21%	10%	18%	16%

Figure 7

Marijuana use in four Vietnam units, 1970.

As the figures indicate, drug-use levels in Vietnam were higher than at any location in the world. The HumRRO survey indicated that over half the soldiers in Vietnam tried marijuana at least once and that nearly 14 per cent smoked it every day. The Army also conducted studies of marijuana use in Vietnam during 1970 and found even higher levels. Surveys of over 4,600 men in the 173rd Airborne Brigade, the 25th Infantry Division, the 4th Infantry Division, and an Engineers battalion in Can Tho are summarized in Figure 7.

The most striking feature of the HumRRO survey was the finding that nearly 10 per cent of the Army's soldiers used heroin or opium on a daily basis. The Army's urinalysis screening of all men leaving the war zone, started in mid-1971, showed an addiction rate of only 5 per cent, but the ease with which GIs could evade detection made these figures unreliable. The Defense Department launched a thorough examination of the problem in September of 1971 in lengthy interviews with 450 returning GIs, and found heroin use even more extensive than indicated in the HumRRO report. Forty-four per cent of the men contacted said they had tried at least some type of narcotic while in Vietnam; 35 per cent reported trying heroin. Twenty-eight per cent of the interviewees used narcotics more often than once a week, and an astonishing 20 per cent stated they became addicted while in Vietnam. The same study disclosed that 93 per cent of those who used heroin had their first contact with the drug while in Vietnam, thus confirming that heroin use increased primarily during service in Vietnam. The same pattern of narcotic use within the combat zone was discovered in a 1969 study conducted at the Cam Ranh Bay replacement center, which found that only 6.3 per cent of men entering the country used opium, compared with 17.4 per cent of those who had completed their combat tour. Vietnam was clearly the breeding ground for the heroin epidemic in the U. S. Army. Indeed, the use of all types of drugs increased during assignment to Vietnam. The Cam Ranh Bay report also noted that marijuana use among new troops was 31.4 per cent but among one-year veterans was 50 per cent. The investigation of 482 enlisted men in an Engineers battalion at Can Tho likewise observed a steady increase in drug use according to length of time served in Vietnam. While many soldiers used drugs

before arriving, service in Vietnam was the primary impetus
for increased drug use within the military.

Top military officers are fond of the fiction that such drug
abuse was concentrated only in rear-echelon areas, that men
in combat remained highly motivated and uninterested in
drugs. In fact, the reverse was true, with several of the Pentagon's own surveys confirming that drugs were most frequently
used in infantry units. The world-wide HumRRO study
showed that nearly 25 per cent of soldiers in the "Infantry,
Gun Crews" classification had tried narcotics, the highest percentage of any of the eight major occupational groupings. The
same report measured the use of marijuana while on duty,
discovering that 17.5 per cent of servicemen in the infantry
classification had smoked while on duty, a rate nearly double
that of any other job group. Similarly, the Army's own study
of the 25th Infantry Division stated: "More persons in combat units use marijuana than in other type units." Finally,
the Army's survey within the 173rd Airborne included random questioning of 494 frontline GIs. Thirty-five per cent
smoked pot more than once a week (compared to 31 per cent
for the entire thousand-man sample), and 19 per cent smoked
every day (compared to 16 per cent overall); two thirds of
these infantry troops admitted using marijuana while on field
duty. It's difficult to determine what impact, if any, such
marijuana use had on actual combat performance, but it
would seem likely that it slowed reaction time and created
troublesome tensions between first-termers and senior commanders. Infantry units with 10–15 per cent of their men
constantly stoned on pot could not have been very efficient
or highly motivated. Easier to guess is the disruption caused
by heroin addiction. No Army can function properly with 10
per cent of its troops using hard narcotics on a regular basis.
As was pointed out in an official September 1971 Report on
Drug Abuse Treatment to the Commander in Chief of Pacific
forces: "because of the nature and extent of heroin usage/
dependency among U.S. forces in Vietnam, the military mission has been significantly effected [sic]." The plague of drug
abuse signaled an Army demoralized to the point of collapse.

II

For soldiers already in the combat zone, there was little point in anti-war protest action. Opposition to the war was not a matter of politics but of survival; signing petitions or attending rallies was less important than simply avoiding personal injury. Moreover, the lack of security within most American units and the nearly total isolation of bases in Vietnam further hindered the development of political activities. Thus it is not surprising that no known GI newspaper appeared at any time during the war, or that very few anti-war protests of any kind took place. New York *Times* correspondent R. Drummond Ayers, reporting on conversations with infantrymen in the summer of 1969, quoted a young private who aptly summed up the common GI attitude: "I just work hard at surviving so I can go home and protest all the killing."

One of the few occasions when peace actions were noted in Vietnam was during the 1969 Moratorium mobilizations. Hal Wingo of *Life* magazine interviewed nearly one hundred GIs in the combat zone and found "unexpected cheers" and "open and outspoken sympathy" for the Moratorium demonstrations. Other journalists in Vietnam at the time reported a number of small anti-war protests from the troops themselves, including a seminar attended by soldiers in Quang Tri and an incident near Da Nang where approximately fifteen members of a combat unit wore black armbands while on patrol. A more formal action took place in November, when Captain Alan Goldstein and others at Long Binh collected 136 names on a petition supporting the aims of the Moratorium demonstrations. A few weeks later, on Thanksgiving Day, over one hundred servicemen from the 71st Evacuation Hospital and the 44th Medical Detachment at Pleiku abstained from the traditional turkey dinner as a protest against the war. One of the boldest anti-war protests in Vietnam occurred several weeks later, on Christmas Eve, in downtown Saigon. Approximately fifty soldiers, many of them in uniform, gathered in JFK Square and distributed leaflets urging fellow GIs to stop all fighting and declare a cease-fire during the Tet holiday on February 6. MPs quickly broke up the assembly, however.

The only other known incidents of anti-war protest in Viet-

nam occurred during 1971, at Chu Lai and in the Saigon
area. As the July 4 holiday approached, GIs in Chu Lai issued
a call for a mass GI rally and picnic at local beaches on the
afternoon of the Fourth. The action apparently was not very
well organized, however, and although a crowd of over one
thousand soldiers showed up, the supposed "Independence
Day Peace Rally" quickly turned into a huge picnic, and became not a political demonstration but the largest pot party
in the history of the Army. A much more serious and effective
action was that organized by Vietnam Veterans Against the
War in the fall. In September, a group of servicemen in the
Saigon area began circulating a petition to Congress expressing "opposition to further United States Military involvement
by air, sea, or land forces in Vietnam, Laos, Cambodia or
other countries of South East Asia."

Through the work of James Mohler, James Carlson, and
other sailors in the Saigon area and with support from the
VVAW national office in New York, the petition drive
quickly spread to soldiers and airmen at Pleiku, Cam Ranh,
and other locations. Hundreds of signatures were collected
within a few weeks in the Saigon area alone, and with
VVAW members throughout Vietnam involved, it appeared
the drive might obtain thousands of names. Military authorities quickly stepped in, however, and through arrests, discharges, and the usual forms of intimidation, managed to
crush the effort. Carlson was arrested on October 10 at Ton
Son Nhut; Jim Mohler was discharged for "substandard personal behavior" (despite an unblemished record); and Army
Sergeant Bob Stanfill was physically assaulted by an NCO
for circulating petitions in Saigon's 90th MP Company. Other
activists encountered similar repression, and in the process
many signed petitions were confiscated. The actual number
of signatures collected during the short-lived effort was never
accurately determined. David Addlestone, attorney for most
of the men involved, personally saw over one thousand names
and estimated that the total number throughout the country
was near two thousand. The effort demonstrated substantial
anti-imperialist sentiment among troops in Vietnam.

III

Opposition to the war among men in Vietnam commonly involved not political protest but the simple and direct expedient of avoiding combat. Mutiny is a potent and evocative term, but it accurately describes what in fact took place frequently among American soldiers in Vietnam. On October 23, 1970, veteran Vietnam correspondent John Saar published an illuminating article in *Life* about a combat unit on patrol near the Cambodian border: "You Just Can't Hand Out Orders" portrayed the successes of a young company commander who enjoyed the confidence of his men precisely because he accepted their loathing for the war and managed to avoid combat. The article popularized a new phrase, "working it out," to describe the emergence of battlefield democracy: commanders frequently had to conform orders to the wishes of their men, usually by avoiding situations likely to produce casualties. The practice was unobtrusive and subtle, but by all accounts it was widespread, particularly during the latter stages of the war. Reporters for *Newsweek*, the New York *Times*, *Saturday Review*, and other publications filed dispatches of minor combat refusals and of infantry platoons purposely evading enemy engagements. There's no way to determine the frequency of such low-key combat avoidance or its impact on U.S. offensive capabilities. These minor acts must have occurred often, though, for we have evidence of a substantial number of larger, more formal combat refusals —occasions on which the caldron of rank-and-file disaffection boiled over into mass insubordination. The latter stages of the Vietnam War produced no fewer than ten major incidents of mutiny.

On August 26, 1969, the New York *Daily News* bannered the startling and historic headline "Sir, My Men Refuse to Go"—the first reported incident of mass mutiny in Vietnam. "A" Company of the 3rd Battalion/196th Infantry had been pushing through the Songchang Valley south of Da Nang for five grueling days and had suffered many casualties. On August 24, Captain Eugene Shurtz ordered the sixty men remaining in the company to move out again and proceed down the dangerous slope of Nuilon Mountain. The exhausted, disgruntled men simply refused to go, all sixty of them. The

bewildered young captain radioed headquarters of his predicament, and within hours a senior commander and a senior
NCO arrived on the scene to talk with the men. Captain
Shurtz was relieved of his post, and the command's representatives began the tense job of threatening and persuading
the men to move out as ordered. After several more refusals,
most of the sixty men grudgingly and halfheartedly followed
the sergeant, who had started to advance by himself. According to the military code, mutiny in time of war is the cardinal
offense, punishable by death; yet none of the men who balked
on that August day in the Songchang Valley received even
a reprimand.

Later in the year, in November, another mutiny incident
came to light at Cu Chi, near the Cambodian border.
Twenty-one men of the 1st Platoon, B Company, of the 2nd
Battalion/27th Infantry refused to advance. All the men were
hardened combat veterans and were nearing the end of their
twelve-month tour of duty. When Captain Frank Smith ordered them into enemy-held territory, the GIs apparently felt
the risks were no longer worth it and defied the command.
The story was reported in the Cleveland *Press* by correspondent Tom Tiede, who termed the rebellion "not without precedent in these late days of the Vietnam war." Several months
later, another mutiny took place, this time before CBS television cameras. Newsman John Lawrence was accompanying
Captain Al Rice and the men of C Company, 2nd Battalion,
7th Cavalry on patrol in War Zone C during April 1970.
The going was tough, with frequent enemy contact, and the
inexperienced new commander seemed determined to prove
himself under fire. When the captain ordered his men down
the center of a dangerous jungle path presumed to be surrounded by NLF forces, however, the men balked. The soldiers objected that a direct advance would almost certainly
draw fire and produce casualties, and they argued instead for
an alternate route. Incredibly, the viewing audience was
treated to a live performance of "working it out" as the enlisted men informed the captain that his order was nonsense
and they would not obey.

The Nixon administration's invasion of Cambodia in May
of 1970 sent thousands of American GIs rushing into yet another foreign country, and also led to two further incidents
of insubordination. On May 7, sixteen soldiers stationed at

Fire Base Washington refused to advance with their units into Cambodia. The men were from two companies of the 3rd Battalion/22nd Infantry. Four days later, the action was repeated when a small group of GIs at 4th Infantry headquarters in An Khe refused to board helicopters. The rebellion involved men from the 3rd Battalion/8th Infantry.

Another mutiny incident occurred in December of 1970, when not only low-ranking enlisted men but their superiors joined together to refuse an order sent from higher authority. On the evening of December 29, Lieutenant Fred Pitts and twenty-three men of C Company, 2nd Battalion/501st Infantry pulled into what they considered a secure night defense position. During the night, however, the unit received an order from the battalion commander to move on to another position. Pitts objected that such an advance was not only unnecessary but would endanger lives. After meeting with his men and talking over the situation, Pitts formally refused the order. The outraged colonel called the platoon sergeant to the radio, but he, too, rejected the command. The next morning, both men were removed from the unit for disobeying a direct order. Pitts later pleaded guilty and received only a suspended sentence—a remarkably lenient punishment, considering the offense.

The March 1971 South Vietnamese invasion of Laos came at a time when the American Army was already in an advanced state of decline. U.S. infantry units were heavily committed to the operation, providing firepower and rear support for the ARVN columns advancing along Route 9, and the unwanted combat burden inevitably led to further rebellions, including one of the most significant and widely publicized mutinies of the war. Troop B of the 1st Squadron, 1st Cavalry, had been assigned to clear Route 9 near Lang Vei and was running into intensive North Vietnamese and NLF opposition. When Captain Carlos Poveda ordered two platoons to advance against heavy fire on March 20 to retrieve a damaged helicopter and armored vehicle, the men of the troop decided, as Sp/4 Randy Thompson later put it, "the reason given wasn't a very good one"; the platoon refused to move. Lieutenant Colonel Gene Breeding, the squadron commander, quickly arrived and attempted to talk the men into complying with the orders. The colonel lined up the troop and ordered the sergeant major to take the names of those who still would not advance. Fifty-three soldiers refused. Not only all of B Troop but the entire squadron was pulled back from the operation, apparently to prevent the mutiny from spreading. Captain Poveda was relieved of command, and the men of B Troop were reassigned; but no disciplinary action was taken against any of the rebels. Another mutiny occurred during the Laotian invasion, according to Congressman Paul McCloskey (R-Calif.), when an entire platoon of the 1st Brigade, 5th Mechanized Division, also refused to advance into combat.

By the latter part of 1971, the American war effort was clearly coming to an end; the Congress, the people, and even the President were in apparent agreement that the ground war was a hopeless and futile venture. For the remaining troops, counting the days until their rotation date, the risks of combat seemed even more senseless than before, and the Army thus witnessed two additional mutiny incidents in the war's final months. The first involved men of B Company, 1st Battalion/12th Infantry, dug in against North Vietnamese artillery at Fire Base Pace, near the Cambodian border. On October 9, Captain Robert Cronin ordered fifteen men of the 3rd Platoon into enemy-controlled territory outside the base perimeter. Convinced that the patrol would be tantamount to suicide, six of the men refused the order. The next day, as the rebels were threatened with court-martial, GIs in the other platoons rallied to their support and agreed that they, too, would not advance. At this point, the story becomes uncertain due to the role of reporter Richard Boyle, who had arrived at Pace a few days earlier. Army officials and some independent observers say that Boyle in fact set up the mutiny and the subsequent protest. Boyle, on the other hand, in his book *Flower of the Dragon* and in a thirty-minute tape of the incident, claims that he merely tried to help the grunts. Regardless of who initiated the action after the refusal in the 3rd Platoon, sixty-five of the one hundred men in B Company signed a petition circulated by Sp/4 Al Grana requesting Senator Ted Kennedy to protect them from what they considered needless danger.

The final reported mutiny in Vietnam occurred at Phu Bai during the April 1972 Easter offensive. When troops of C Company, 2nd Battalion/1st Infantry of the 196th Brigade were ordered into trucks to patrol enemy territory, about one hundred of the GIs refused to advance, considering the mission too dangerous. After some discussion, about half the men agreed to board the trucks, but approximately forty-five soldiers remained adamant. At this point, Lieutenant Colonel Frederick Mitchell, the battalion commander, arrived at the scene to talk with the men. After being transferred back to a rear base, the group finally agreed to advance. The men were convinced not by threat of court-martial but by learning that their refusal would endanger "A" Company; to protect their buddies, the soldiers reluctantly moved into the field.

For every incident reported here, numerous other rebellions probably took place along isolated, unobserved jungle trails. During his year of legal-defense work in Saigon, David Addlestone heard of literally dozens of combat refusals, with nearly every case ending not in punishment but in negotiations between commanders and GIs. And for every instance of defiance in combat, hundreds of minor acts of insubordination occurred within base camps and rear stations. The mutinies we have described represented only the tip of a much larger iceberg of rebellion throughout the Army in Vietnam. With disaffection at the stage where soldiers openly refused to engage in combat, the Army's effectiveness as a fighting force was in serious doubt. It may have been, for example, that the South Vietnamese rout in Laos in March of 1971 was at least partly caused by the reluctance of American support evidenced at Lang Vei. On a more general level, such combat refusals must have played at least some role in restraining U.S. operations. The knowledge that dangerous or unpopular missions could lead to mutiny undoubtedly prompted commanders to think twice about ordering certain actions. These mutinies were unmistakable signs of an Army on the verge of collapse.

IV

Of all the troops in Vietnam, the most rebellious were the blacks. As was the case throughout the armed forces, black GIs in Vietnam were militant leaders of the GI resistance, posing great problems for American commanders. David Addlestone claims that by the time he arrived in Saigon, in November of 1970, black radicalism had already seriously hin-

dered U.S. fighting capabilities, with brothers very seldom
trusted in combat, apparently for fear they might turn their
guns around. It is one of the ironies of Vietnam that minority
troops, who in the early stages of the war constituted a major
portion of the American infantry, by 1970 were often not
even trusted with weapons. In the mid-1960s, blacks were welcomed into the front lines (through the lowering of entrance
standards and Project 100,000) as a crucial source of manpower for sustaining the Vietnam intervention, but by 1970
they were no longer considered reliable in combat.

Black unrest in Vietnam began well before the period of
troop withdrawals, erupting with explosive fury in the summer of 1968. The month of August witnessed two of the largest prison rebellions of the Vietnam War period, both led
by black GIs. On the weekend of August 16, troops within
the Da Nang Marine brig rioted in protest over prison regulations. The Marine inmates seized control of the central area
of the compound and held out against armed guards for
twenty hours. Seven prisoners and a guard were injured in
the clash, and one entire cell block was heavily damaged by
fire. As command officials attempted to remove seventy inmates from the prison a few days later, violence flared up
again. A force of 120 riot-equipped MPs was required to quell
the renewed fighting and finally restore order to the troubled
brig. Just two weeks later, the huge American prison at Long
Binh erupted in perhaps the bloodiest and most savage military revolt of recent history. LBJ, as the jail was known in
GI parlance, was overcrowded (719 men crammed into a
space reserved for 502), had no interior plumbing, and was
staffed by inexperienced, overworked guards. The oppressive
conditions were no doubt the root cause of the uprising, but
little is known of what immediately sparked the violence or
how the fighting developed. Hundreds of inmates clashed
with MPs for several hours, and many of the stockade buildings were destroyed by fire. According to press statements at
the time, fifty-eight prisoners and five MPs were injured in
the fighting, including twenty-three who required hospitalization. One soldier, Private Edward Haskett of St. Peters-
burg, Florida, was killed in the riot. Afterward, nearly two
hundred blacks banded together and staged a no-work strike.
A smaller group barricaded themselves within a section of the
stockade and refused to surrender. More than a month later,

twelve blacks still held control of a small enclave. During their occupation, the militants reportedly simulated African dress and customs and transformed their tiny holding into a kind of liberated African state. When the incident finally ended, six of the blacks were charged with murder.

In our earlier discussion of mutinies, we mentioned only those incidents involving primarily white GIs. As black nationalism increased, though, and over-all morale deteriorated, similar acts of insubordination occurred among blacks. At least two examples of black refusal came to light during 1970, both involving frontline infantry units. When A Company of the 1st Battalion/506th Regiment returned to Camp Evans near the A Shau Valley after a combat patrol in the spring, rising racial tensions erupted in a near tragedy. Fighting broke out during the company's first night at camp, and as tensions flared the men went for their weapons and squared off against each other with loaded rifles. Further violence was somehow avoided that night, but the next day fifteen blacks refused to report for duty. Six of the blacks were eventually persuaded, but nine refused to give in and were charged with disobeying a direct order. Six months later, in November, another group of blacks, this time at Camp Eagle, near the DMZ, defied orders to join a combat operation. Claiming that they would be endangered by racist commanders, Willie Moten and six others of C Company, 3rd Battalion/187th refused to move into the field. There is no telling how many other similar incidents took place out of view of reporters and investigators.

In Vietnam, as elsewhere, the growth of black pride led to self-imposed segregation and the emergence of numerous black solidarity groups. Although most of these associations were informal and social in nature, on some occasions blacks joined together for political aims. One such group, the so-called "Black Liberation Front of the Armed Forces," was led by Eddie Burney, a committed black nationalist and Black Panther Party supporter stationed with the 4th Transportation Command at Long Binh. Chanting "Free Angela Davis" and "Free the Brothers in LBJ," forty of the men demonstrated in Long Binh in the spring of 1971 to commemorate the birthday of Martin Luther King. As with many black organizers, Burney was tapped as a special enlisted assistant to his commanding officer—an apparent attempt to co-opt his activities. Eddie continued to resist, however, and after three courts-martial, was punitively discharged. Another example of black organizing was the "Black Brothers Union," active during 1971 at Cam Ranh. Led by Sp/4 Joe Hardy, the Union worked to eliminate discrimination in on-post facilities. In January 1971 the group presented a report to the post inspector general complaining of racist practices at the base enlisted men's club. When the report and a subsequent follow-up request failed to bring results, the Union organized a black boycott of the club in April. Still no changes were made, however, and, as racial tensions inevitably worsened, the club was ripped by a tragic explosion a month later. A fragmentation grenade was thrown into the crowded bar, resulting in injury to thirty-one people; BBU member Sp/4 Leon Prince was jailed for the incident but later acquitted for lack of evidence.

No section of Vietnam witnessed more black unrest than the I Corps region, in the northern part of South Vietnam, where soldiers lived in primitive garrison bases constantly threatened by guerrilla attack. A tragic example of the extreme racial tensions in the area came in a fatal dispute between Gerald McLemore and a group of whites following a racial brawl at Chu Lai in September of 1970. After returning to his quarters later in the evening, McLemore was disturbed by angry whites threatening and taunting him from outside his "hooch." Grabbing his M-16, McLemore rushed outside, where he saw a grenade in the hand of one of the soldiers, and in a panic gunned down Sp/4 Bruce Thomas. The grenade held by Thomas went off, but it turned out to be just a harmless smoke device. McLemore was later tried and convicted of manslaughter. Further unrest surfaced at Chu Lai a few months later when, in early December, forty blacks marched on the commanding general's headquarters to protest discriminatory field assignments. Serious trouble also erupted at nearby Da Nang. This sprawling American base was the scene of a major race riot and a week of virtually open racial warfare in early 1971. Perhaps the most severe unrest occurred at Camp Baxter, near the DMZ. New York *Times* correspondent Donald Kirk visited the outpost in 1971 and, referring to "intermittent demonstrations, a couple of killings, secret meetings and threats," described the camp as in a state of siege. The details of the event are sketchy, but in the early part of 1971 a major racial clash occurred at the base that left at least one black GI dead. When MPs were called in after the riot, they discovered that many GIs were carrying illegal arms and that blacks and whites had assembled secret arms caches of ammunition, grenades, and machine guns to defend themselves from further attacks. At the March 1971 funeral for the black riot victim, two hundred brothers staged a black power demonstration. Racial incidents were prevalent at bases throughout South Vietnam. In a very real sense, the American Army was fighting on two fronts, one against the Vietnamese guerrillas in the jungles and the other against embittered militants within its own ranks. The strain of black resistance was a key factor in crippling U.S. military capabilities in Vietnam.

V

On April 20, 1971, Senate Majority Leader Mike Mansfield began the proceedings of Congress by dramatically introducing his colleagues and the nation to the most macabre development of the Vietnam War: fragging. In a trembling voice, Mansfield grimly told of a young first lieutenant, a West Point graduate from Montana, who was murdered by his own men at Bien Hoa on March 15, just four weeks before his scheduled return to the States. In the brief comments following Mansfield's disclosure, Senator Charles Mathias of Maryland captured the shock and dismay of those present:

In every war a new vocabulary springs up . . . but in all the lexicon of war there is not a more tragic word than 'fragging' with all that it implies of total failure of discipline and depression of morale, the complete sense of frustration and confusion and the loss of goals and hope itself.

The Army began keeping records on assaults with explosive devices in 1969. Through the end of 1970, over three hundred incidents had taken place, resulting in seventy-three deaths and injury to nearly five hundred people. By July of 1972, as the last American troops were leaving Vietnam, the total number of incidents had reached 551, with eighty-six soldiers dead and over seven hundred injured. In effect, these are the casualty figures for the Army's "other war" in Vietnam, its battle with the insurgents in its own ranks. As startling as these totals may be, fraggings were in fact more frequent than the Pentagon's figures imply. One quite obvious deficiency is that the statistics include only assaults with explosive devices and omit the vast number of shootings with firearms, which, given greater availability, probably occurred more often. David Addlestone reports that Army lawyers with the 173rd Airborne told of periods during 1970 and 1971 when violent attacks were almost a daily occurrence. In fact, assaults against commanders during the Vietnam War probably reached into the thousands. The Pentagon figures do indicate a sharp rise in the rate of fragging, with the number of incidents increasing each year from 1969 to 1971, despite troop withdrawals:

Calendar Year	Number of Assaults	Deaths
1969	96	39
1970	209	34
1971 (first 11 months only)	215	12

Figure 8
Confirmed fragging incidents.

Military spokesmen sometimes claim that many of these incidents involved attacks among low-ranking enlisted men, particularly blacks against whites, but the Pentagon's own figures show that the great majority of fraggings were aimed at those in positions of authority. Statistics supplied to the House Appropriations Defense Subcommittee for the period January 1969 to August 1971 show that, of 435 identified fragging victims, approximately 80 per cent were officers and NCOs. Fragging was the GI's ultimate means of resistance, a deadly and effective weapon against military authority and dangerous or oppressive policies. A few examples will show the powerful impact of fragging.

In 1970, former Marine Sergeant Robert Parkinson of Sunland, California, appeared before a Congressional Subcommittee on Juvenile Delinquency. A crippled man, the sergeant told how two years earlier, in Vietnam, he had attempted to crack down on widespread drug use within his unit; how he began to receive threats and eventually had to arm himself; and how on September 23, 1968, a fragmentation grenade exploded under his bunk, shattering his foot and causing severe internal injuries. The sergeant's tragic experience was not unique, even at this early stage of the war. Lieutenant Colonel Anthony Herbert told interviewers for *Playboy* magazine of similar attacks within his battalion of the 173rd Airborne before he took command in early 1969:

> There had been two attempts on the previous commander's life. There had been quite a few fraggings in that battalion, of both officers and senior enlisted men. One man had both legs blown off; seven people had been wounded by a grenade, and a Claymore mine had been thrown right at the tactical-operations center—a mine to kill the staff, for Christ's sake.

On some occasions, the bitterness and rage of GIs erupted in random and indiscriminate violence, directed not at military authorities but at anyone who happened to be in the way, fellow GIs included. We have already noted the tragic blast that left thirty-one injured at Cam Ranh in the spring of 1971. An even larger incident occurred earlier, in February of 1970, within the Maintenance Battalion of the Force Logistics Command near Da Nang. On the evening of Thursday, February 5, a grenade was tossed onto the crowded patio of the local enlisted men's club, injuring sixty-two people and killing one serviceman. Both blacks and whites were among the victims, and most observers thus discounted racial motivations. Information about the incident is sketchy, but it was apparently sparked by a general shakedown within the unit earlier in the day, presumably in search of drugs. Whatever the cause, all suspects in the case were Marine enlisted men.

Most fraggings were aimed at eliminating the abusive practices of individual commanders. On November 9, 1970, an incendiary grenade was thrown into the quarters of several notoriously rigid NCOs of the 2nd Battalion/17th Artillery at Nha Trang. The sergeants escaped unhurt, but presumably they got the message from the grunts to ease up. A similar incident occurred several months later within the 538th Transportation Company at Long Binh. The unit seethed with discontent over the policies of the first sergeant, and talk of fragging was blatant. In April of 1971 the sergeant finally

fell victim to an attack, later blamed on Sp/4's Richard Buck-
ingham, a member of VVAW, and Richard Strain. Fraggings
also took place under combat conditions. In his January 1972
article in *Saturday Review*, Eugene Linden recounted an episode in an armored cavalry unit near Khe San in the spring
of 1971. After four months in the bush, the company was
scheduled to return to Khe San, when the commander, at
the last minute, volunteered his men to stay out on patrol.
That night, three Claymore mines were stolen and placed under what was thought to be the commander's armored track
vehicle. The captain was elsewhere, though, and the explosion injured (apparently accidentally) four enlisted men
sleeping nearby. Linden also reported on a fragging involving
black radicals at Camp Eagle during the Laotian invasion in
March of 1971. The commander of a supply unit at the camp
had attempted to discipline several militants for drug use, but
after jailing one of the blacks, the captain was wounded in
his sleep by a Claymore mine slipped under his bunk. Similarly, in a 1972 article for *Life* magazine, John Saar wrote
of a fragging in the fall of 1971 in which grunts attempted
to blow up their overly zealous commander but accidentally
killed the wrong officer. In an unannounced urinalysis test
immediately after the slaying, 25 per cent of the men were
detected as heroin users and removed from the unit.

The ultimate impact of fragging lay not with any one particular incident but with its general effect on the functioning
of the Army. For every one of the more than five hundred reported assaults, there were many instances of intimidation
and threats of fragging which often produced the same result.
The unexpected appearance of a grenade pin or the detona-
tion of a harmless smoke grenade frequently convinced commanders to abandon expected military standards. Once a commander was threatened by or became the actual target of a
fragging, his effectiveness and that of the unit involved were
severely hampered. Indeed, as internal defiance spread within
many units, no order could be issued without first considering
the possibility of fragging. The ardent young West Point
graduate, eager to succeed in combat and push his men to
medal-winning heroics, was a doomed figure. The majority of
grunts in Vietnam had but one aim, to return home safely,
and few were willing to risk their lives for a hopeless cause.
As violent and ruthless as it may have been, fragging was an

essential tool of soldier democracy, the means by which men thrust into Vietnam against their wills were able to resist military authority. It was the final manifestation of a breakdown in the U.S. mission in Vietnam and signaled an Army at war with itself.

VI

The plague of disaffection and defiance within the ranks, most dramatically evidenced in fragging, crippled the infantry and left the once-proud American Army helpless—more a liability than an asset to U.S. purposes. This was perhaps best illustrated by the Army's attempted solution to the problem of fragging. By 1970, many commanders in Vietnam apparently felt that enlisted men could no longer be trusted with weapons and began a policy of restricting access to explosive devices and rifles. Information from various separate sources and conversations with Vietnam veterans confirm that in many units grenades and firearms were taken from all but those on guard duty and on combat patrol. Sp/5 William Fischer, then of the 440th Signal Battalion in Mannheim, related in June 1970 (at an anti-war gathering in London's Lyceum Ballroom) how several months earlier in Vietnam a colonel refused to arm the men in his camp, despite an NLF attack, because he was "afraid of incidents." Similarly, in 1971, members of "Better Blacks United," an anti-racist organization centered in Tuy Hoa, disclosed that commanders restricted the possession of arms among blacks and white radicals. Correspondents for *Time*, the Washington *Post*, and other journals likewise observed instances of troops being denied access to weapons. Thus soldiers were stripped of the very weapons with which they had been sent to fight. Limiting possession of weapons may have prevented some fraggings, but it also undermined the U.S. role in Vietnam. An Army so utterly demoralized clearly was incapable of functioning as a credible military force.

Military officials and some journalists have asserted that the Army did not seriously fall apart until after extensive withdrawals began—that troops grew restless because they were taken out of combat and thus became bored. Such arguments raise a "chicken and egg" dilemma: did resistance force the Pentagon to withdraw, or did withdrawal create dissent and unrest? The actual process was no doubt a dialectic combination of the two, each process playing on the other to produce constantly deteriorating troop morale and an ever-increasing rate of withdrawal. Nonetheless, too little attention has been directed to the question of just what influence the Army's collapse in Vietnam had on Nixon-administration disengagement policies. It's hard to pinpoint a date when turbulence within the infantry reached a critical state, but my own guess would be that by early 1970 morale problems were already beginning to create grave difficulties. Several combat refusals had already been reported, drug-use levels were approaching 50 per cent, and fraggings were spreading rapidly; black and white troops throughout the services were loudly clamoring for an end to the war and greater personal freedoms. David Hackworth's description of the 173rd Brigade at An Khe, even as early as 1969, suggests an Army rapidly approaching collapse:

> Pound for pound, the Brigade was garbage. Discipline was lax, the troops were slovenly, mentally as well as physically. It was obvious that in An Khe at least they were no match for either the Viet Cong or the North Vietnamese regulars. As the sergeant had said, they preferred pot, two to one. But marijuana was only an expression of a deeper, more serious failure. . . . They called the hierarchy 'motherfuckers' and printed 'fuck the Green Machine' on their jackets and hats.

There seems little doubt that troop withdrawals were in fact speeded up because of the GI revolt. Military officials were compelled to act in order to preserve the Army as an institution and prevent even further internal disintegration. This was done not only because of fragging and mutiny in Vietnam itself but because of the generalized crisis throughout the armed forces at the time: the plummeting re-enlistment rates, soaring desertions, and rising dissent which threatened to destroy the American military apparatus. Against such a background, it's not surprising that voices were raised to submit to the pressures for withdrawal. Stewart Alsop, a veteran journalist with reputed close connections to Pentagon officials, penned an extraordinary *Newsweek* editorial, in December 1970, reporting a "growing feeling among the Administration's policymakers that it might be a good idea to accelerate the rate of withdrawal." The main reason cited for this view, according to Alsop, was "that discipline and morale in the American Army in Vietnam are deteriorating very seriously." Similar sentiments were attributed to Pentagon officials a few weeks later in a *Time* magazine article on GI dissent: "Officers from Chief of Staff William C. Westmoreland on down are known to be arguing that they are not being pulled out fast enough." Washington *Post* reporters also found appeals for accelerated withdrawal rates among many leading officers who "believe that a continued presence provides little help for the Vietnamese but exacerbates the problems of drugs and disaffection." There were also reports in early 1971 that then-Secretary of Defense Laird returned from an inspection tour of Vietnam "shocked and distressed by the high level of marijuana use and the low level of morale" and urged a more rapid reduction in ground troops. The Nixon administration claimed and received great credit for withdrawing the Army from Vietnam, but in fact it was the rebellion of low-ranking GIs that forced the government to abandon a hopeless and suicidal policy.

CHAPTER 3

THE GI MOVEMENT

The fraggings, mutinies, desertions, and other symptoms of collapsing morale we have examined would alone qualify the Vietnam period as the most disruptive in American history. These were not the only serious problems faced by the military, however. The Indochina war also produced a phenomenon of wholly different quality, a challenge never before experienced within the armed forces: a sustained movement of organized political opposition and resistance. A few previous books have alluded to the GI movement, but till now no attempt has been made to seriously examine its development, largely because reliable sources are not generally accessible. Drawing on my own involvement in the movement and on various internal documents and files, I have been able to reconstruct here the outlines of the historic struggle for peace and justice within the ranks. Our chronicle begins in the present chapter with the story of the movement's birth and early development within the United States. Before proceeding, though, we should understand some of the unique problems of GI organizing.

Political activism is difficult even under the best of circumstances, but within the Draconian legal structure of the military it can be suicidal. Restrictions on a soldier's civil liberties are nearly absolute. Public assembly, distribution of literature, the wearing of political symbols—all such means of political expression are strictly forbidden on post. Indeed, there is very little a soldier can legally do anywhere. Even off-post demonstrations are prohibited if in a foreign country, if the serviceman is in uniform, or if his activities "constitute a breach of law and order." GIs who attempt something even so innocuous as a newsletter, risk arrest merely distributing it on base. Beyond these formal strictures, however, rank-and-file organizers are imperiled by extralegal harassment and punitive administrative measures—options easily available in an isolated and authoritarian bureaucracy such as the military. It would probably be safe to assert, and our history will provide numerous examples, that nearly every serviceman seriously attempting to resist war and injustice has suffered some sort of privation. Whether it be the loss of a security clearance, removal from a job, transfer to some isolated post, discharge under less than honorable conditions, or outright imprisonment, GI activists have paid a stiff price for their commitment. The certain knowledge of such consequences has deterred many would-be participants.

The rigidity of the military environment has also contributed to another feature of the movement: its cyclical, transitory nature. The history of the GI movement exhibits a consistent pattern of political groups rising and falling in rapid succession—with organizations spontaneously arising, growing to maturity, and then quickly disappearing, often in less than a year. Even where political groups appear well established and possess more or less stable facilities, cadre and membership change frequently, resulting in recurring periods of low activity. Of course, military repression has played a major role in this. Leading organizers and spokesmen repeatedly have been transferred, discharged, or jailed; in some cases, the entire staff of an organization has been eliminated at one time. Even without such obstruction, though, servicemen's groups have experienced problems of turnover because of the very nature of military life. People in the armed forces seldom spend an extended period at any location and often are relocated several times in one year, especially in the Army. Consequently, GI groups have been notoriously impermanent. In the uncertain and transitory atmosphere of the military, political organizations have proved difficult to maintain.

That resistance emerged despite such encumbrance adds further dimension to our view of the military's internal crisis. The young people forced into the ranks by the Vietnam build-up expressed a sometimes articulate, sometimes desperate, opposition to an unwanted mission. Reflecting a society steeped in social upheaval and growing radicalism, they rejected the constraints of hierarchy to speak out and act on what they believed. The GI movement imbued the military with the voice of a troubled citizenry, providing a measure of democratic restraint on the otherwise unresponsive and imperious institutions of war.

I

The GI movement was born of the U.S. intervention in Vietnam, and its development closely matched the declining fortunes of that effort. In the early stages of the war, before the American military hubris was shattered by the 1968 Tet offensive, opposition to the war was limited, confined largely to isolated acts of conscience. The first known incident took place in November 1965, when Lieutenant Henry Howe of Fort Bliss participated in a small civilian peace demonstration in downtown El Paso. For this innocuous act, and because he carried a placard reading "End Johnson's Facist [sic] Aggression," Howe was court-martialed and sentenced to two years hard labor at Fort Leavenworth—a harsh portent of the military's reaction to internal dissent. The first public refusal of orders to Vietnam came on June 30, 1966, when privates James Johnson, Dennis Mora, and David Samas—the so-called "Fort Hood 3"—announced they could not participate in an immoral war. One of the most famous early incidents occurred in October 1966, when Army doctor Howard Levy refused to train Green Beret medics at Fort Jackson, on the grounds that Special Forces units were responsible for war crimes in Vietnam. Levy's historic court-martial became a *cause célèbre* as his attorneys attempted a defense based on both the illegality of the Vietnam War and the Nuremberg principle requiring non-participation in war crimes. The military court, of course, rejected the arguments and sentenced Levy to three years at Fort Leavenworth (he served twenty-six months). The first known example of black defiance came in July 1967 (during the Detroit ghetto uprising), when Camp Pendleton Marines William Harvey and George Daniels called a meeting to question why black men should fight a white man's war in Vietnam. When Harvey, Daniels, and twelve other Marines requested captain's mast to discuss the matter with their commander, the two were arrested and charged with insubordination and promoting disloyalty. In November of that year, they were found guilty and sentenced to six and ten years respectively.

As U.S. efforts in Vietnam encountered increasing public criticism during 1967, some leaders of the growing peace movement recognized that emerging anti-war feelings within the ranks could become extremely important if focused into effective, ongoing political action. The first attempt to provide such direction was launched in late 1967: the GI coffee-house movement. The founder of the first coffeehouse projects was Fred Gardner, a writer and former editor of the *Harvard Crimson*, who, after a tour of active duty as a reservist, became convinced that increasing numbers of GIs were unhappy with military life and needed an alternative to the barracks—a place independent of military influence where they could meet and freely exchange ideas about the war and the Army. With ten thousand dollars of his own money and the aid of one co-worker, Donna Mickleson, Gardner set out for Columbia, South Carolina (near Fort Jackson) and in late 1967 opened a Main Street storefront called the "UFO," not to be confused with the more established USO located nearby. The operation consisted of entertainment, food, and stereo music, with a low-key emphasis more on culture than politics. This first coffeehouse struck a responsive chord, for within a few months of opening, an average of six hundred GIs a week were visiting the place, and anti-war activities were beginning to develop. The first group protest action at Fort Jackson came in February 1968, a few weeks after the opening of the UFO—just days after the start of the Tet offensive. On the evening of February 13, thirty-five uncertain but determined soldiers gathered in front of the main post chapel for what had been advertised as a silent protest service against the war. The group was stopped by a squad of MPs, however, and all but two left quickly. The remaining privates, Robert Tater and Stephen Kline, were unceremoniously dragged away and placed in confinement. News of the incident created a sensation within the peace movement and prompted leaders of the (old) Mobilization Committee to End the War in Vietnam to view soldier dissent with great optimism. Rennie Davis and others launched a "Summer of Support" project to raise funds for additional coffeehouses, while Gardner and a number of supporters left Columbia to establish two more projects, the "Oleo Strut," in Killeen, Texas (near Fort Hood), and "Mad Anthony Wayne's," in Waynesville, Missouri (near Fort Leonard Wood). From the very beginning, these and other coffeehouses, immersed in heavily pro-military localities, faced an uneasy and perilous existence.

A prime example is the case of the Fort Knox coffeehouse, which civilian and GI activists tried repeatedly but unsuccessfully to open during 1969. The Muldraugh, Kentucky, municipal council passed a special amendment to the city charter requiring that commercial licensees be of "good character and repute"; local police and Military Intelligence officials repeatedly entered the premises to harass and frighten away GI clients; and the Meade County Quarterly Court canceled the one-year lease and evicted the organizers. When the group responded to this last challenge by raising the necessary ten thousand dollar bond and appealing the decision, a grand jury issued indictments for conducting a public nuisance and for health-code violations, and five of the organizers were jailed. After other arrests and an exhausting series of legal battles and countersuits, the group finally abandoned its plans. The Fort Knox incident was by no means an isolated example; almost every other coffeehouse experienced similar troubles. Summer of Support people attempting to open a center in Leesville, Louisiana (near Fort Polk) were refused a license and drummed out of town. The "Shelter Half," opened in the fall of 1968 in Tacoma, Washington (near Fort Lewis) was continually harassed by local police for noise and vagrancy violations and in late 1969 was almost declared "off limits" by Fort Lewis authorities (a designation later withdrawn under threat of suit). Some coffeehouses actually became the targets of physical assault, presumably by right-wing vigilante groups. The Fort Dix coffeehouse, for example, was wracked by a bomb explosion on February 14, 1970, which left three injured. It had been the fourth attack in five months, and although the state police barracks stood directly across the street, no suspects were ever found. Similarly, on April 29, 1970, the "Green Machine" coffeehouse, near Camp Pendleton, in California, was attacked with .45-caliber machine-gun fire, wounding Marine Pfc Jesse Woodward. Despite such difficulties, which continued throughout the history of the GI movement, rank-and-file dissent grew rapidly.

II

Often short-lived and appearing in the form of barely readable mimeographed sheets, GI newspapers have been the fundamental expression of political opposition within the armed forces. Colonel Robert Heinl estimated in the spring of 1971 that "some 144 underground newspapers [were] published or aimed at U.S. military bases," and in March of 1972 the Department of Defense gave the total number of such papers as 245. My own, independent investigation indicates that the cumulative total as of this writing is near three hundred. (For a more detailed analysis of the GI press and a comprehensive list of 259 known newspapers, see Appendix B.) One of the first was *Vietnam GI*, published by Vietnam veteran Jeff Sharlet and other Chicago activists in late 1967. With press runs exceeding fifteen thousand, *Vietnam GI* was distributed to soldiers by draft-resistance groups in Chicago, Boston, the Bay Area, and numerous other locations. Thousands of GIs received the paper in bus stations, induction centers, and elsewhere, but the backbone of *Vietnam GI* was a remarkable mailing list of some three thousand servicemen in Vietnam. Perhaps the first newsletter authored solely by GIs was *Act*, published during January of 1968 in Paris by "resisters-inside-the-army (RITA)," a loose association of politically active deserters from American bases in Europe. Within the United States, the first GI-initiated radical journals began appearing during the summer of 1968. One of the earliest of these was *Strikeback*, published by soldiers at Fort Bragg; like many GI papers, though, it lasted only a few issues, disappearing by the end of the year. Another fleeting effort was *Pawn's Pawn*, which surfaced briefly at Fort Leonard Wood but faltered along with Mad Anthony's coffeehouse. Two of these pioneer efforts proved more enduring, however, and were among the most successful of the entire GI movement: *FTA** at Fort Knox and the *Fatigue Press* at Fort Hood first appeared in the summer of 1968 and continued to publish more or less regularly for four years.

Another early newspaper was *The Bond*, the voice of the first formal organization of the GI movement, the American Servicemen's Union (ASU). The ASU was founded and is still headed by Andy Stapp, a socialist who purposively entered the Army in 1966 to organize among soldiers. With fellow militants Sp/4 Dick Wheaton, Private Paul Gaedke, and others, Stapp agitated among Fort Sill enlisted men through-

---

* No Army barracks is free of this pervasive *graffito* inscription, representing the standard recruitment lure of "fun, travel and adventure" and the disgusted soldier's reply, "Fuck The Army."

out 1967. At its formation, in December of 1967, the ASU proclaimed its purpose as the building of a world-wide GI union to unite all low-ranking enlisted people in a common struggle against the military. Its eight-point program demands the right to refuse illegal orders, the election of officers, collective bargaining power for enlisted men, rank-and-file control of court-martial boards, and other far-reaching changes in military service. While never enjoying the degree of success claimed by chairman Stapp, the ASU has been quite influential at many bases. ASU organizers were among the first activists at Fort Sill, Fort Benning, and a number of other bases.

The appearance of coffeehouses and a burgeoning GI press, in an atmosphere of mounting disillusionment over stalemate in Vietnam, set the stage for the first significant GI action. The Army's huge armored training center at Fort Hood experienced a particularly rapid deterioration of troop morale, especially among combat returnees, and throughout the Vietnam period witnessed extensive unrest and drug use (the base's copious marijuana supplies earned it the sobriquet "Fort Head"). The civilians who opened the Oleo Strut in the summer of 1968 thus met with an enthusiastic response; with the founding of *Fatigue Press*, a long history of successful GI activism began. The first political gathering of Fort Hood soldiers occurred in Killeen on July 5, 1968. A "Love-In" and countercultural festival was held in Condor Park, featuring rock music and anti-war speeches; approximately two hundred soldiers attended, most of them white. The atmosphere at the base grew considerably tenser in the following weeks, however, as thousands of troops were prepared for possible use against civilian demonstrators at the Democratic National Convention in Chicago—culminating in a dramatic and important act of political defiance among black troops. On the evening of August 23, over one hundred black soldiers from the 1st Armored Cavalry Division gathered on base to discuss their opposition to Army racism and the use of troops against civilians. After a lengthy, all-night assembly, which included a visit from commanding general Powell, forty-three of the blacks were arrested for refusal to follow orders. The action of the blacks was spontaneous and unrelated to the work of the white soldiers (reflecting a common pattern of parallel but separate development of dissent among blacks and whites), but the Oleo Strut GIs supported the brothers and helped with their legal defense. Because of widespread support for the resisters, especially among blacks, the Army's treatment of the Fort Hood 43 was not as harsh as it might have been; most received only light jail sentences. Far less lenient, though, was the command's treatment of Pfc Bruce Peterson, one of the principal activists at the Strut during this time and the first editor of *Fatigue Press*. Apparently hoping to make an example of Peterson and deter would-be followers, local police and military authorities hounded him constantly, trying to find a pretext for taking punitive action. Finally, in August, he was arrested for possession of a minute amount of marijuana, with bail set at an incredible twenty-five thousand dollars. Although the only grass found was residue in the lint of his trouser pockets and this was destroyed during the laboratory analysis, Peterson was found guilty and sentenced to eight years at hard labor! It was not until two years later that the conviction was overruled and he was finally released.

The San Francisco Bay Area has been in the vanguard of most of the radical movements in the United States during the past decade, and the GI movement was no exception. With the support of two local GI newspapers, *The Ally* and *Task Force*, area servicepeople were among the first to speak out in 1968. On April 27 a group of forty active-duty people marched at the head of an anti-war demonstration in San Francisco, the first time GIs led a civilian peace rally. Two months later, also in San Francisco, nine AWOL enlisted men (five soldiers, two sailors, one airman, and one Marine) publicly took sanctuary at Howard Presbyterian Church in moral opposition to the war. After a forty-eight-hour "service of celebration and communion," they were arrested by MPs on July 17. In the fall, the growing network of GI activists in the area laid plans for the largest servicemen's peace action to date—an active-duty contingent for the scheduled October 12 anti-war rally in downtown San Francisco. Among the efforts to mobilize area soldiers and distribute literature about the march was Navy nurse Susan Schnall's daring feat of dropping leaflets from an airplane onto five area military bases (for which she was later court-martialed). As the demonstration date approached, military authorities became nervous that a large number of GIs might become involved, and, in a manner that became standard whenever protests were planned, sought to prevent servicemen from attending. A communication from the Military Airlift Command in Washington, later anonymously released to *The Ally*, depicted the military's attitude toward even lawful dissent: it urged that "this demonstration be quashed if possible because of possible severe impact on military discipline throughout the services." On the Saturday of the actual march, soldiers at the nearby Presidio were detained for mandatory company formations, while special maneuvers and other diversions were held at several West Coast bases. Despite such obstruction, two hundred active-duty GIs and some one hundred reservists marched at the head of the demonstration, in what was the largest gathering yet of the expanding GI movement. Two days later, in an incident partly inspired by the show of antiwar strength on October 12, twenty-seven inmates of the Presidio stockade held a sit-down strike to protest the shooting death a few days earlier of fellow prisoner Richard Bunch and to call attention to unbearable living conditions—what became known later as the Presidio mutiny.†

III

As the GI movement emerged, civilian radical organizations played an important role in helping to sustain rank-and-file dissent. One of the first agencies to recognize the changes taking place within the Army was the Student Mobilization Committee (SMC) and its closely allied counterpart, the Young Socialist Alliance (YSA). Through leafleting and support work among soldiers, and sometimes through the efforts of members within the services, the SMC and YSA aided the development of GI organizations at a number of bases. One of the first examples of this co-operation was the GI-Civilian Alliance for Peace (GI-CAP) and the newspaper *Counterpoint* at Fort Lewis. Aided by SMC activists, GI-CAP developed into one of the most successful early GI-movement groups, with as many as fifty servicemen at regular weekly meetings. On February 16, 1969, the Alliance sponsored a peace rally in downtown Seattle, with two hundred active-duty people leading a crowd of several thousand. A few months later, the servicemen formed their own organization apart from the civilians and continued their work as an all-

† For a sensitive and penetrating account of the Presidio incident see Fred Gardner's *Unlawful Concert*.

GI group. The YSA also exerted influence on the GI move-ment through the in-service activities of members who con-sented to being drafted so that they could organize from within.

The greatest triumph for the YSA, and the incident that more than any other focused public attention on soldier dis-sent, was the case of the "Fort Jackson 8." In a highly volatile, racially mixed basic-training brigade, skillful political tactics and a vigorous civilian publicity and legal-defense campaign led to important gains for the GI movement. The Fort Jack-son movement began modestly in the early part of 1969 when Private Joe Miles (a YSA member before being drafted) in-vited fellow black soldiers to listen to taped speeches by Mal-colm X and to discuss the need for a GI organization. When the command heard of these sessions, the participants quickly fell victim to petty harassment and punishments. Miles himself was shipped out to Fort Bragg in February in a highly unusual one-man levy, on just three hours' notice. These reprisals only served to solidify the growing number of dissidents, however, and led to a significant increase in the level of opposition. Blacks were joined by white GIs in the formation of an organization called "GIs United Against the War in Vietnam" (a name that would be used by many other groups during the history of the GI movement). As their first act, the newly united soldiers drew up and circulated a peti-tion to the base commander, General James Hollingsworth, requesting permission to hold an on-base meeting to discuss the Vietnam War. After more than three hundred signatures were collected (in a few short weeks), Privates Steve Dash and Joe Cole attempted to present the petition to the general on March 2. Not surprisingly, they were rebuked by a sub-ordinate and told that the Army did not recognize the right of collective bargaining. Anticipating the command's denial of their request, GIs United had decided earlier to take the matter to court, and on March 16 their attorneys (among them Leonard Boudin of New York) announced that they would enter federal court to force Army compliance with freedom-of-speech provisions of the First Amendment. The filing of the suit proved an effective political tactic, attracting local GI support and drawing national press attention to the growing dissent movement at Fort Jackson.

With tensions between GIs United and the command

mounting, the situation reached a climax during an incident on March 20. On that evening, about one hundred members of Basic Training Company B-14-4 were lounging and wrestling on the barracks lawn, with perhaps another one hundred soldiers watching from barracks windows. What started out as a leisurely after-dinner gathering, though, quickly turned into a political meeting, as GIs United members José Rudder and Andrew Pulley, spotting an ideal opportunity to reach a large audience, began to rap to the assembled soldiers about Army harassment and the war. The brigade duty officer came by and attempted to "restore order" but was derided and cursed at by the increasingly unruly crowd. After a few tense minutes, the trainees dispersed, and what the Army later labeled a riot came to an end. The next day, nine leaders of GIs United were arrested (one was later released when it was disclosed that he had acted as an undercover agent). With support for the "Fort Jackson 8" growing on base and throughout the country, all charges against the accused were dropped within a few weeks.

The transfer of Joe Miles, meanwhile, merely compounded the Army's difficulties, for it led to the founding of another GI organization, at Fort Bragg. Soon after arriving in North Carolina, Miles successfully formed a second chapter of GIs United. With most of its support among Vietnam veterans, the group held a number of on-base meetings and was able to gain over a hundred signatures on a petition supporting the Fort Jackson 8. One of its first major activities was a federal court suit filed on May 19 seeking on-post distribution of their newspaper, *Bragg Briefs*. Four days later, Miles was once again shipped out in highly unusual circumstances—this time to Fort Richardson, Alaska, the U. S. Army's equivalent of Siberia. (With indomitable spirit, Joe then helped form another GIs United group, at Fort Richardson, and aided with the newspaper *Anchorage Troop!*.) The Fort Bragg organization grew rapidly despite (or because of?) such repressive tactics, and by July claimed a core membership of fifty soldiers, half of them Vietnam veterans, and had opened a headquarters at the "Quaker House," in Fayetteville.

As rank-and-file dissenters surfaced at an increasing number of bases, the YSA and other groups established formal civilian support operations, providing a measure of continuity to an otherwise unstable and precarious movement. Heart-

ened by the Fort Jackson case, the SMC in June 1969 launched
the *GI Press Service,* a newsletter designed to be a world-wide
information exchange and co-ordinating center for GI organizations. The *GI Press Service* exerted considerable influence
during the early stages of the GI movement, but it served
primarily to mobilize GI involvement in peace demonstrations and did not provide much support to local groups. The
previously mentioned American Servicemen's Union likewise
offered legal aid and information services to servicemen, but it
never enjoyed a widespread following (its claims of ten thousand paid members notwithstanding). Too often, its strident
rhetoric and sectarian political perspective turned off GIs
otherwise attracted to the ASU program and the idea of a
servicemen's union. The most important agency for providing
material aid to GIs was the United States Servicemen's Fund
(USSF). Evolving out of the coffeehouse-support work of
Fred Gardner and Donna Mickleson, USSF became the primary fund-raising and sustaining organization for dozens of
GI papers and coffeehouses throughout the world. With "Support Our Soldiers" offices in New York and Oakland, USSF not
only offered financial aid but assisted with films, entertain-
ers, speakers, legal defense, and staff workers. Another influential support organization emerging in 1969 was the Pacific Counseling Service (PCS). Initially known as the West
Coast Counseling Service, the group's first office was set up
in Monterey, near Fort Ord, by Unitarian minister Sid Peterman. Offering trained legal assistance to victimized servicemen,
the Monterey office in its first six months handled some
seven hundred legal cases and helped 120 soldiers obtain
conscientious-objector or other-type discharges. In October and
November of 1969 the group expanded, establishing additional offices in San Francisco, Oakland, and San Diego—with
a combined staff of twelve people (predominantly clergymen
and veterans) and an average weekly caseload of 150 GI complaints. Combining legal counseling with political support
work, PCS played a crucial role in the development of the
GI movement in the West.

IV

Bolstered by this support network, active-duty political
groups appeared at an increasing number of bases throughout

the country. By the summer of 1969, approximately thirty-five servicemen's newspapers were publishing within the United States, with additional journals surfacing every month. The new organizations, no longer as isolated or vulnerable as many of the earliest efforts, emerged as one of the most dynamic forces within the American peace movement, and during the Vietnam Moratorium actions in the fall of 1969, displayed growing unity and political strength. On October 11, nearly one hundred Fort Bragg soldiers, mostly Vietnam veterans, marched in a Moratorium demonstration in Fayetteville. On October 15, protests occurred in San Antonio and Colorado Springs. At Fort Sam Houston, approximately 150 soldiers signed a petition sponsored by the new paper *Your Military Left* requesting facilities for a meeting on post. Their plea was rejected, though, and the Moratorium gathering was held instead in downtown San Antonio. At Fort Carson, Vietnam veterans Tom Roberts and Curtis Stocker, editors of *Aboveground,* encountered a series of command restrictions aimed at preventing them from attending an evening demonstration in Colorado Springs. Despite the obstruction, later documented in an official Fort Carson memorandum leaked to the New York *Times,* the two managed to elude their would-be captors and joined seventy-five fellow soldiers for the anti-war observance in Acacia Park. A few days later, on October 20, the ASU chapter at Fort Lewis called a meeting at an on-post service club to discuss the war and the need for GI organizing; the gathering was broken up by MPs, however, resulting in the arrest of thirty-five GIs and three civilians.

As the country prepared for the second wave of Moratorium actions, in November, an extraordinary full-page ad appeared in the New York *Times* Sunday edition of November 9. A statement calling for an end to the war and support for the planned November 15 mobilization in Washington, D.C., was signed by 1,366 active-duty servicemen. Included among the signees were 189 soldiers in Vietnam, 141 GIs at Fort Bliss, and people on over eighty additional bases and ships throughout the world. The statement had a dramatic impact within the peace movement and was at least partly responsible for the success of the events on the following weekend. The huge November 15 peace rally in Washington (attended by some 250,000 people) was led by a contingent of over two hundred GIs, many of them associated with the local GI paper, *Open Sights*. The next day, fifty of the servicemen joined in a picket line at the Court of Military Appeals Building to protest the injustices of military law. A simultaneous rally in Los Angeles on the fifteenth also was headed by active-duty servicemen, including fifty Marines from Camp Pendleton.

The November Moratorium also witnessed a series of important actions by one of the most dynamic new groups of the GI movement, Fort Bliss "GIs for Peace." The organization was formally launched on August 17, 1969, when several hundred soldiers, many of them assigned to the Defense Language Institute (DLI), gathered in El Paso's McKelligan Canyon to proclaim the following purposes: to promote peace, secure constitutional rights for servicemen, combat racism, improve enlisted living conditions, and provide aid to the local chicano community. Through *Gigline*, an unusually well-written and articulate GI paper, the activists quickly attracted widespread local support—and as a result, encountered serious repression. Paul Nevins, a drafted Ph.D. student and the group's first chairman, was shipped out to Germany; *Gigline*'s first editor received abrupt orders to Vietnam; and three other leading organizers were suddenly transferred to different bases, just hours before a scheduled Moratorium protest. In all, ten soldiers received transfer orders in the organization's first five months of existence. New members always rose to fill the vacuum, though, and the group's activities proved remarkably successful. One of their first actions involved an anti-war protest at the traditional Veterans Day parade in El Paso. As weapons and marching units filed by in the November 11 pageant, nearly one hundred GIs boldly gathered across from the reviewing stand behind a huge banner reading "GIs for Peace." The response from soldiers forced to march in the parade proved embarrassing to the assembled commanders: hundreds flashed the "V" for peace sign or raised clenched fists in solidarity with the demonstrators. On Moratorium day, the group urged students at DLI to boycott the noon meal and gather for a period of meditation at a nearby chapel. Nearly a dozen plain-clothes men and officers showed up at the church to intimidate the protesters, but sixty soldiers braved the threats and carried out the prayer meeting as planned. The neighboring enlisted mess hall, meanwhile, was three fourths empty—despite the rare attendance of a huge contingent of officers. The anti-war up-surge culminated the following Saturday, when several hundred Fort Bliss soldiers marched at the head of a peace rally in downtown El Paso.

The third series of Moratorium protests, scheduled for December, produced two additional GI demonstrations, including one of the largest and most militant gatherings in the history of the GI movement. At Fort Bragg, a growing GIs United Against the War sponsored another rally in Fayetteville, this time attended by two hundred soldiers and two hundred civilians. The more significant action, however, came on December 14 in Oceanside, California. In the largest Moratorium demonstration in the country on that day, an estimated one thousand servicepeople joined a crowd of four thousand in a march and rally near Camp Pendleton. The event united black, white, and chicano GIs behind a strongly anti-imperialist and anti-racist program and marked the founding of an important new GI organization, Movement for a Democratic Military (MDM). Operating out of the "Green Machine" coffeehouse in Vista, Camp Pendleton Marines launched the paper *Attitude Check* and established MDM as an openly revolutionary organization. Their program called for the right to collective bargaining, constitutional rights for all servicepeople, abolition of the court-martial system and its replacement with a jury and court of peers, the end of officer privileges, the elimination of racism, freedom for all political prisoners, and an immediate pullout from Vietnam. During a visit to the area in February 1970, Marine Commandant General Leonard Chapman labeled MDM "a serious threat to the defense of this country." Because of internal disputes, however, Pendleton MDM faltered, and by the summer of 1970 split into factions, with a new paper, *All Ready on the Left*, replacing *Attitude Check*. Despite these difficulties at Camp Pendleton, the idea of MDM proved attractive to other radical servicemen. During the first half of 1970, the group's program and name were adopted at six other locations: San Diego, Long Beach Naval Station, El Toro MCAS, Fort Ord, Fort Carson, and Great Lakes Naval Training Center.

As GI organizing flourished, the factionalism that hindered MDM became evident at other bases, with several separate organizations often existing on one post at the same time.

Partly, this was the inevitable result of the rapid and spontaneous development of GI groups and the repressive, secretive atmosphere in which they were forced to operate. In some cases, though, it reflected sectarian differences among the new GI activists and their civilian supporters. At Fort Dix, for example, three groups were active during 1969 and 1970: *Shakedown* was published by GIs and SDS members affiliated with the local coffeehouse; *Ultimate Weapon*, founded by drafted YSA member Allen Meyers, maintained firm ties with the GI *Press Service*; and *SPD News*, circulated within the Special Processing Detachment,‡ closely followed policies of the ASU. Fort Knox holds what must be the record, however; for a time during the first half of 1970, four different soldier groups existed. One committee, consisting primarily of blacks, was quickly suppressed in early March when an on-post meeting of forty brothers was broken up by MPs and the group's leaders were placed in the stockade. Another, much smaller group, of whites, published the newspaper *EM-16*. The paper was edited by Progressive Labor Party member Private Mark Smith and apparently had only a limited circulation. A more established group of GIs who had worked on the coffeehouse effort continued to publish the old standby *FTA*. They were no doubt the most popular of the four. The final group, considering *FTA* too radical, adopted a more moderate, liberal tone with the newspaper *In Formation*.

No such divisiveness hindered soldier organizing at Fort Bliss. By adopting a broad, non-partisan approach, GIs for Peace successfully united a large number of servicemen and, despite a lack of civilian aid, carried on an extensive program of anti-war activity. One particularly effective demonstration occurred during a January 1970 visit to El Paso by Army Chief of Staff William Westmoreland. When the former Vietnam commander arrived in the city on the fifteenth to deliver an address, he was greeted by a picket line of eighty local soldiers. To avoid an embarrassing public confrontation, the general was forced to sneak in the back entrance of his hotel. The largest GIs for Peace gathering, indeed one of the largest in the history of the GI movement, was a March 15 rally in El Paso's McKelligan Canyon. Approximately two thousand

‡ SPD units were minimum-security detention centers for AWOL and other minor offenders.

people, including more than eight hundred servicemen, came together for a festival of political speeches and rock music, in a massive display of local anti-war sentiment.

V

As GI organizations proliferated and gained in strength during the spring of 1970, a number of groups attempted to focus GI resistance into co-ordinated national action. In March, the American Servicemen's Union national office in New York issued a call in *The Bond* urging enlisted men to organize a world-wide GI strike on April 15. While the actual results fell hopelessly short of expectations (reflecting the ASU's limited base of support), important actions did take place at Fort Lewis, Fort Dix, and Fort Carson. In the Fort Lewis stockade, over one hundred prisoners joined the strike action by boycotting the mess hall. At Fort Dix, seventy-five men in the SPD unit went on sick call together. At Fort Carson, a similar sick-call strike was held at a main post dispensary, assisted by an on-post visit by actress Jane Fonda. While the ASU scheduled strike actions on the fifteenth, *GI Press Service* urged its readers to join local demonstrations sponsored by the Student Mobilization Committee on April 18. Here again the appeal was largely ignored, although significant GI protests did occur in at least two locations. In Texas, one hundred soldiers from Fort Hood traveled to Austin for a mass peace rally held at the University of Texas. The eighteenth also witnessed the first GI demonstration ever in the state of Alaska. Organized by Fort Greely and Fort Wainwright soldiers working with the paper *Green Machine*, an anti-war rally in Fairbanks attracted more than one hundred servicemen. After gathering in the downtown area, the group of nearly five hundred demonstrators marched to the gates of nearby Fort Wainwright; among the speakers was a veteran GI organizer who flew up from Anchorage for the occasion: Joe Miles.

These initial efforts at co-ordination failed because of the sponsors' limited resources and because objective conditions were not yet favorable. Just one month later, though, on May 16, public furor over Cambodia and Kent State and support from the national peace movement resulted in success—the first effective national GI-movement action. In early 1970, the New Mobilization Committee, the largest civilian peace organization, established a special "GI Task Force" to mobilize the growing number of anti-war GIs and plan for nationwide demonstrations at military bases on Armed Forces Day, traditionally a day for honoring the military. When the Task Force initially issued its call, there was considerable doubt whether servicemen would participate. The unprecedented upheaval of the time, however, swelled the growing insurgency within the ranks and produced an overwhelming GI response. Demonstrations took place at twelve Army and Marine Corps posts, as well as a number of Air Force and Navy bases; in all, seventeen actions were held across the country, many at posts with no previous history of dissent. The huge anti-war upsurge forced the military to cancel regularly scheduled Armed Forces Day exhibitions at twenty-eight bases. The May 16 actions, summarized below, mark a major advance in GI organizing:

- At Fort Devens, about twenty GIs join several hundred civilians for the first rally ever attempted at this base. The paper *Morning Report* appears for the first time.
- Seventy-five soldiers and five hundred civilians gather for an anti-war march and rally outside Fort Meade.
- The first anti-war demonstration in the history of Anniston, Alabama, draws fifty Fort McClellan servicepeople and two hundred civilians.
- At Fort Benning, one hundred GIs and some three hundred civilians attend a "people's tribunal" on American war crimes.
- In Fayetteville, North Carolina, Rennie Davis, Jane Fonda, and Mark Lane address a crowd of 750 Fort Bragg soldiers and three thousand civilians in the largest Armed Forces Day rally in the country.
- At Fort Hood, over seven hundred soldiers march through the streets of Killeen and rally in a nearby park.
- At Fort Bliss, GIs for Peace and local students demonstrate against the war at the local University of Texas campus.
- The first anti-Vietnam protest in Manhattan, Kansas, attracts over one thousand people, including four hundred soldiers from Fort Riley.
- An MDM-sponsored rally in Colorado Springs draws thirty Fort Carson GIs and several hundred civilians.
- Tom Hayden raps to approximately two hundred Ma-

rines and several thousand civilians in a rally near Camp Pendleton.

▶ Fort Ord MDM sponsors a march and rally of more than three thousand people. Extra work assignments and riot-duty mobilizations limit the GI contingent to only one hundred.

▶ A festival and series of workshops near Fort Lewis draw sixty soldiers and two hundred civilians.

The events of Armed Forces Day not only demonstrated widespread anti-war sentiment within the ranks but sparked continuing political activity at many bases. Several groups made their initial appearance during the time, and a number of others experienced an increase in active-duty involvement. Perhaps just as importantly, the May 16 actions had great impact on the civilian community. The spectacle of simultaneous soldier demonstrations at twelve separate bases finally convinced people that sweeping changes were occurring within the Army and aroused renewed appreciation of the potential of GI resistance. As Abbie Hoffman quipped to the crowd at Fort Meade: "Behind every GI haircut lies a Samson."

One further attempt to focus and unify the anti-war movement within the ranks involved a second petition drive organized by *GI Press Service*. After the success of the November 1969 New York *Times* statement, the editors of *GI Press Service* embarked on an ambitious campaign to collect an even greater number of signatures and publish them in local newspapers across the country. Because of a lack of funds, the effort had to be abandoned after the summer of 1970, but in the few short months it was circulated, the plea for American withdrawal received massive support. The petition was signed by more than 1,740 servicemen from over one hundred bases and ships, including 364 soldiers at Fort Bliss, three hundred men in Vietnam, and eighty-four Marines at Iwakuni, Japan. That so many signed this second petition is particularly significant since, after the publicity generated by the first effort, many base commanders attempted to suppress the drive. I myself experienced such difficulties in June 1970 in a confrontation that led to important GI organizing work at Fort Hamilton.

Most of the members of the 26th Army Band stationed within the Fort Hamilton complex at Fort Wadsworth were professional musicians who had enlisted for duty as bandsmen to avoid a draftee infantry assignment in Vietnam; many were decidedly anti-military and outspoken in their views against the war. When the second *GI Press Service* petition came to our attention, thirty-five of the fifty-five men assigned to the unit agreed to sign. The Fort Hamilton commander, Major General Walter Higgins, would not allow such activities, however, and through a series of threats, forced the group to withdraw their names. An uneasy peace then prevailed for a few weeks, until an incident at a July 4 parade in New York led to renewed confrontation. Five women—four wives of band members and my fiancée, Monica—showed up at a parade in which the band was performing to demonstrate against the war. The action sparked a near riot among irate onlookers and generated considerable adverse publicity. Needless to say, the commanders at Fort Hamilton were outraged, and a few days later began a crackdown on the unit, imposing numerous restrictions and petty harassments.

The command's efforts backfired, however, for the band members decided to fight back. Thirty-six of us signed an Article 138 complaint (a seldom used but sometimes effective provision allowing servicemen to seek redress of grievances against superiors) and let it be known that we would not give in to further threats. When the command responded by issuing transfer orders to three of the most active dissenters (myself included), the group decided to take the matter to court and on July 23 filed a class-action suit in the Eastern District federal court in Brooklyn. From this point on, a sort of continuous confrontation took place. Nearly all military functions ceased, as the command was busied with legal defense and the enlisted men pursued the offensive: filing additional court actions, writing to Congress, and establishing a GIs United chapter. Although I was in fact transferred to Fort Bliss on July 24, the federal court agreed to maintain jurisdiction over the matter and review the facts. (In February 1971, Judge Jack B. Weinstein found that the transfer had been unconstitutional and ordered that I be returned to Fort Hamilton. The decision was overturned by the 2nd Circuit Court of Appeals in June 1971, however, and a further appeal to the Supreme Court was denied in early 1972.) The remaining GIs continued the fight, although eight of them also received orders during the first month. A newspaper, *Xpress*, was founded, and GIs United members participated in various peace demonstrations in the New York area. One of the group's most unusual and daring activities occurred at a civilian-sponsored demonstration on October 31. Led by Sp/4 Verne Windham, ten Fort Hamilton GIs marched up the streets of New York at the head of thousands of demonstrators—undoubtedly the movement's first anti-war Army band.

VI

While an increasing number of GIs articulated their opposition to the military through the standard methods of demonstrations, petitions, and the like, other soldiers expressed their political antagonisms through less sophisticated, often violent means. This was particularly so among inmates of military prisons. During the Vietnam period, nearly every major stockade erupted in some sort of rebellion, often resulting in serious property damage or personal injury. Army prisoner population tripled during the course of the war, by the end of 1969 totaling seven thousand—the majority non-white. Most of this increase resulted from opposition to the military and its mission in Vietnam. The Army's 1970 MacCormick Commission found that over 80 per cent of stockade inmates were charged with AWOL. An incredible 58 per cent were being held in pretrial confinement—held by their commanders' arbitrary power to imprison those considered undesirable. The commission admitted that every facility contained political activists, variously labeled as "antiwar, anti-army prisoners" and "determined dissidents." Inevitably, these men reacted with rage to the scandalous conditions within military prisons. Untrained and alienated guards, inadequate psychological aid and counseling, dilapidated and unsanitary buildings, poor medical and food services, an almost complete lack of rehabilitation, excessive brutality, and overcrowding led to frequent uprisings. The pattern of events in most of the revolts was dismally similar, and it would be too repetitive to describe them all here. Rather, we shall recount a few of the more significant incidents as an illustration of the explosive bitterness rampant in Army stockades.

One of the largest uprisings during 1968 occurred at Fort Bragg on July 23. Outraged at the beating of a black inmate, a group of black and white GIs seized control of the stockade and held out for over forty-eight hours before surrendering to armed troops from the 82nd Airborne. During 1969, a serious wave of rebellions erupted at Army bases throughout the country. The first occurred at Fort Carson on May 13, when blacks in the maximum-security section overpowered guards, constructed barricades, and kept three white MPs as hostages. A force of forty MPs was required to quell the rebels. On June 5, another uprising occurred at Fort Dix, when one hundred fifty prisoners took over three of the twelve buildings in the stockade and touched off a number of fires. Among the so-called "Fort Dix 38" later court-martialed on arson and riot charges were veteran activist Terry Klug and several other leading ASU organizers. The prison at Fort Riley witnessed particularly severe disruption, with three major uprisings in a period of just four months—on April 6, June 22, and July 21. The last involved more than two hundred men, who refused to participate in a work detail and then set fires to various parts of the prison. Two other stockades witnessed major revolts during this time, but in these instances violence was avoided. At Fort Ord, inmates who were denied access to reporters visiting the stockade called a protest meeting attended by one hundred fifty of the prisoners. On May 20, most of the five hundred soldiers in the prison joined in a non-violent boycott of the mess hall to publicize their demands for better conditions. Similarly, on June 14, one hundred fifty inmates in the Fort Jackson stockade staged a non-violent sit-in to protest the beating of a fellow prisoner.

Of all the military prisons in the country, none has a reputation of being more oppressive or has witnessed more rebellions than the Camp Pendleton brig. The prison was seriously overcrowded throughout 1969, with as many as nine hundred twenty men crammed inside a space designed for seven hundred fifty; beatings by untrained guards were frequent. Several incidents already had occurred prior to the summer of 1969: on December 7, 1968, and again on January 6 and April 19. On June 22, another violent brawl took place, this time leaving over twenty Marines injured. The climactic incident, however, came in September. An article had appeared in *The Nation* early in the month, provocatively titled "Andersonville by the Sea," which documented the inhumane conditions in the brig. The prison commander publicly refuted the charges and welcomed investigators to visit the prison to see for themselves. When reporters arrived, however, they were not allowed to speak to the inmates. On the night of September 14, a few hours after the reporters had left, the enraged prisoners vented their frustrations. One hundred fifty men from "B" Company surrounded a supply hut and burned it to the ground. When MPs arrived and counterattacked against B, "C" Company erupted and began smashing furniture, throwing equipment, and ripping out telephone wires. With fires raging and MPs firing tear gas at the two companies, "A" Company joined the rebellion. By the time the uprising was quelled, later in the night, the entire prison was a shambles.

As the Army's morale crisis deepened, the flood of drug users, returning AWOLs, and other military offenders completely swamped already overcrowded stockades and forced the establishment of minimum-security Special Processing Detachments. A limbo for men about to be discharged, SPD units contained many of the same kinds of people and had many of the same oppressive conditions as the stockades. They often became centers of GI resistance (underground papers circulated within several) and, not surprisingly, witnessed numerous rebellions. In one mid-1970 period, four major uprisings took place within a few short months. The first incident occurred on May 22, when GIs in the SPD unit at Fort Knox barricaded themselves in their barracks and refused to disperse until commanders agreed to negotiate their demands for better conditions. Two months later, the huge Fort Dix SPD witnessed a dramatic confrontation between minority troops and white commanders. On Wednesday evening, July 22, after a long series of racial injustices, 250 black and Spanish-speaking soldiers held a special meeting and marched to the unit Operations Room. The brothers were met along the way by a huge contingent of armed MPs, however, and, after some tense moments, decided to return to their barracks, thus averting what would certainly have been a bloody clash. The next few days saw continued meetings among the blacks, a series of isolated minor assaults, and the arrest of a number of leading organizers. Armored patrols and a 6 P.M. curfew were imposed, and a special, 175-man riot-control unit from Fort Meade was brought in to supplement local MPs. Peace was finally restored only when most of the men in the unit were granted thirty-day leaves and sent home. Blacks also played a leading role in an August 6 action at Fort

Belvoir, Virginia, when fifty GIs marched to the post MP headquarters to secure the release of an arrested black soldier. The fourth SPD incident occurred at Fort Ord. On August 12, MPs entered the unit to apprehend two detainees for slovenly appearance. Friends of the soldiers quickly came to their defense and began pelting the MPs with rocks and other debris, which led to the arrival of additional MPs and the start of a full-scale uprising. In the ensuing chaos, two mess halls were burned to the ground and a number of other buildings were damaged.

In addition to these prison revolts, violent uprisings of a general nature occurred at numerous bases, usually originating near enlisted barracks areas and labeled by military authorities as "race riots." While this characterization attempted to portray the incidents as indiscriminate clashes among low-ranking GIs, in fact most were of an anti-authoritarian nature; like many of the prison conflicts mentioned above, they often pitted black enlisted men, and whites as well, against white MPs and NCOs. One incident of this sort occurred at Fort Bragg on August 11, 1969, when a minor scuffle at a base enlisted men's club turned into a huge brawl. When armed MPs (all but one of them white) were called in to quell the disorder, the tense situation exploded in bitter fighting, involving some two hundred men and reportedly resulting in the hospitalization of twenty-five soldiers. Two of the largest outbreaks of the Vietnam period took place within a few days of one another in July 1970. On July 26, some two hundred soldiers at Fort Hood, most of them black, launched a major rebellion, closing off a six-block area of the base and clashing with MPs for several hours. Forty GIs were arrested in the incident, and a number of important buildings were damaged, including several re-enlistment offices. Four days later, a second massive rebellion erupted at Fort Carson. On July 30, approximately two hundred soldiers, again mostly black, took over a section of the post and pelted MPs with rocks, bottles, and other debris. The rebels dispersed before MP reinforcements arrived, and no arrests were made.

Perhaps the most tragic uprising of recent years took place on July 20, 1969, at Camp Lejeune. Occurring a few days prior to a scheduled embarkation of the 2nd Marine Division to the Mediterranean, the fighting left fourteen injured and resulted in the death of one white Marine, Corporal Ed

Bankston of Picayune, Mississippi. Arising out of a dispute over discrimination at a base enlisted men's club, the brawl soon turned into a black-versus-white melee near the 1st Battalion, 6th Marines, barracks area. Black and Puerto Rican GIs involved, most of them Vietnam veterans, later laid the blame for the incident not on any one particular act but on the accumulated frustrations of months of command harassment. Their interpretation was corroborated by the division's "Ad Hoc Committee on Equal Treatment and Opportunity," which had issued its findings months before the July 20 outburst. Obtained by the New York *Times* several weeks after the riot, the report contained the warning, apparently unheeded, that "an explosive situation of major proportions" existed on post. Although the committee was composed of seven officers and had been appointed by the base commanding officer, it found that "many white officers and NCOs retain prejudices and deliberately practice them"; the report verified that many off-base facilities were segregated and that black recruits were subjected to excessive harassment from MPs.

The differing responses to the Camp Lejeune riot, by the Marine Corps on the one hand and the black enlisted men on the other, is instructive of the gap separating the two groups in a supposedly homogeneous military organization, and helps explain why black GIs and white commanders remained at odds—despite official claims of improved relations. In a frantic law-and-order crackdown, the Camp Lejeune command installed huge bright lights and armed sentries along troop paths between barracks; three reaction forces were also created—equipped with tear gas, walkie-talkies, and loaded guns. Twenty-six Marines involved in the July 20 incident were flown back to the States from the Atlantic cruise for criminal action—twenty-four black and two Spanish-speaking men, but no whites. The blacks, meanwhile, apparently assuming that little if any satisfaction would come from official quarters, set up their own organization, the "Council of Concerned Marines," to defend themselves against command reprisals and continued racial abuse. Among the Council's activities were a petition campaign to free those arrested for the riot and an effort to form a network of elected representatives from the black minority within each company. At the same time, Marines aboard the U.S.S. *LaSalle* on cruise off the coast of Spain also organized to defend themselves. An organization was formed to work as an independent shore patrol for blacks (as protection from abuse by white MPs) and to press for more black representation in shipboard affairs. In the 2nd Marine Division, as in so many military units, a virtual state of war raged between minority servicemen and their white superiors.

Before continuing with our saga, it's important to look at the pattern of official reaction to resistance. Did repression increase or decrease with time? What impact did reprisals have on the level of unrest? These are crucial questions for understanding the GI movement, but they are not easily answerable, because of the military's decentralized handling of personnel matters. The services traditionally have relied on the discretion of local commanders in dealing with morale and disciplinary problems, and as a result their response to emerging GI dissent followed no consistent plan. Left to their own devices, officers generally reacted clumsily to anti-war protest and tended to be excessively harsh in dealing with resisters. As the movement gained in strength and service morale plummeted, though, the Pentagon recognized that a coherent policy was necessary and accordingly began to develop a more sophisticated response, on the one hand permitting certain innocuous forms of protest and cultural expression, and on the other unobtrusively isolating and discharging leading activists. One of the first signs of a slightly more conciliatory attitude was the introduction, in September 1969, of DoD Directive 1325.6, which set forth minimal guidelines on allowable dissent. More extensive innovations came during 1970, as the services launched a wide range of reforms and Project Volunteer experiments designed to remove the "irritants" of enlisted life. Thus, by the middle of 1970, the military had embarked on a policy of co-opting rather than bludgeoning GI resisters, hoping that new approaches would dissipate the swelling dissension in the ranks.

CHAPTER 4

ARMED FARCES

Most measures introduced to ameliorate the crisis came too late and were woefully inadequate. Indeed, many were merely formal acknowledgments of changes that had already taken place. New haircut regulations were announced, for example, only when commanders realized they could no longer enforce previous standards. Similarly, reveille was eliminated because soldiers were refusing to get up in the morning. At Fort Bliss, I remember, the 6 A.M. turnout had dropped to less than 50 per cent when the new regulation arrived. So it was with most of the Army's new policies. A few meager changes were made in obsolete personnel procedures, but the root grievances of enlisted life remained untouched. The arbitrary power of commanders, a repressive and undemocratic legal structure, and military racism received little attention. Moreover, the most important question—the purpose of the armed forces—was not even addressed. Servicemen were still being forced to fight in a discredited intervention few supported. As we shall see in the present chapter, beer in the barracks and an extra inch of hair could not erase opposition to Vietnam, nor halt growing GI resistance.

I

A key example of the strength of the GI movement was the rapid growth of organizing activity at Fort Lewis. When the original GIs United group and *Counterpoint* disappeared near the end of 1969, a new paper, *Fed Up*, began circulating at the post. The local ASU chapter also remained active and continued to enjoy substantial active-duty support. On January 21, 1970, for example, the Union sponsored a "trial of the military" at the University of Washington campus, which attracted over one hundred GIs and nearly fifteen hundred civilians. In the summer of 1970, the "GI Alliance" was formed (with the aid of PCS) and a second paper began appearing in the area, the *Lewis-McChord Free Press*. In addition to these major efforts, several smaller, short-lived sheets surfaced within individual companies and battalions during the middle of 1970. Two unit newspapers that attempted to expose and mobilize opposition to discrimination and harrassment in the 1st/3rd Air Cavalry were *First of the Worst* and *B-Troop News*. Yet another paper published briefly at the time was *Yah-Hoh*, the work of a unique group, "Hew-Kacaw-Na-Ya," composed of American Indian servicemen and -women. As a major Indochina embarkation point, Fort Lewis also witnessed considerable anti-war resistance, including a June 26, 1970, incident in which six conscientious objectors publicly refused orders to Vietnam.

Most major organizations experienced an occasional lull because of cadre turnover, repression, etc., but in nearly every instance new activists rose to sustain the struggle—as I found in my own experience at Fort Bliss. When I arrived in Texas, in July 1970, GIs for Peace was in a state of disarray, with the chairman and most of the active members discharged and no activities scheduled. Meetings soon began, however, and within a few months a GI coffeehouse had been set up in downtown El Paso, *Gigline* was again circulating, and the core membership had increased to twenty-five soldiers. On October 31, a major peace rally was held at the local University of Texas campus, with over four hundred GIs joining several hundred civilians to hear featured speaker Rennie Davis. Several months later, on March 21, 1971, GIs for Peace engaged in another successful action, this time countering a pro-war "Honor POW Day" held in El Paso. The POW Day sponsors (among them several officers at Fort Bliss) had expected a crowd of fifteen thousand people to kick off a massive "tell it to Hanoi" campaign. Because of the vigorous publicity and educational drive mounted by local peace forces, however, only a few hundred people actually showed—including approximately one hundred GIs for Peace members who had come to distribute anti-war literature.

An increasingly important element in sustaining political activity at Fort Lewis, Fort Bliss, and elsewhere was the growth of civilian support. By the end of 1970, this aid had become established in a number of major organizations. The most important of these continued to be the United States Servicemen's Fund (USSF), which during 1970 raised more than one hundred fifty thousand dollars to support the GI movement. After closing temporarily in August of 1970, the Servicemen's Fund reorganized in December and operated continuously until mid-1973. During 1971, USSF widened its influence, reaching out to an even greater number of servicemen's groups, including many in the Air Force and the Navy, and sponsoring the U.S. and East Asian tours of the Jane Fonda FTA Show. The Pacific Counseling Service also expanded during this time. Originating at four California locations during 1969, PCS extended its services to two other West Coast cities and made preparations for sending counselors to Asia. In May of 1970, an office was established in Tokyo, through the aid of "Beheiren," the Japanese Vietnam Peace Committee; four additional Asian offices were opened soon afterward. By May of 1971, PCS employed forty full-time staff workers at eleven project offices at the following U.S. and overseas locations:

San Francisco	Tokyo, Japan
Oakland	Iwakuni, Japan
Monterey	Koza, Okinawa
Los Angeles	Quezon City, Philippines
San Diego	Kowloon, Hong Kong
Tacoma	

In August of 1970, ex-Green Beret Sergeant Don Duncan and Jane Fonda launched a new civilian support operation in Washington, D.C., the GI Office. Acting as an unofficial ombudsman service, the Office helped channel GI grievances to Congressional workers and assisted with legal complaints. Another new organization providing legal aid was the "Lawyers Military Defense Committee" (LMDC), sponsored by the American Civil Liberties Union. The Committee's first office was established in Saigon at the end of 1970 and received nearly one thousand requests for service in its first year of operation. A second office opened in Heidelberg in 1972 and continues today as an important part of the struggle for GI rights in Germany. In 1971, the National Lawyers Guild also increased its support operations, opening the "Tricky Dix" project at Fort Dix and sending a number of lawyers to assist GI organizers in the Philippines and Okinawa. One of the most influential support groups of the GI movement was the "Chicago Area Military Project" (CAMP) and its newspaper *Camp News*. Founded in early 1970 as a counseling service for midwest groups, CAMP quickly enlarged its scope of interest; by early 1971, *Camp News* had emerged to replace *GI Press Service* as a world-wide GI-movement newsletter. For over three years, it carried on extremely valuable co-ordination and political-education work and served as the most authoritative information source available on servicemen's dissent.

One result of this support was an increase in the number of civilians working directly with soldiers at the local level. Recently discharged GIs, and in some cases outside civilian radicals, formed collectives and, often with the aid of USSF, provided legal counseling and other services to active-duty organizers. A number of observers, most notably Fred Gardner, have been highly critical of such arrangements, claiming that civilians often exploit GIs for sectarian political purposes and stifle spontaneous dissent. To a certain degree the criticism is valid, but it is also true that civilian workers impart needed stability and legal expertise to GI projects. Indeed, in some cases their presence sparked substantial political activity among servicemen. At Fort Ord, for example, a civilian collective in March 1971 started a new base paper, *P.O.W.*; within a few months, a new GI group emerged, the "United Soldiers Union." Similarly, civilians helped establish an important new organizing center and coffeehouse near Fort Campbell, in Clarksville, Tennessee. The center, known as the "People's House," was immediately successful, attracting over two hundred soldiers in its first six weeks and publishing the newspaper *People's Press*. The group's first major action occurred on April 10, when approximately three hundred people, many of them active-duty, demonstrated at the Clarksville federal building against the jailing of Lieutenant William Calley. The protesters demanded that the leaders responsible for the war, not low-ranking servicemen, be tried as war criminals.

With the growth of civilian support and a consequent greater degree of unity and self-awareness among base projects, the GI movement displayed increasing strength and political sophistication. For many groups, a simple anti-war perspective gave way to a broader anti-imperialist emphasis and a more thorough understanding of the failings of American society. One of the first indications of this co-ordination and heightened political awareness came early in 1971, with GI-movement support for the lettuce boycott organized by chicano farm workers in California. When Cesar Chavez's United Farm Workers (UFW) union called for a national boycott against firms refusing to negotiate, the Defense Department tripled its purchases from Bud Antle, Inc., and other non-union growers, in a conscious attempt to crush the strike. (The same strikebreaking tactics had been used during the UFW grape boycott several years earlier.) As word of the Pentagon's intervention against the strikers spread within the armed forces, the GI movement responded with a major appeal to support the Farm Workers. Nearly every GI group in the States distributed information about the strike and urged participation in the boycott. Several projects exerted pressure on local commanders to purchase only union lettuce, and throughout the country thousands of "Lifers Eat Lettuce" stickers (distributed by *Camp News*) began appearing at numerous bases. One of the more active campaigns against non-union lettuce occurred at Fort Lewis, where servicemen set up a daily picket line at the main gate and circulated petitions in support of the Farm Workers. On February 24, a petition with over five hundred fifty GI signatures was presented in Washington to Senator Henry Jackson. The UFW drive marked a major advance in the evolution of GI resistance. For the first time, soldiers and workers united in common political struggle, a classic alliance with profound implications for radical social change.

II

The GI movement in the Army reached its peak during the spring of 1971. The growing anti-military insurgency within the nation, dramatically evident in a massive upsurge in civilian peace action and the national emergence of "Vietnam Veterans Against the War" (VVAW), kindled an intense outpouring of soldier resistance. Nowhere was this more evident than in the center of anti-war activity at the time, Washington, D.C. Operating out of the "DMZ" coffeehouse, area soldiers published the paper *Open Sights* and established a wide network of organizers at local bases (including groups editing *The Oppressed* at Walter Reed Army Medical Center and *Liberated Castle* at Fort Belvoir). Throughout the Washington mobilizations—beginning with the encampment of some two thousand VVAW members in April, culminating in the giant peace rally of April 24, and continuing until the "Mayday" disruption in early May—active-duty GIs were deeply involved. When Vietnam veterans were threatened with forcible removal from the Mall on April 20, members of the 82nd Airborne Brigade (many of them combat returnees themselves) told the veterans they would refuse orders to interfere with their brothers. A few days later, on April 23, hundreds of enlisted people participated in the anti-war memorial service sponsored by the Concerned Officers Movement in Washington's National Cathedral. Despite Pentagon press announcements that those attending in uniform would be prosecuted, over three hundred servicemen and -women came to the ceremony in uniform; another four hundred showed up in civilian clothes. The next day, an estimated crowd of over three hundred thousand people marched against the war in the streets of Washington. Leading the demonstration was a contingent of over five hundred GIs, including groups from as far away as Fort Hood and Fort McClellan; many hundred more were among the vast crowd.

The Mayday civil disobedience actions planned for the following week posed a serious physical threat to government operations, and as a result, tens of thousands of policemen and soldiers were prepared for riot-control duty. Many of the GIs supported the aims of the demonstrators, however, and played a vital role in aiding their plans, providing counterintelligence on the nature of the riot-duty force. Because of its extensive support at area bases and its contacts with other GI projects, the DMZ was able to find out in advance which units were being prepared for civil duty and to monitor their preparations and movements. Leaflets were distributed at every affected base, including Fort Lee, Fort Eustis, and Quantico Marine Station, informing GIs of the aims of the protesters and asking that troop-movement information be called in to a central switchboard. The DMZ bustled with activity during this period and was able to provide an extremely accurate account of what military units were being mobilized. As it turned out, the government was able to control the fifteen thousand demonstrators without resort to military units and thus was saved the risks of calling out young servicemen against civilians. Nonetheless, the Mayday events raised serious questions about the reliability of American troops in politically sensitive riot-control operations.

GI projects endorsed the Mayday actions not just in Washington but at bases throughout the country. The GI Alliance at Fort Lewis displayed this solidarity in one of the most extraordinary undertakings of the GI movement—a mass sick-call strike. Like previous strike efforts, however, the May 3 sick-in encountered elaborate command countermeasures and repression and failed to attract the support necessary to halt post activities. In many units, officers came to work several hours early to check personally those going to sick call; and special medical dispensaries were set up inside barracks buildings. Threats, petty harassments, and extra duty were imposed on many potential GI Alliance supporters. Despite such measures, several post dispensaries reported three times the normal number of soldiers at sick call. Several training companies were forced to cancel duty because too many men were absent, and throughout the base GIs in various units boycotted the mess hall and engaged in other minor acts of resistance. While failing to disrupt base operations, the May 3 strike did demonstrate widespread defiance among enlisted men and was a sign of the increasing militance of the GI movement. The tactic was and still is a theoretically sound means of revolutionary struggle, but, as the Fort Lewis people later acknowledged, it could succeed only if supported by an elaborate network of activists in every barracks and small unit—a level of organization seldom if ever achieved within the GI movement.

As in 1970, the traditional pro-military displays of Armed Forces Day became the target of co-ordinated protests from GIs at many different bases. In 1971, however, a stronger and more politically advanced movement organized the May 15 demonstrations without outside assistance and successfully carried out the largest united action of the Vietnam period. On "Armed Farces Day," as it was called, political gatherings occurred at nineteen separate posts, including nine Air Force and Navy bases (see Chapter 6). The largest soldier actions of the day occurred at Fort Lewis, Fort Bragg, Fort Bliss, and Fort Hood. In Tacoma, Washington, the GI Alliance

climaxed its vigorous spring campaign with a people's fair attended by over seven hundred local servicemen from Fort
Lewis and McChord AFB. Armed Farces Day also attracted
major support at Fort Bragg, where over three hundred soldiers braved heavy rainstorms for a march and rally in Fayetteville. The day before, twenty-nine members of the local Concerned Officers Movement had published an ad in the
Fayetteville *Observer* endorsing the aims of the protest. At
Fort Bliss, GIs for Peace continued to prosper, with a festival
of some six hundred GIs and seven hundred civilians at Mc-
Kelligan Canyon. A fourth major action occurred at Fort
Hood, where the newly formed "Spring Offensive Committee"
sponsored a march and rally in Killeen. Among the more than
five hundred soldiers present were thirty men who had traveled all the way from Fort Polk, Louisiana.

The upsurge of GI dissent continued into the weeks following Armed Farces Day, with Memorial Day protests in Beaufort, South Carolina, and in Washington, D.C. At Beaufort,
fifty Marines and a hundred fifty civilians conducted a memorial service for the war dead, laying a black wreath on the
grave of a Vietnam veteran. The action marked the founding
of a new GI paper, *Chessman II*, distributed among Marines
at Beaufort Marine Corps Air Station and nearby Parris Island
Marine training center. On the same day, the GI group at
Walter Reed Hospital, in Washington, joined with VVAW
in sponsoring an anti-war service at an on-post chapel. Approximately two hundred soldiers joined in the ceremony.

III

The Oleo Strut/*Fatigue Press* project was one of the most
consistently successful organizations of the GI movement.
When the CBS television network produced a documentary
on GI dissent in late 1971, they selected Fort Hood as the
subject of their inquiry. The choice was an appropriate one,
for few groups could match it either in mass participation
or innovative political tactics. In the summer of 1971, for
example, they managed to link the struggles of stockade inmates and regular soldiers in an important display of the
strength of GI organizing. The episode grew out of a huge
uprising in the Fort Hood prison on December 20, 1970.
Sparked by the refusal of guards to provide medical care for

a sick prisoner, the rebellion left much of the stockade destroyed and required the intervention of some one hundred riot-equipped guards. More than six months later, Fort Hood authorities suddenly decided to prosecute inmates Kevin Harvey and John Priest for their role in the December 20 incident. The move created a furor at the base and prompted the newly formed "Ft. Hood United Front" (successor to the Spring Offensive Committee) to embark on a vigorous political defense campaign. A petition demanding release of the two men was drawn up and signed by nearly one thousand soldiers in a matter of weeks. On September 12, approximately seventy-five people attended a "Free Harvey and Priest" picnic at Stillhouse Lake. Afterward, thirty of the demonstrators were arrested in a confrontation with local police, which focused further attention on the Harvey and Priest case. Three days later, all charges against the two were dropped, largely due, according to their military defense lawyers, to the efforts of the United Front.

Perhaps the most significant and imaginative program developed at Fort Hood during 1971 was a boycott of the Tyrrell's jewelry store in downtown Killeen. The Tyrrell's shop, part of a nationwide chain with locations in many military towns, was notorious for its exploitive sales practices, including use of the military command system to extract credit payments. After hearing numerous complaints from area soldiers, the Fort Hood committee decided that action against Tyrrell's might be an important way to better serve people on base and work for direct change in local conditions. The boycott was announced in May, with the following set of demands: 1) stop sidewalk solicitation and high-pressure tactics, 2) stop the exploitation of homesickness, 3) end the use of the military as a collection agency, and 4) take down the hypocritical "Vietnam Honor Roll" (of customers who "have given their lives in Vietnam"). When picketing began, in late May, the effort met with immediate success, attracting many new GIs to the group. By the third night of the action, June 1, about fifty people were participating in the picket line, and Tyrrell's sales volume had dropped to zero. Not surprisingly, local authorities were infuriated and quickly tried to quash the action. Ten of the demonstrators (eight of them GIs) were arrested on charges of conducting an illegal secondary boycott, with bail set at $2,200 each. The group responded by organizing another mass picketing for June 30, in defiance of police threats. On that day, over one hundred GIs showed up at the store expecting that they, too, would be arrested. Instead, the store managers and town officials decided to avoid another embarrassing confrontation, preferring to close the shop; the GIs scored an easy victory. The next night, the store was back in operation but so, too, were the boycotters, with forty GIs and civilians again walking the picket line.

Following the Oleo Strut's success with the Tyrrell's action, GI organizations in other parts of the country began adopting the boycott themselves. Picket lines appeared near Fort Bragg, in Norfolk, in Oakland, and at Newport. In June, various GI groups in the Southern California area announced that they, too, were joining in the boycott. By the end of the summer, stores near eleven separate bases were being picketed, and the national operations of the Tyrrell's chain were being seriously affected. At several bases, local stores acceded to some of the GIs' demands. In late September, the Tyrrell's regional manager in Southern California approached the PCS office in San Diego (acting as co-ordinator of local boycott efforts) and agreed to negotiate some of the GI demands. In October, the New York USSF office also was contacted by a Tyrrell's attorney seeking to establish national negotiations. The Tyrrell's boycott was the beginning of a recognition within the movement that basic GI grievances were becoming increasingly important to the new soldiers entering the Army. As fewer men faced the threat of combat and the number of service projects declined, the GI movement changed its primary focus from the war and imperialism to the conditions of enlisted life—a point we shall examine more fully in Chapter 7.

While withdrawals from Vietnam in the long run sapped the strength of soldier resistance, the immediate effect was to exacerbate the internal crisis, by increasing the number of disgruntled combat veterans at stateside bases. Indeed a principal reason for continued dissent within the Army in 1971 was the contagious defiance of military authority that returnees spread to other troops. The General Accounting Office confirmed this in a 1972 study that stated that Army operations had been seriously disrupted by the reassignment to stateside units of Vietnam veterans, described as "extremely difficult to motivate." One of the main centers for combat veterans was Fort Bragg, and accordingly the *Bragg Briefs* organization and "Haymarket" coffeehouse prospered. Approximately fifty GIs were regular members of GIs United, and *Bragg Briefs* enjoyed an on-post circulation of over seven thousand. One measure of the group's influence came in March 1971, when approximately seventeen hundred Fort Bragg soldiers signed a petition requesting on-post facilities for the Jane Fonda anti-war entertainment show. Another illustration of the disruptive role of Vietnam veterans occurred during the redeployment of the 173rd Airborne Brigade to Fort Campbell in September. The return of the battle-hardened unit was marked by a lavish welcome-home ceremony, including a personal visit from Secretary of Defense Melvin Laird. When the Secretary arrived, however, he was greeted by an anti-war petition signed by 250 of the men (collected in just four days) and by a picket line of thirty GIs outside the main gate.

Another important example of the persistence of anti-war organizing was the emergence, in the summer of 1971, of a new soldier group at the isolated desert outpost of Fort Huachuca, Arizona. Soon after launching the appropriately titled paper *Where Are We?* the all-GI organization embarked on one of the most unusual actions of the GI movement. In an unprecedented decision within the Fort Huachuca command, the group was granted a request to solicit for an anti-war petition on post and to set up tables for this purpose in front of the main PX. It was the first time any GI group had succeeded in obtaining permission to exercise First Amendment petition rights on base. It probably will remain the last, too, for the effort met with astounding success. On the appointed day, July 31, 540 people signed the petition, including 143 Vietnam veterans and twenty-three officers. The *Where Are We?* staff reported that at times during the day GIs were queued up in long lines waiting to sign. Subsequent requests to repeat the petitioning were denied, and the petition thus had to be circulated surreptitiously thereafter. When it was finally presented to Representative Morris Udall in the fall, 811 active-duty servicepeople had signed it.

One of the most vigorous new organizations appearing during the summer was the GI Co-ordinating Committee (GICC) in San Antonio—founded in late July at a meeting of some two hundred servicemen from Fort Sam Houston and nearby Air Force bases. The Committee's first action came in early August, with a three-day series of anti-war actions to commemorate the bombing of Hiroshima and Nagasaki; on the last day, one hundred fifty GIs participated in a march in downtown San Antonio. A month later, GICC played host to a performance of the Jane Fonda Show which attracted some fifteen hundred servicemen. In the fall, the group continued its activities with another, more ambitious series of political protests. On October 13, approximately seventy-five GIs and airmen joined two hundred other people for an anti-war march through downtown San Antonio. On November 6, fifty servicemen traveled to Houston for a regional peace rally, and on November 20, seventy-five soldiers joined a march called by the local chicano community to protest police brutality.

The GI Co-ordinating Committee also was one of four Army groups that sponsored anti-war activities on Veterans Day 1971—as Vietnam veterans and other soldiers attempted to recapture the original meaning of Armistice Day. In San Antonio, over one hundred fifty soldiers and airmen marched from Mannke Park to the gates of Fort Sam Houston for a short memorial service, and then to nearby Brackenridge Park for a speech by Tom Hayden. At Fort Campbell, over two hundred GIs, many of them from the 173rd Airborne, also marched to the gates of the base for an anti-war rally. At Fort McClellan, GIs and WACs sponsored a rally at the entrance to the post and a march to a nearby park which attracted seventy-five servicepeople and fifty civilians. The most extraordinary event of the day occurred in Killeen, where the Ft. Hood United Front again displayed great strength— and again clashed with local authorities. When city officials refused to grant their request for parade permits, the United Front decided to proceed with plans for an October 25 demonstration. On the day of the march, about two hundred people assembled in front of the coffeehouse, with another three hundred waiting hesitantly nearby; most were active-duty soldiers. As soon as the demonstrators stepped off, however, Killeen police moved in and began mass arrests. In all, 118 people were placed in jail, including ninety-one servicemen.

IV

The Veterans Day actions marked the end of the era of mass anti-war demonstrations within the ground forces. As the Army's role in Vietnam ebbed and enlisted manpower levels dropped, the resistance movement entered a difficult, new period. By the fall of 1971, the changing nature of enlisted service and the evolution of the air-war strategy began to alter the GI movement, reducing the level of soldier participation and forcing many projects to grope for new political directions. In the search for new approaches, the Ft. Hood United Front again assumed a vanguard role, demonstrating that political action could be sustained in a "peacetime" Army if properly focused on the basic grievances of enlisted life. Continuing their emphasis on local issues and recognizing the vital importance of the struggle against racism, the Front, in November 1971, began a major effort to combat discriminatory policies and, in an important but rarely achieved political alliance, managed to join forces with a vigorous new organization of black activists.

The effort was sparked by a visit to Fort Hood by Congressional Black Caucus member Louis Stokes (D-O.) and the subsequent formation of the all-black "People's Justice Committee." After a November 15 meeting with the congressman, black GIs decided that little or no immediate relief would come from official quarters. Led by activist Wes Williams, the brothers met later that evening at the Oleo Strut and agreed that their only defense against discrimination lay in an independent political organization. Because of the effective leadership of Williams and a strong anti-racist commitment among members of the United Front, the two groups established a close working relationship. On December 4, they cosponsored a small rally urging freedom for political prisoners, attended by one hundred fifty people. As with so many GI activists, Williams' successful organizing made him the target of command efforts to contain his activities, first through co-optation and then by repression. The base commander, General Seneff, tried to persuade him to lead a command-administered racial-harmony program. Williams refused, though, and shortly afterward was handed court-martial charges for possession of marijuana. Wes's trial became a major political case, as the People's Justice Committee, with help from the Oleo Strut, leafleted extensively throughout the base. Because of the flimsy nature of the charges and the widespread support for Williams on post, he was acquitted, and quietly discharged a few days later. Despite his departure, the two groups maintained close relations and worked together more or less harmoniously for nearly six months.

Despite the political advantages of GI unity, the black-white alliance forged at Fort Hood did not spread elsewhere. In 1971, as throughout the GI movement, minority troops and whites continued to pursue separate paths, with the burden of resisting racism and repression in most cases falling on blacks alone. On October 26, about one hundred fifty mostly black soldiers in the Fort Gordon stockade engaged in a major rank-and-file rebellion. When prison officials refused to grant emergency leave to one of the inmates, the angry soldiers, fed up with mistreatment and racial discrimination, began a four-hour rock-throwing melee. A barracks building was burned to the ground and several prisoners were injured. A few weeks later, black enlisted men and women at Fort McClellan also became embroiled in a militant confrontation with authorities. On the night of November 13, a group of over one hundred blacks, most of them WACs, gathered to protest racist insults to which several of them had been subjected earlier in the evening. The group marched past the officers' quarters area and demanded a special meeting with command officials for the following Monday morning. Approximately 140 blacks (half of them WACs) showed up for the November 15 assembly but quickly became frustrated and impatient with the command's sophistry. The angry crowd shouted down a race-relations officer and a black major. The militance of the blacks panicked the assembled commanders, and MPs were called in to arrest the entire 140-person group.

The winter of 1972 marked the inevitable decline of GI organizing in the Army. The winds of change sweeping through the military at last weakened the basis of GI support and swept away many leading servicemen's organizations. By spring, several previously successful groups had vanished: Fort Bliss, Fort Huachuca, Fort McClellan, Fort Jackson, and other bases were now without rank-and-file protest. Of the groups that remained, many were in a state of turmoil, adopting different organizational approaches and searching for new political tactics; as mentioned earlier, many projects began to concentrate on local concerns. In April of 1972, however, the decline of anti-war protest among soldiers was interrupted by the intensive American bombing of North Vietnam. As the Nixon administration escalated U.S. involvement in response to the NLF Easter offensive, some bases experienced a brief resurgence of mass activity.

At Fort Sam Houston, ten GIs, all of them conscientious objectors and activists with *Your Military Left*, were arrested on April 14 for disrespect and insubordinate remarks about American bombing in Indochina. The next evening, three hundred servicemen from the area attended a benefit concert to raise funds for legal services for the objectors and to protest the air war. After the benefit, many of those attending joined a candlelight march and vigil to support the ten soldiers. At Fort Hood, the Oleo Strut/*Fatigue Press* project temporarily recovered from a period of declining fortunes to engage in one last anti-war campaign. A petition demanding an immediate end to the war was circulated and signed by over twelve hundred GIs.

As American bombs fell on Indochina with increasing severity, clouded in a shroud of Pentagon secrecy, a handful of GI-movement activists and Vietnam veterans in the New England area established an unprecedented world-wide intelligence network, dubbed the "Ad Hoc Military Buildup Committee," to monitor the mobilization of American forces. Hoping to enlighten the American people on the extent of the U.S. attack, the Cambridge-based Committee began a massive information-gathering operation among anti-war servicemen throughout the United States and Asia. Drawing on communications from civilian counselors and GIs in Japan, Okinawa, the Philippines, Thailand, Hawaii, and some twenty-five bases in the United States, the Committee was able to disclose secret American military preparations before they were publicly announced. On April 13, for example, the group reported that the 548th Reconnaissance Group, at Hickam AFB in Hawaii, had been "drawing up extra large targeting charts for Hanoi and Haiphong." The notice preceded by two days the barbarous attack against those cities. Through its extensive contacts among GI anti-war groups, the Committee was able to accurately predict the movement of 33,000 men, 650 planes, and over forty ships into the war zone during its two weeks of operation. Like the Mayday actions in Washington a year earlier, the Committee's work indicated that the loyalties of many troops lay not with their commanders but with the people.

Despite this response to the air-war escalation, the overall trend of dissent in the Army was unmistakably downward. The "winding down" of the war, which relieved soldiers of further responsibilities in Vietnam; a decline in enlisted manpower levels, with the size of the Army reduced nearly fifty per cent in three years; and extensive Volunteer Army reforms, eliminating many of the Spartan customs of military life—all played a major role in the transformation of the GI movement. The principal cause of the decline, however, was the Pentagon's December 1971 decision to permit thousands of low-ranking soldiers early discharges. In a drastic campaign to rid itself of potential resisters, the Army announced that overseas returnees and troops with less than six months service need only ask to receive an immediate honorable discharge. For many disgruntled soldiers, the offer was like a dream come true, and tens of thousands of them rushed to take advantage of the program, causing a further steep drop in manpower levels. Most of the people affected—Vietnam veterans and short-timers—were precisely those with the strongest political commitment, and their sudden departure undermined many GI organizations. While the "early out" program and the end of ground combat in Vietnam thus decimated resistance within the Army, the movement continued to grow among sailors and airmen, as we shall see in Chapter 6.

CHAPTER 5

OVER THERE

The crisis within the ranks has been a pervasive and deep-rooted phenomenon, extending to every segment of the military and to every major outpost in the world. The same kind of resistance that appeared in the United States has developed wherever servicemen are stationed, particularly within the Army's 190,000-man garrison force in Germany. While generally following the patterns of dissent in the States, the GI movement in Europe has displayed unique features which reflect specific local conditions. Political activity is considerably more difficult than in the United States, because of the military's stringent personnel policies overseas: all political demonstrations, no matter what the nature, are forbidden. Dissent is also hindered by the physical and cultural isolation of American bases and the almost complete lack of off-base civilian support. Black soldiers face particularly oppressive circumstances in Europe, totally cut off from black civilians and isolated in a completely white, often racist German population. Indeed, discrimination against non-whites is notorious among many native landlords and bar owners. All enlisted people face special hardships in Europe, because of poor housing conditions and dilapidated barracks, frequent assignment to field duty, and a more rigid enforcement of military discipline. These conditions, coupled with opposition to the Indochina intervention, sparked a long history of GI resistance within the Seventh Army in Germany.

I

The GI movement abroad started slowly, almost imperceptibly, with very little of the individual heroism or public demonstration that occurred in the United States. Without media coverage and unaided by a sympathetic civilian peace movement, such acts would have been self-defeating. Instead, resistance in Europe first became evident in desertion. Beginning as early as 1966, American soldiers in Germany began streaming from their bases in mass numbers, first to Amsterdam for passage to France, and later to Sweden. Throughout 1967 and 1968, thousands of GIs deserted their units, often causing severe personnel shortages; some units, such as the 509th Airborne Battalion, in Mainz, experienced a 10–20 per cent AWOL rate. By mid-1967, these desertions became increasingly political, with troops not merely hiding from authorities, but speaking before the press and spreading the word to other soldiers. Out of these efforts evolved the first GI organizing activity in Europe: *RITA Notes*, appearing in 1967, and *Act*, published in Paris in January of 1968. Written entirely by "self-retirees," often with a press run of up to twenty-five thousand, these early sheets related the experiences of and reasons for desertion, and informed GIs where they could receive help. While those associated with *Act* also encouraged on-base political action, other early GI exiles, particularly those associated with a second Paris-based paper, *Second Front*, contended that desertion was the only means of political resistance within the Army and that active-duty organizing was impossible. For a time, a major ideological debate raged over the question, but the matter was resolved before long by the appearance of the first GI newspapers and anti-war demonstrations among troops in Germany.

A number of political actions occurred during 1968 and 1969, but they were generally small, clandestine affairs and received little public notice. One of the first to attract press attention took place in May of 1969 at Kaiserslautern. Despite threats of immediate arrest, approximately fifty soldiers gathered across from the Daenner Kaserne enlisted barracks and distributed leaflets urging fellow troops to oppose the war. Afterward, the GIs published two issues of a newspaper entitled *The Ash*, one of several underground papers that emerged in mid-1969. In Baumholder, members of the American Servicemen's Union published the Baumholder *Gig Sheet*. Other papers appearing at the time included *Graffitti*, edited by Sp/4 Bruce Scott in Heidelberg; *Speak Out*, published in Hanau; and *Venceremos*, written by members of the 97th General Hospital, in Frankfurt. As the pace of activity accelerated, another public protest occurred, in September

1969, at Grafenwöhr, with over one hundred GIs gathering for a series of meetings to oppose the war and the military justice system. During the Moratorium demonstrations in October, an anti-war meeting and film-showing in Augsburg attracted one hundred GIs. In November, a group of German and American civilians working with the paper *We've Got the brASS* in Frankfurt opened the first GI coffeehouse in Europe, "The First Amendment." The center met with an enthusiastic response, on Sundays becoming a favorite gathering place for the growing number of anti-war soldiers in southern Germany.

The most militant and effective political organizing in Germany occurred among black soldiers. By the winter of 1970, blacks at nearly every base in the country had formed independent black organizations, usually intended as cultural or educational associations but often acquiring political character during periods of crisis. As the number of these groups increased, so did efforts to establish some sort of co-ordination. Through the work of Sp/5 Lincoln Ashford and others, a central "Defense Committee" was set up, with representation at some twenty-five different posts and as many as one hundred GIs at monthly meetings. Three of the most active local chapters were the "Black Action Group," from the Panzer Barracks at Stuttgart; the "Black Dissent Group," from Smiley Barracks at Karlsruhe; and "Unsatisfied Black Soldiers." The latter group, centered in the Mannheim/Heidelberg area, was by far the largest, with numerous supporters at Patton, Coleman, Mannheim, and Turley barracks. They published the paper *About Face* and were principal sponsors of one of the most important events of the GI movement.

During the spring of 1970, the blacks issued a "Call for Justice," asking soldiers throughout Germany to assemble at the University of Heidelberg on July 4 for a meeting to discuss the grievances of enlisted men. Nearly one thousand active-duty servicemen, most of them black, showed up for the Heidelberg conference, the largest gathering of the GI movement in Europe. The July 4 assembly was important not only for the large number of GIs involved but for the remarkable political awareness displayed by those attending. The proclamation issued at its conclusion was a clear and detailed statement of the demands of black soldiers:

1. All GIs out of Southeast Asia now.
2. Withdraw all U.S. interests from African countries.
3. Establish an investigating committee to review all cases of GIs, especially black and Puerto Rican, in the Mannheim stockade.
4. Establish a committee of EMs to approve all confinement orders of GIs.
5. Establish a record review board to eliminate discriminatory policies. Abolish the present promotion board.
6. Abolish the present IG [inspector general] system, and replace it with a civilian advisory board.
7. Establish an effective committee to advise about-to-be-discharged GIs on what is really available in educational and occupational opportunities.
8. Hire more blacks in civilian jobs connected with the Army.
9. Initiate noncredit college preparatory classes to help GIs, regardless of color, to pass college entrance exams.
10. Equal and adequate housing for black GIs with families.

The meeting not only provided great impetus to black organizations but inspired some white soldiers as well. At Patton Barracks, for example, whites formed "Soldiers for Democratic Action" and began publishing the paper *Call Up*.

The growing radicalism of blacks in Germany became dramatically evident in a series of major rebellions in the spring and summer of 1970. As in the United States, tensions between white authorities and black GIs exploded in frequent confrontation. Perhaps the largest of these uprisings occurred on March 13, 1970, in the notoriously brutal and overcrowded Mannheim stockade. Following the beating death of a fellow prisoner, hundreds of inmates, most of them black, took control of the prison, setting fire to numerous buildings and causing tens of thousands of dollars' worth of property damage. The rebels were subdued only after local MPs were reinforced by some one hundred German policemen armed with dogs and fire hoses. Two months later, growing friction within the 1st Battalion/26th Infantry, at the Hohenfels training area, resulted in another major incident. Blacks in the unit had tried repeatedly but unsuccessfully to bring demands for better treatment before higher authorities. On May 21, when seventy-five of the brothers were denied a request to see

division commander Brigadier General Marshall Garth, sub-
merged frustrations erupted in violence. That evening, a fragmentation grenade exploded inside a crowded mess hall, injuring ten soldiers. Commanders attempted to blame the assault
on leading black organizer Sergeant James Hobson, but testimony at the trial of this former Chicago gang leader and Vietnam veteran showed that, in fact, he had attempted to re-
strain the brothers. A few days later, on May 24, violence
also flared in the 3rd Infantry Division at Schweinfurt—
sparked by a German merchant's refusal to serve blacks. The
angry troops went on a rock-hurling, window-smashing spree
and touched off a brawl at the Ledward Barracks enlisted
men's club. Later, one hundred fifty blacks and armed MPs
squared off in front of 1st Brigade headquarters, but further
conflict was avoided. Fighting also occurred at McNair Barracks, in Berlin, on August 20. A scuffle between a white
NCO and a black GI at an enlisted men's club turned into
a bitter clash between MPs and black troops, reportedly injuring some twenty-five soldiers. Alarmed at this growing black
revolt, the Pentagon dispatched Deputy Defense Secretary
Frank Render and a fourteen-member commission to Europe
in the fall of 1970 to investigate the complaints of minority
troops. The Render team returned with alarming accounts of
"acute frustration" and "volatile anger" among blacks, and reported that at Mannheim and Karlsruhe they encountered
groups openly advocating armed struggle within American
cities.

While military commanders often portray rank-and-file con-
vulsions as solely the result of racial divisions, in fact the roots
of enlisted resistance go much deeper, with whites often shar-
ing the same bitterness and outrage as blacks. The spread of
anti-war, anti-military feelings and the oppressive conditions
of GI life in Germany led to militance among whites as well
as blacks—as strikingly illustrated by events at Nellingen in
the summer of 1970. The arrival of a zealous new commander
and an increase in harassment and disciplinary measures in
the 903rd HEM Company created a virtual war within the
unit. On July 21, after a soldier was unjustly placed in pretrial
confinement, a Molotov cocktail exploded outside the company orderly room. When the new captain responded by jailing two men as suspects, the GIs fought back with two additional fire-bombings, on August 10th and 24th, which

damaged the commander's office. Similar unrest developed in most of the other units at Nellingen as well, as evidenced in an increasing number of incidents of minor sabotage, such as flattenings of officers' tires and telephoned bomb threats. After months of mounting dispute over racism and harassment, resistance at the base reached a climax on September 21. Following a weekend of growing friction and frustrated attempts to negotiate with officers, black and white GIs threatened to blow up the entire base. Their warnings were not idle threats, for two fire bombs had already gone off in the early morning at an MP station near the base gate. Frightened commanders responded by mobilizing truckloads of MPs and imposing a 6:30 P.M. curfew. At about 9 P.M. that evening, however, approximately one hundred GIs deliberately broke the curfew and marched through the base shouting "Revolution" and "Join Us" to fellow GIs. Several hours later, the men returned to their barracks—but only after a pledge by provost marshal Lieutenant Colonel R. McCarthy that no action would be taken against them. Although repression and reprisals against leading activists continued, the events at Nellingen set an important precedent for black-white unity. As one black soldier told a reporter for *Overseas Weekly*: "There is no racial problem among E-5s and below . . . that's one thing our demonstration proved."

Similar examples of resistance took place at numerous other bases. On September 1, 1970, *The Wall Street Journal* published a startling tale of drug use, black militance, and dissent in one of the Army in Europe's elite nuclear missile units, the 1st Battalion/81st Artillery, at Neu Ulm. On August 20, the unit was wracked by a serious sabotage attack in which four five-ton trucks were fire-bombed, causing fifty-five thousand dollars damage. In late September, white soldiers joined Puerto Ricans and blacks in a series of united protests against command harassment and discrimination at Bad Hersfeld. Approximately fifty of the men, on one occasion, staged a no-work strike and demanded that commanders listen to their grievances. A few weeks later, blacks and whites again joined together, in the 3rd Medical Battalion at Aschaffenburg. At a meeting on October 9, some one hundred soldiers agreed to boycott work unless their demands concerning command harassment and unbearable living conditions were accepted. An actual strike was averted only after the base commander agreed to meet with the men and discuss their complaints. At the Mannheim stockade, similar demands ended in open confrontation, with inmates forced to actually carry out a threatened strike. When names were called for morning work formation on October 6, more than one hundred GIs refused to move; the action reportedly resulted in speedy improvements in stockade conditions. On December 22, 1970, yet another uprising occurred, this time among troops of the 36th Infantry at Ayers Kaserne, Kirch Goens. Fed up with harassment and the command's refusal to acknowledge their grievances, nearly two hundred men went on a violent rampage, setting off artillery simulators near the battalion headquarters building, assailing the officer of the day, and smashing windows at the base officers' club. These incidents, and dozens of others, signaled an Army on the verge of collapse, rent by virtually open rebellion among large numbers of black and white troops.

II

By the beginning of 1971, the GI movement in Europe had grown to massive proportions. Dozens of GI organizations were in operation, including at least ten underground newspapers and a large number of black study groups; sabotage and rebellion were occurring at bases throughout Germany. Even top military officials in Washington were beginning to take note of the Army's deterioration. Senator Stuart Symington reported to the Senate Armed Services Committee in 1971 that he had seen signs of serious disintegration during his visit to bases in Germany earlier in the year. Commenting on widespread drug usage and anti-war protest, Symington remarked: "My impression is that the morale of the armed services in Europe is in very bad shape." Representative Dan Daniel (D-Va.) of the House Armed Services Committee gave a similar assessment to his colleagues following a journey in the summer of 1971. Daniel spoke of a "noticeable decline in discipline and morale since I was there two years ago" and relayed reports from officers in the field of "threats against . . . enforcement of disciplinary rules." The Washington *Post*'s survey of the state of the Army quoted an officer in Nuremberg who succinctly summed up the military's predicament in Germany: "There is no control. The word is, 'Don't harass the troops.'"

Outside of Vietnam itself, the Army probably encountered more internal turmoil in Germany than anywhere else in the world. The level of resistance climbed steadily during the latter stages of the war, reaching a peak in the summer of 1971. An official Army report on "group dissent against authority" listed a total of fifty-four instances of insubordination from October 1970 through September 1971, with the rate of such acts accelerating from one every two weeks in late 1970 to two a week in the summer of 1971. Coupled with this growing rebellion was a fantastically high rate of drug use, usually involving powerful Moroccan hashish. Surveys conducted at the time by Major Forrest Tenant, a 3rd Infantry Division surgeon and leading expert on drug usage, showed that 46 per cent of Army troops had smoked hash at least once and that 16 per cent used it on a regular basis.

Overseas Weekly aptly captured the atmosphere in Germany at the time with the banner "GIs Declare War on the Army"—part of an April 11, 1971, feature on GI organizing and guerrilla assaults against military installations. In one episode at Karlsruhe, twenty black and white GIs of the 78th Engineers Battalion launched a co-ordinated raid against the battalion commander's office and trucks of the highly sensitive Atomic Demolition Maintenance Section. Using Molotov cocktails and a pickax, the group managed to burn the headquarters of the commanding and executive officers and damage twenty-three trucks, thus delaying the scheduled beginning of field exercises the next morning. The article also told of an earlier incident at Nuremberg, where men of the 3rd Battalion/17th Artillery incapacitated fourteen self-propelled cannons and forty-five other vehicles by pouring sugar into the fuel tanks. While such sabotage attacks happened frequently, the resistance movement in Europe also witnessed many examples of mass organizing. One of the most dramatic and politically effective protests occurred among troops of the 77th Artillery at Camp Pieri, in Wiesbaden. In March of 1971, approximately seven hundred of the twelve hundred men at the camp signed a petition protesting discrimination, excessive harassment, and intolerable living conditions, and demanding major changes in base policy. The petition contained an ingenious provision which guaranteed its sponsors an immediate hearing: a pledge not to re-enlist unless the improvements were made (an idea other GI groups might do well to copy). Several hundred of the men also attended a gathering in the post gymnasium and cheered a call for a mass GI strike.

Another important example of enlisted resistance, an action demonstrating the continued militance of blacks and the political importance of GI solidarity, was the "Darmstadt 53." On Sunday, July 18, 1971, a minor clash between blacks and whites broke out in a mess hall of the 93rd Signal Battalion in Darmstadt. Although an official Army fact sheet later admitted the incident had been "deliberately instigated by white soldiers," the only person arrested after the disturbance was a black soldier. Soon afterward, a band of thirty angry blacks descended on the MP station and demanded the brother's release. To avoid violence, the MPs were forced to comply. The next day, however, the battalion commander, Lieutenant Colonel David Partin, ordered the jailing of another black soldier, an Sp/4 named Dixon. That afternoon, fifty-two blacks from the 93rd and the 7th Evacuation Hospital attempted to meet with Partin, asserting that Dixon was no more guilty than any of them and that if he was to be jailed they all should be locked up. The colonel refused to see the men and ordered them to disperse. When the brothers ignored his commands, Partin summoned his mostly white riot squad, arrested the entire group, and herded the men into a truck. The command tried to dispose of the matter quickly by offering the blacks non-judicial punishment, but twenty-nine of the men refused to give in, demanding full court-martial proceedings. With the help of civilian activists, the brothers stayed together and built a massive defense campaign. They secured civilian attorneys from France and the United States and successfully obtained two trial postponements, on August 30 and October 4. In addition, for the first time in the history of the GI movement in Germany, they attracted massive press coverage and public attention to their case. On October 22, with officers attempting to fend off defense attorneys and a corps of fifty newsmen, the Commander in Chief of the Army in Europe, General Michael Davison, personally intervened and ordered the charges dropped. The incident became the subject of considerable controversy during hearings before a subcommittee of the House Armed Services Committee, as conservative congressmen sought to find out why the rebels had been released. Army officials explained that a primary consideration in General Davison's decision was the "poor state of discipline" within the unit, implying that a public trial of the twenty-nine defendants was abandoned to prevent further disruption.

Although the Darmstadt incident received a great deal of public attention, it was only one of many acts of defiance among enlisted people in the latter part of 1971. Two of the largest actions occurred at Fulda and Augsburg. In September, approximately two hundred soldiers gathered in the Fulda area to protest poor living conditions and demand that base facilities be improved. The command not only ignored their requests but arrested fifty-six of the men and brought them before court-martial. In Augsburg, a similar but more militant demonstration proved successful. In late November, some eighty blacks of the 1st Infantry Division staged a sit-in at the headquarters of Brigadier General Charles Simon, threatening to strike unless their demands were met. The action forced the general to take measures against discrimination on base and to investigate prejudice among local German proprietors.

As in the United States, the GI movement in Europe withered during the winter of 1972, primarily because of the Army's "early out" program. The sudden departure of thousands of low-ranking troops decimated most organizations and virtually eliminated GI resistance. The calm lasted only a few months, however, for despite liberal reform measures and the increasingly volunteer make-up of the enlisted ranks, the movement soon reappeared. Few of the Army's new policies altered the root injustices of GI life, particularly the racism and repressive discipline so prevalent in Germany. Moreover, as Max Watts and other close observers of the movement have emphasized, political opposition among servicemen always came chiefly from enlistees, not draftees, and the end of the draft, therefore, increased the potential for GI resistance. Not surprisingly, then, after an initial shock caused by the disappearance of enlisted cadre, the GI movement slowly re-emerged in the spring and summer of 1972. At first, much of the new activity was unorganized and isolated, but new GI organizations and papers quickly developed—*New Testa-*

ment at Schweinfurt, *FighT bAck* in Heidelberg, and *Wiley Word* in Neu Ulm, to name just a few. Several severe sabotage attacks took place, including two major arson incidents at Wiley Barracks; black uprisings continued, the largest a bloody street clash with German police in Stuttgart; and a number of anti-war demonstrations occurred, among them marches in Schweinfurt on May 29 and Frankfurt on October 28. In general, though, protest occurred less frequently and with less intensity than in previous years, reflecting the impact of the "early out" program and the preoccupation with rebuilding organizations. At the end of the year, however, the movement received a major boost with the opening in Heidelberg of the Lawyers Military Defense Committee, which for the first time brought independent legal aid to servicemen in Europe. The office quickly saw action, too, for in January of 1973 commanders launched a massive crackdown on drug use and internal opposition. As we shall see in Chapter 7, the attempted repression resulted in a major increase in GI resistance.

III

The Pacific theater consists of a vast array of relatively small, isolated outposts scattered across thousands of miles of ocean—principally in Hawaii, Japan, Korea, Okinawa, and the Philippines. Considerable political activity appeared among the soldiers and Marines stationed there, but the limited numbers of these troops, their extreme isolation from one another and from civilian society, and the military's rigid ban on overseas demonstrations inhibited the emergence of large-scale resistance. The GI movement in the Pacific, at least among ground forces, thus never approached the levels achieved in Germany or the United States.

The earliest known protests outside Indochina did not occur until the summer of 1969. The first of these took place in Hawaii in August, when the tranquillity of this central headquarters for all Pacific operations was rocked by two separate GI rebellions. On August 5, airman Louis "Buff" Parry took refuge in the Church of the Crossroads in Honolulu and began what would soon become the largest sanctuary action of the GI movement. A few days later, Parry spoke at an August 9 peace rally in Honolulu and entreated GIs in the audience to launch a mass strike against the military. Soon other servicemen began streaming to the church. By the fifteenth, twelve servicemen were involved; by August 20, the number had grown to twenty-four, including eight Vietnam veterans and a number of GIs who had flown in from the States. In all, a total of thirty-four GIs participated in the sanctuary, which lasted thirty-eight days, until broken up by MPs on September 12. Trouble also developed in Hawaii among black Vietnam veterans stationed at Kaneohe Marine Corps Air Station. In early August, the brothers attempted to present commanders a list of grievances concerning discrimination and harassment. Not only were their complaints ignored, but three leading spokesmen were arrested. On Sunday, August 10, in a highly charged atmosphere of increasing racial tension and bitterness, fifty of the black Marines vented their feelings during evening flag-lowering ceremonies. When retreat was sounded, the brothers stood up and in unison raised the black power salute. The display immediately touched off a massive four-hour brawl, which spread over the entire base and eventually involved some 250 Marines. Sixteen men were injured, three requiring hospitalization.

The events at Kaneohe were repeated literally dozens of times during the course of the war at Army and Marine Corps bases throughout Asia. As in the United States and Germany, blacks in the Pacific area carried on a long and bitter struggle against racism and military repression. A look at just a few of the incidents for which data are available underscores the depth of this black rebellion:

► On August 30, 1969, several hundred blacks attack MPs and military-intelligence agents in the Four Corners Section of Koza, Okinawa. Several military vehicles are set afire and overturned, and two of the investigators are injured.

► In May of 1970, fifty soldiers at Po'ch'ŏn, South Korea, call a meeting to protest command racism; afterward, five buildings are burned to the ground, resulting in $50,000 damage.

► Six hundred brothers gather on January 15, 1971, the birthday of Martin Luther King, at a recreation hall of the 2nd Infantry Division near the Korean DMZ.

► A few months later, on the May 19 birthday of Malcolm X, more than fifty blacks stage a sit-in outside Eighth Army headquarters in Seoul.

▶ On the night of May 22, 1971, four grenade explosions
rip through Camp Humphreys, South Korea, destroying
a section of the runway and a helicopter, and injuring
four people. Three blacks from a militant group protesting racism are arrested for the attack.

Ironically, these last two outbursts came only a short while
after Deputy Defense Secretary Frank Render returned from
a Far East inspection visit to warn of pent-up rage and frustrations among minority servicemen and of the serious potential for violent upheaval.

The main center of political activity among troops in Asia
was the huge American Marine base at Iwakuni, Japan. The
outpost, southwest of Hiroshima, witnessed several major uprisings and possessed one of the most consistently successful
GI organizations in Asia. The first anti-war activity at Iwakuni
surfaced in late 1969, inspired by the Moratorium demonstrations in the United States. Corporals Lonnie Renner and
George Bacon along with other Marines formed a local chapter of the American Servicemen's Union and, in January 1970,
began publishing the newspaper *Semper Fi*. From these
modest beginnings the group grew rapidly, thanks in part to
valuable assistance provided by "Beheiren," the Japanese Vietnam Peace Committee. Long before their counterparts in the
United States, Beheiren recognized the importance of resistance among American servicemen and for years carried on
an extensive program of aiding deserters and leafleting servicemen on furlough from Vietnam. When Marines at Iwakuni
began organizing from within, therefore, Japanese civilians
quickly came to their aid. One of *Semper Fi's* earliest actions
was an April 12 "Love-In" attended by approximately fifty local Marines, at the traditional Japanese Cherry Blossom Festival. The group also was one of the few organizations outside
the United States to participate in the first Armed Forces
Day, in 1970. During the May 16 observances, many Marines
on post wore black armbands, while from outside the base,
peace messages were broadcast to the troops on a loudspeaker
system set up and operated by Beheiren. Because of the success of the original *Semper Fi* group, military authorities
launched a crackdown on the principal organizers. On June
2, 1970, Corporal Renner was hurriedly transferred back to
the United States, while Bacon was given similar orders to
Vietnam. The actions only served to solidify the group and

extend its influence, however; both Bacon and Renner were hailed as heroes at their departure by cheering supporters. Indeed, a Japanese press report at the time estimated that the *Semper Fi* organization had 350 active supporters at the base. Far from being crushed, the group remained active throughout 1970 and following years, and is still in operation today.

Iwakuni was also the scene of a number of GI rebellions. On July 4, 1970, a few weeks after the attempted suppression of *Semper Fi*, a major uprising rocked the local brig. Many of the prisoners were members of the ASU who had been active with *Semper Fi* or who had refused orders to Vietnam. On the evening of the fourth, after fruitless efforts at petitioning for improved stockade conditions and an end to repression, the inmates declared their own independence. They occupied the main detention center and set fire to several buildings, holding out against armed guards for some fourteen hours. The largest uprising occurred in late 1971, when black and white Marines at the base engaged in a savage New Year's Eve brawl. Beginning with a scuffle at an enlisted men's club, fighting quickly spread throughout the base, involving several hundred troops and resulting in a number of serious injuries. In the aftermath of the incident, fifty-seven blacks were investigated or charged for their role in the fight. No whites were implicated.

GI resistance appeared at other Army and Marine Corps bases in the Pacific but never as extensively as at Iwakuni. Organizations existed at Camp Drake, Japan (*Kill for Peace*); in the 2nd Infantry Division (*Korea Free Press*); at Fort Buckner, Okinawa ("GIs United Against the War"); and at a number of other locations. In general, these were limited efforts, however, frequently lasting only a short while. The most important political activity in the Pacific theater developed not among soldiers and Marines, but among sailors and airmen. In the latter stages of the Indochina intervention, U. S. Navy and Air Force bases in Asia witnessed a massive swell of enlisted resistance. In the next chapter, we examine this crucial aspect of the GI movement.

CHAPTER 6

RESISTING THE AIR WAR

In *Nineteen Eighty-four*, George Orwell envisioned war as no longer an annihilating mass struggle but "a warfare of limited aims." In the lurid world of the future, military conflict would become a continuous affair without victory or defeat, fought "on the vague frontiers . . . or round the Floating Fortresses," involving "very small numbers of people, mostly highly trained specialists." In many ways, this Orwellian nightmare has taken form with chilling accuracy in American policy toward Indochina, particularly the Nixon doctrine of low-profile, automated bombardment. The early 1970s policy of winding down ground operations while increasing the level of bombing and specialized warfare was a major step toward making war less objectionable and thus numbing the populace into acceptance of continuous conflict. In April of 1971, Fred Branfman wrote that the "New Totalitarianism" of automated warfare—fought without conscripts by a "smaller tighter military force composed as much as possible of technicians"— would eliminate opposition among an indifferent public and a powerless Congress, leaving the guerrillas of Indochina to stand alone against American technological might. As student unrest and the anti-war movement dwindled in the second half of 1971, many came to share the assessment that opposition to the air war could not be sustained. Nor was any resistance expected from the servicemen involved, who, it was assumed, had willingly volunteered for their jobs and, sheltered behind radar scopes and in repair shops, would function as obedient professionals. The notion proved wrong, though, for these "highly trained specialists" did in fact rise up in opposition to the new technological warfare. In the Brechtian vision, they retained their essential humanness and with dignity and conscience resisted the emergence of automated war. In this chapter, we recount the history of this vital struggle in the Navy and the Air Force.

1. Seasick Sailors

I

Resistance within the Navy began during the early stages of the Vietnam intervention, but the movement generally failed to achieve a mass following until 1971. Much of the initial activity involved isolated acts and only small-scale organization. The first known anti-Vietnam War incident within the Navy occurred in October 1967, when four sailors deserted from the carrier U.S.S. *Intrepid* while on leave at Yokosuka, Japan. The four—Richard Bailey, John Barilla, Craig Anderson, and Michael Lindner—were assisted by local peace activists and escorted through the Soviet Union to Sweden. In another early protest, petty officer Dennis Ciesielski in late 1967 refused to sail with the U.S.S. *Dewey* as it left Norfolk for Vietnam. Ciesielski was sentenced to a year in the brig for his action, but he returned in 1969 to help establish the first GI paper in the Norfolk area, *Rough Draft*. One of the very first anti-war newspapers in the Navy, *OM*, appeared in the early part of 1969 in Washington, D.C. Although the work of a single sailor, Roger Priest, the paper became the subject of considerable public furor when the late Congressman L. Mendel Rivers found himself the subject of its barbs and decided it was a "gross abuse of the constitutional right of free speech." Soon after the House Armed Services Committee chairman complained to Navy officials about the paper, Priest was charged with fourteen violations of the UCMJ, including soliciting desertion and sedition. After a year of legal battles, he was drummed out of the service with a bad-conduct discharge.

The Movement for a Democratic Military (MDM), which surfaced in Southern California and elsewhere in the early part of 1970, drew much of its initial support from sailors. One of the earliest servicemen's organizations in the Navy was San Diego MDM, which operated out of the "Waiting Room" coffeehouse and published the newspaper *Duck Power*. MDM groups also emerged at Long Beach Naval Station, with the paper *Out Now*, and, in the Alameda/San Francisco Bay area, *Up Against the Bulkhead*. Perhaps the most active MDM chapter appeared near Chicago at the

Navy's central recruit-training facility, Great Lakes Naval Training Center. Aided by activists with the Wisconsin Draft Resistance and Chicago Area Military Project, sailors at the base circulated the paper *Navy Times Are Changin* and opened a counseling and organizing center known as the "People's Place." On May 16, 1970, the group sponsored an Armed Forces Day rally near the base, attended by fifty sailors and nearly five hundred civilians. MDM also staged a "liberation festival" near the base on September 19, which drew a crowd of over five hundred sailors and civilians.

With a militant stand against racism and in support of Third World struggles, MDM enjoyed a substantial following among both blacks and whites at Great Lakes. During the summer of 1970, the sailors joined together in a major confrontation with authorities. On July 9, commanders arrested four black WAVES and illegally placed them in confinement. After hearing of the incident, blacks and whites met and decided on a co-ordinated campaign of direct resistance to free the women. More than a hundred of the brothers marched to where the women were being held and formed a circle around the building, refusing to move until the WAVES were released. As military policemen rushed to the scene, whites in other parts of the post engaged in various acts of sabotage, painting "MDM" and "All Power to the People" on trash dumpsters and causing some ten thousand dollars property damage. After a night of spreading enlisted defiance, authorities released the women. In the weeks following the incident, more than nine hundred enlisted men and women at Great Lakes were discharged or transferred to other bases, cleaning out the entire transient personnel unit and several other barracks.

While most rank-and-file resistance within the military came from enlisted people, a certain amount of political opposition also occurred among junior officers. The principal organizational vehicle for this was the Concerned Officers Movement (COM), founded in Washington, D.C., in the spring of 1970. Although involving men and women from all services, COM was established by and drew much of its initial support from naval officers. Indeed, two of the group's charter members, Lieutenants (Junior Grade) Jim Pahura and Gordon Kerr, worked in the Pentagon headquarters of the Chief of Naval Operations. Through an articulate journal entitled

COMmon Sense, first published in May 1970, the group developed numerous contacts in the Washington area and quickly built a large network of concerned officers. On September 26, 1970, they held a press conference in the capital to issue an anti-war statement signed by eighty active-duty officers. The COM statement, like their newsletter and other declarations, shunned the revolutionary demands and militant tactics of enlisted organizations such as MDM and pleaded simply for the right to speak out against military policy. Despite their moderate stance, many COM members encountered harassment from higher authorities and often were either forced out of their jobs or handed early discharges; the Washington chapter alone lost at least eight members in its first six months of existence. Nonetheless, the organization touched the consciences of thousands of young officers and by 1971 encompassed some three thousand members in more than twenty local chapters.

One of the most active COM chapters was "Concerned Military," formed in August of 1970 in San Diego. At the time of the September 26 announcement in Washington, the group held a similar press conference in San Diego to present an identical statement signed by twenty-nine active-duty officers. Concerned Military grew from a core of sixty officers into a mass organization of enlisted men and women, officers, veterans, and civilians, and for nearly two years played a crucial role in the resistance movement within the Seventh Fleet. Another active COM chapter was situated in Norfolk. As part of a major educational campaign, the group rented a billboard directly outside Norfolk Naval Base with the message "Peace Now." On December 7, 1970, nineteen officers submitted a letter to the editor of the Norfolk *Pilot* calling for immediate withdrawal from Vietnam. A COM chapter even emerged at the U.S. naval station in Keflavik, Iceland, with publication of the newspaper *Stuffed Puffin*.

The issue of war crimes and the applicability of the Nuremburg principle to the American armed forces were extremely important to the Concerned Officers Movement, particularly after the disclosures of the My Lai massacre. When the Pentagon fixed blame for the incident solely on Lieutenant William Calley, six COM members held a press conference in Washington on November 23, 1970, urging that the Calley trial be halted and announcing the formation of a "Citizens Com-

mission of Inquiry" to investigate the criminal responsibility
of senior American commanders. The officers and their civilian supporters asserted that U.S. operations in Vietnam were
criminal by their very nature and that national policy leaders,
not low-ranking servicemen, should be held accountable for
American atrocities. On January 12, 1971, the Washington
officers held another press conference announcing their request for an official Pentagon investigation into the conduct
of U.S. military officials. On January 20, officers in Los Angeles held a similar press conference stating that they, too, were
calling for an inquiry into the responsibilities of their commanders. The COM campaign against war crimes was an
extremely important step toward recognizing the need for a
code of individual responsibility within the American military.
If future My Lais were to be prevented and the armed forces
held accountable to the standards of law, American servicemen, like their counterparts in France and elsewhere, would
have to be guaranteed judicial avenues for refusing criminal
orders.

II

By the first half of 1971, the breakdown of the Army in
Vietnam forced the Pentagon to accelerate its policy of winding down the war and substituting naval and air bombardment for ground forces. While the tactic helped to prevent
a complete collapse in the Army, it led to a major jump in
resistance within the Navy. As the fleet incurred growing responsibility for sustaining the Indochina intervention, enlisted
men responded with a steadily mounting campaign of political
opposition. An early indication of these stirrings within the
Navy came on Armed Forces Day 1971, when protests occurred near five major Navy bases (compared to only one,
a year earlier). At Portsmouth, New Hampshire, the newly
formed "Service People for Peace and Justice" sponsored a
march and rally in that town attended by over one hundred
active-duty servicemen and several hundred civilians. In
Pennsylvania, civilian activists with the Philadelphia Draft
Resistance and servicemen from the local naval hospital and
shipyard marked the founding of the paper *Destroyer* with
a march and memorial service near Independence Hall. At
Newport, Rhode Island, the staff of *All Hands Abandon Ship*,

founded a year earlier, held a special film showing at the Potemkin bookshop. At Great Lakes, MDM continued its successful activities with an anti-war march and rally at Foss Park attended by two hundred sailors and over one thousand civilians. The most important events of Armed Forces Day, though, took place in San Diego, sparked by an appearance of the Jane Fonda FTA Show. Several weeks before the scheduled May 15 performances, Concerned Military circulated a petition requesting that the show be presented on the deck of the carrier U.S.S. *Constellation* (a courtesy routinely extended to the Bob Hope USO Show). Although nearly fifteen hundred members of the crew signed the appeal, Captain Harry Gerhard flatly rejected it. Nonetheless, the show's performances in San Diego were a huge success, attracting over four thousand people, a majority of them servicepeople.

The FTA Show appearance coincided with and helped spur a pioneering organizing effort that laid the groundwork for a major surge of resistance within the Seventh Fleet. As the Navy's combat responsibilities increased in the spring of 1971, Concerned Military and other San Diego-area activists (among them former draft resister David Harris) began a massive campaign against the counterinsurgency mission of the *Constellation*. Recognizing the vital role of aircraft carriers in the Indochina intervention, a broad coalition known as the "Harbor Project" launched an extensive educational and organizing effort aimed at mobilizing opposition among the ship's crew prior to its scheduled October departure. For months, the coalition worked vigorously, disseminating information against the air war in general and against the function of the *Constellation* in particular. On one occasion soon after the drive began, Captain Gerhard illegally confiscated hundreds of letters sent to the ship as part of a mass mailing, an action that prompted 112 servicemen to request an official military court of inquiry into the commander's action. The culmination of the Harbor Project was an unofficial vote held just prior to the *Constellation*'s October 2 sailing date. Over fifty-four thousand San Diego people voted, including sixty-nine hundred active-duty men and women; 82 per cent of the civilians and 73 per cent of the servicepeople participating voted for the *Connie* to stay home. Just before the ship's departure, nine sailors sought sanctuary in Christ the King Church in San Diego and publicly refused to go to Vietnam.

The Harbor Project was extremely important in generating public awareness of the Navy's growing role in the air war and in laying the groundwork for more significant carrier actions to follow, what became known as the SOS (Stop Our Ships/Support Our Sailors) movement.

On the night of September 28, as the *Constellation* project was reaching a climax, twelve sailors met below decks on the U.S.S. *Coral Sea* and decided to initiate a similar SOS movement aboard their own ship. Their first act was to circulate a petition to Congress protesting the ship's deployment. The statement gained over two hundred signatures in just three days but was immediately confiscated by the executive officer. Undaunted, the SOS group printed additional petitions and again circulated them throughout the ship, this time gathering approximately twelve hundred signatures—one fourth of the entire crew. The petition read in part:

> in our opinion there is a silent majority aboard this ship which does not believe in the present conflict in Vietnam. . . . As Americans we all have the moral obligation to voice our opinions. We the people must guide the government and not allow the government to guide us. . . .

As the movement aboard ship gained momentum, the sailors received support from large numbers of civilian activists in the San Francisco Bay Area. The huge civilian peace rally in San Francisco on November 6 was used as a forum to focus attention on the struggle aboard the *Coral Sea*. At 5 A.M. on November 9, as the crew returned from pre-embarkation leave, over one thousand anti-war civilians gathered at the main gate of Alameda Naval Station to distribute anti-war literature and talk with the men about opposing the ship's mission. The following day, three junior officers publicly tendered their resignations and strongly condemned the war effort. On the morning of the *Coral Sea*'s departure, November 12, fifteen hundred civilians again demonstrated before dawn at Alameda to support the dissenting sailors. When the ship sailed that day, thirty-five sailors stayed behind.

Organizing did not stop with the ship's departure from California. The *Coral Sea*'s arrival in Hawaii in late November coincided with a special performance by the FTA Show, then beginning its alternate-USO journey to U.S. bases in the Far East. Approximately fifty sailors from the ship attended a meeting with the show's cast, and several hundred crew members were among the more than four thousand people who attended the FTA Show performance in Honolulu. When the ship pulled out to continue its journey to East Asia, another fifty-three sailors were missing. Dissent continued in the West Pacific with publication of a shipboard underground newspaper entitled *We Are Everywhere*. On January 4, 1972, crew members arranged a special meeting with New York *Times* journalists Iver Peterson and Nancy Moran, who were visiting the ship on official assignment at the time. Nearly one hundred dissident sailors showed up for the designated meeting to show the strength of the SOS movement. (Peterson's subsequent January 9 release mentioned only that "several" crewmen had to "juggle doubts" about their role in the war.) Further protest took place on January 15, when Secretary of the Navy John Chaffee came aboard for an inspection visit and was greeted with an anti-war petition signed by thirty-six crew members.

As more sailors found themselves assigned to the West Pacific and heard of the protests aboard the *Constellation* and the *Coral Sea*, the SOS movement spread. In late 1971, sailors aboard yet another huge American carrier, the U.S.S. *Kitty Hawk*, launched an anti-war movement below decks, and, with the help of Concerned Military in San Diego, published their own newspaper, *Kitty Litter*. As the ship's February 17 sailing date approached, the enlisted activists obtained several hundred signatures on an anti-war petition, but as in earlier cases most of the copies fell into the hands of commanders and were confiscated. One hundred fifty crewmen also attended a downtown San Diego rally led by singer-activist Joan Baez to protest the Navy's role in the air war. When the ship departed, nine members of the crew refused to sail and took sanctuary in San Diego churches. *Kitty Litter* continued to circulate even while the ship was at sea, through a carefully prepared mailing list of several hundred supporters compiled by the organizers on board. The protests aboard these huge carriers, three of the premier warships of the U. S. Navy, signaled that a rebellious mood was brewing within the fleet and that increased reliance on naval operations in Vietnam would encounter serious internal opposition.

III

The increasing pace of naval air-war activity suddenly burst into full-scale mobilization with the massive expansion of bombing and the mining of North Vietnamese ports in April of 1972. The Nixon administration's response to the liberation fighters' Easter offensive drastically changed the nature of Navy involvement. During the remainder of the year, as many as four carriers (out of a total of fourteen) were on combat station in the Tonkin Gulf at one time, with an equal number committed to the area on rotation. Normal fleet routine was completely disrupted, with practically all of the Pacific fleet thrown into the fray, as well as many ships normally assigned only to the Atlantic. For the crew members involved, the escalation created severe hardships. The average workload during aircraft carrier flight operations is an incredible one hundred hours a week. With sailors often not even able to obtain eight hours sleep, much less time for leisure, and with "on line" deployments lasting as long as forty-five days, the carriers' crews were strained to the very limits of human endurance—at a time when many thought the war should have been long since over. The men of the Navy found themselves suddenly thrust to the center of activity in a war many never expected or wanted to join. Not surprisingly, the result was a major upsurge in resistance.

Within a two-month period, four major aircraft carriers were urgently dispatched to the South China Sea, each encountering opposition from crew members and local civilian activists. The first carrier to be affected was the U.S.S. *Midway*, which left Alameda in April, several months ahead of schedule. As the departure date approached, sixteen enlisted members of Fighter Squadron 151, part of the ship's Carrier Group Five, signed a letter to President Nixon opposing involvement in Vietnam. In San Diego, meanwhile, crew members of the U.S.S. *Ticonderoga* organized a movement called "Stop It Now" (SIN). Three sailors refused to leave with the ship when it departed in mid-May, and on-board protest meetings held at sea reportedly drew as many as seventy-five participants. The June 5 sailing of the U.S.S. *America* from Norfolk encountered opposition from local civilians. In a symbolic attempt to stop the ship, thirty-one peace activists formed a "people's navy" of thirteen kayaks and canoes and steered their way in front of the huge hulk as it prepared to pull away. When the Coast Guard moved in to clear the demonstrators, hundreds of sailors on the deck of the *America* jeered and pelted the cutters with garbage in a clear show of support for the protesters. The June departure of the U.S.S. *Oriskany* from Alameda led to further sailor and civilian protest activity in the Bay area. On the second of June, two hundred civilians rallied in support of dissident sailors at the east gate of the base. When the ship left, on June 6, an estimated twenty-five crew members refused to sail, including a group of ten men who turned themselves in to naval authorities on June 13 and issued a bitter public denunciation of U.S. imperialism. Their widely publicized statement held that "the only way to end the genocide being perpetrated now in South East Asia is for us, the actual pawns in the political game, to quit playing."

The Navy's showpiece carrier, the U.S.S. *Enterprise,* also experienced dissent among its crew. The movement began when a number of sailors published and circulated two thousand copies of *SOS Enterprises Ledger,* an ingenious underground newsletter closely modeled after the ship's official paper, the *Enterprise Ledger.* A petition opposing the war and demanding GI rights was drawn up and circulated below decks. Before being signed by even one hundred sailors, though, it was confiscated. As protest activities spread, leading SOS members became the target of repression. In August, twelve known dissidents were questioned by Navy intelligence agents about sabotage incidents aboard the ship and were threatened with revocation of security clearances (a particularly serious concern to men in the Navy's six-year nuclear-propulsion enlistment program). Just before the ship's departure, on September 12, five SOS organizers were escorted off the ship under armed guard, in an apparent attempt to prevent further dissent at sea. At the same time, fifty civilian peace activists formed another "people's blockade" to support the dissident sailors and try to block the *Enterprise.* Late onboard meetings in the Pacific reportedly attracted nearly one hundred fifty sailors.

Dissent aboard the Navy's carriers received invaluable aid with establishment of organizing centers at two of the Seventh Fleet's major ports. In January of 1972, sailors and civilian attorneys from the National Lawyers Guild opened a GI support project in Olongapo City, the Philippines, adjacent to the important support base at Subic Bay. Growing out of the successful appearance of the FTA Show in December of 1971, the Subic Bay project published the paper *Seasick* and provided the thousands of sailors regularly entering and leaving the port with direct exposure to the growing SOS movement. The organization also worked to improve local conditions for sailors on shore leave. In early 1972, for example, five hundred enlisted men signed a petition against police brutality from military Shore Patrol units, an action that succeeded in forcing a number of changes in local police practices. The *Seasick* group's political activities continued until October of 1972, when the project was swiftly suppressed in the wake of the Marcos government's declaration of martial law. At the major Seventh Fleet home port, San Diego, GI and civilian activists responded to the escalation in naval activity by merging the various local anti-military organizations into one major operation, the "Center for Servicemen's Rights." The huge storefront project, with counseling, printing, and meeting rooms, as well as a bookshop and performance area all in one building, provided valuable services to dissident sailors, and continues today as one of the most active and successful GI projects ever established.

The growing air of defiance within the fleet was also evident at the Great Lakes recruit-training center. On May 20, 1972, MDM and the Chicago Area Military Project organized a huge Armed Forces Day demonstration, with four hundred servicemen joining a crowd of more than two thousand. Soon afterward, MDM launched an on-base petition campaign against a speed-up in training requirements resulting from the escalation. With its resources strained to the very limits by Indochina operations, the Navy ordered a step-up in training duty in order to move men into the fleet at a quicker rate. Few sailors wanted to sacrifice for such a purpose, though, and more than six hundred of them signed the MDM petition to Congress demanding an end to the speed-up. Not just at Great Lakes, but throughout the Navy, servicemen became increasingly restive with the oppressive duty conditions caused by the mobilization of fleet resources for an unpopular mission in Indochina.

IV

Because of the suddenness of the April escalation and the stretching of resources to meet the challenge and still carry on other missions, many ships were deployed without proper attention to safety and shipboard conditions. This was particularly so among many of the destroyers and other smaller ships hastily pressed into action in the build-up. As the naval mobilization spread, enlisted resistance began to focus on the deterioration of working conditions within the fleet. The concern of sailors for their safety at sea thus became entangled with the enlarged Indochina war effort and led to protests against conditions that under other circumstances might have been bearable but, for the purpose of bombing Vietnam, were seen as intolerable. One of the first examples of this kind of challenge occurred in Newport with the sailing of the twenty-seven-year-old destroyer U.S.S. *William Rush*. Many crew members were unhappy with the ship's state of repair and doubted its ability to safely complete a scheduled around-the-world cruise. Sixty-nine of the approximately 270 men on board signed a petition asking for a Congressional investigation into the ship's seaworthiness, work conditions, and medical facilities. The effort led to inquiries by three members of Congress and one senator and brought Representative Robert Tiernan (D-R.I.) to the ship for a personal inspection. At the same time, several crew members began to speak out against the ship's scheduled stops in Africa at Angola and Mozambique. Protesting what they considered U.S. support for Portuguese colonialism in these countries, twenty sailors sent a telegram to members of the Congressional Black Caucus demanding that the cruise be stopped and urging a complete investigation of U.S. involvement in Angola and Mozambique. With the help of civilian activists working at the Potemkin bookshop, a rally was held in Newport on April 4 to protest unsafe conditions and the ship's mission in Africa; seventy people, most of them sailors, attended. When the ship left the next day, thirteen crew members stayed behind.

Similar unrest over shipboard conditions occurred in Charleston, South Carolina, when the U.S.S. *Glennon* was hurriedly sent to Vietnam in mid-April without proper repairs and despite a past record of accidents. When the ship put in at Hawaii several weeks later, sixty-three sailors sent a petition to members of Congress asking that the ship not be sent to Vietnam.

The most dramatic incident of this type occurred aboard the munitions ship U.S.S. *Nitro* at Leonardo, New Jersey. A few days before the ship's scheduled departure for Vietnam, several crew members contacted members of Vietnam Veterans Against the War and other civilian anti-war activists in the area to discuss opposition to the war and unsafe conditions. They drew up a list of specific shipboard hazards, including inadequate fresh-water supply, poor sanitation facilities, faulty ammunition-handling machinery, and improper firefighting equipment, and obtained the signatures of forty-eight members of the crew. On the morning of the twenty-fourth, as the *Nitro* prepared to get under way, forty-five of the veterans and civilians assembled a flotilla of seventeen canoes and paddled their way out into the channel to block the ship's passage. As the Coast Guard struggled with the demonstrators, one of the crew members watching from the ship's deck suddenly stood up on the rail, raised the clenched-fist salute, and literally jumped overboard! Four more men then jumped quickly after him, followed by two others. (Shivering and coated with oil, the men were later plucked from the water by a Coast Guard cutter and returned to the ship for punitive action.) One of the seven, William Monks, later explained his actions in these simple but eloquent words:

> I jumped from my ship because of my beliefs against the war and the killing in Vietnam. . . . I also jumped for the many oppressed people in the military that think like myself, but because of the way the military functions, no one ever listens to these people. . . . I see no reason why I should have to fight in Vietnam. I didn't start this war. I have nothing against the Vietnamese people; they never hurt me or my family. . . .

Anti-war protest also appeared on smaller ships in the West Pacific. In May, sailors aboard the submarine tender U.S.S. *Hunley*, stationed at Guam, published the distinctively titled underground newspaper *Hunley Hemorrhoid* (their message for the brass: "We serve to preserve the pain in your ass").

The sailors joined with dissident airmen at Anderson Air Force Base and military dependents on the island to sponsor several anti-war rallies. Also in May, thirty-six sailors from Destroyer Squadron 15, stationed at Yokosuka, sent a letter to President Nixon protesting U.S. involvement in Indochina and warning of a sharp drop in morale among sailors within the fleet.

One further incident, in October of 1972, demonstrated the degree of unrest caused by opposition to the Navy's role in Indochina. When martial law was declared in the Philippines, the Navy used the occasion to crack down on so-called troublemakers and on October 23 loaded more than two hundred enlisted men from eleven different ships onto planes for immediate transfer back to San Diego. Upon arriving, many of the men decided to inform the public about their struggle. On October 24, a racially mixed group of thirty-one enlisted men held a press conference to denounce the deplorable conditions, harassment, and racial prejudice they encountered while at sea. Their statement, excerpted below, provides a powerful insight into the rebellion within the Navy:

> Most of us were on ships on West Pac cruise off the coast of Vietnam. Living and working conditions on the ships were very poor. People had to work 14–16 hours a day. . . . While we were on the line we got 4–6 hours sleep a night. There was a lot of pressure from our superiors. They kept trying to get us to do jobs faster. . . . Their interest is in getting medals and not the welfare of the men. The Captains and the command pushes the men and the machines to the breaking point. As a result the men turn to alcohol and drugs . . . the tension results in racial fighting. . . .

V

With a history of excluding blacks from all but the most menial positions and of using Filipinos only as cooks and stewards, the Navy traditionally has been the most racist branch of the armed forces. It was the last service to integrate, and as recently as early 1971 fewer than 5 per cent of its people were black (the percentage among officers was below 1 per cent). Manpower shortages and new voluntary enlistment policies (embodied in the recruitment slogan: "You can be Black and Navy too"), however, drastically changed the composition of the Navy and resulted in a record 12 per cent black recruits in 1972. Rather than acquiring skills and job advancement, as promised by recruiters, though, the new black enlisted men found themselves, in the words of the House Armed Services Committee, "swallowed up in mess cooking for three months, followed by . . . an endless period of compartment cleaning and chipping paint." With their strong sense of black pride, the new recruits grew restive under these conditions. The friction caused by this sudden influx of minority recruits, coupled with the general pressures of overwork and low morale caused by Vietnam, led to a startling series of black uprisings during the last few months of 1972. The first and most dramatic of these, and the incident which thrust the issue of sailor unrest into public consciousness, occurred in the West Pacific on October 12 and 13 aboard the carrier U.S.S. *Kitty Hawk.*

The huge warship pulled into Subic Bay in October after a grueling eight months at sea for what was to be the final rest before going home. Unexpectedly, the crew was informed that, rather than sailing for the United States, they were returning to combat operations off Indochina. With tensions among the crew already high from growing racial friction during the long period at sea, this disappointment provided the spark for violence. The night before departure, serious fighting erupted at the Subic Bay enlisted men's club, the San Paquito. On the evening of the twelfth, after the first full day of combat in the Tonkin Gulf, the ship's intelligence investigator exacerbated still smoldering tensions by calling in only black sailors for questioning and possible criminal action relating to the brawl at Subic. Outraged at what they considered blatant discrimination, over one hundred blacks gathered for an angry meeting on the after mess deck at approximately 8 P.M. The ship's Marine detachment was summoned to suppress the meeting, and an explosive situation quickly developed. Commander Benjamin Cloud, the executive officer and a black man himself, entered the area and attempted to restore calm by ordering the blacks and the Marines to separate ends of the ship. Moments later, however, Captain Marland Townsend, the commanding officer, arrived and issued conflicting orders. As confusion spread, the blacks and the armed Marines encountered each other unexpectedly on the hangar deck, and a bitter clash quickly broke out. The fighting spread rapidly, with bands of blacks and whites marauding throughout the ship's decks and attacking each other with fists, chains, wrenches, and pipes. In the ensuing chaos, the executive officer and the captain again worked at cross purposes, further adding to the confusion; for a few violent hours, the ship was virtually without effective control. Finally, after a 2:30 A.M. meeting in the ship's forecastle, the fighting subsided. The uprising left forty whites and six blacks injured. Of the twenty-five sailors arrested for the incident, all were black.

Only a few days after the *Kitty Hawk* rebellion, a similar, though smaller, incident occurred on the oiler U.S.S. *Hassayampa*, in Subic Bay. Fighting on October 16 resulted in serious injury to four white crewmen and the arrest of eleven blacks. A serious uprising also took place earlier aboard the amphibious landing ship U.S.S. *Sumter* while off Southeast Asia on September 7. Fighting between black and white Marines resulted in injury to eight people and led to various charges of assault and mutiny against six blacks. Two racial rebellions also erupted in late November at Navy land bases. One clash took place on Midway Island, in the Pacific, when 130 of the 650 sailors stationed at the outpost engaged in a brawl that left five sailors injured. On November 26, at the Camp Allen Navy Correctional Center in Norfolk, thirty-two blacks and one white barricaded themselves inside their dormitories and fought for hours against Marine guards. In addition, racial incidents reportedly took place in January 1973 on the carrier U.S.S. *Intrepid* while in the Mediterranean.

The largest and most significant of these rebellions took place in early November 1972 aboard the U.S.S. *Constellation* —what has been aptly described as "the first mass mutiny in the history of the U. S. Navy." In October, during training operations off the Southern California coast, black crew members formed an organization called the "Black Fraction," with the aim of protecting minority interests in promotion policies and in the administration of military justice. Throughout October, the group held several meetings, including one attended by the ship's executive officer, where programs were developed to defend blacks subjected to court-martial proceedings and to examine the ship's records for evidence of discrimination in non-judicial punishment. As the organization grew in strength, the command, on November 2, singled out fifteen leading members of Black Fraction as agitators and ordered that six of them be given immediate less-than-honorable discharges. At approximately the same time, a notice appeared in the ship's plan of the day announcing that 250 additional men were to be administratively discharged. Fearing that most of these punitive releases would be directed at them and angry at the command's apparent efforts to suppress their activities, over one hundred sailors, including a number of whites, staged a sit-in at the after mess deck on November 3 and demanded that the ship's commander, Captain J. D. Ward, personally hear their grievances. The captain refused to acknowledge them, however, and the dissidents thus continued their strike throughout the day and into the early morning hours on November 4, refusing a direct order to report for muster on the flight deck. As tensions aboard ship mounted, a series of high-level consultations were held among Captain Ward, the Commander in Chief of the Pacific Fleet, Admiral Zumwalt in Washington, and other senior naval commanders. To avert another *Kitty Hawk*, the officials reluctantly decided to cut sea operations short and return the rebels to San Diego as a "beach detachment." Captain Ward pulled the ship into the harbor on the fourth and allowed more than one hundred thirty of the men to go ashore. The *Constellation* returned a few days later to pick up the dissidents, but the men refused to board ship, and on the morning of November 9 staged a defiant dockside strike—perhaps the largest act of mass defiance in naval history. Despite the seriousness of their action, not one of the one hundred thirty sailors was arrested. Several of the men received early discharges, but most were simply reassigned to shore duty.

The *Constellation* incident created an immediate uproar within the military establishment. On November 10, Chief of Naval Operations Zumwalt called eighty leading admirals and Marine Corps generals to an emergency meeting at the Pentagon in which he demanded greater attention to equal-opportunity programs. A few days later, the House Armed Services Committee responded to the crisis by appointing a special subcommittee to investigate disciplinary problems in the Navy. Although dissent and racial unrest were the immediate occasion for this concern, military officials were also be-

coming increasingly worried over a far more serious and menacing phenomenon within the fleet: sabotage.

VI

For every sailor who spoke out or openly resisted, many
others supported the movement silently, unwilling to risk the
consequences of military repression. With even the most
innocuous forms of protest certain to encounter a harsh
response, many enlisted people expressed their bitterness
through covert acts of disruption. For some, sabotage was a
spontaneous, often frustrated reaction to particular command
policies or government action. For others, though, internal
destruction was seen as the most politically effective form of
resistance, as a sure means of directly obstructing an imperious
war machine. As opposition to the air war increased, the surging undercurrent of hostility among enlisted people produced
a growing number of acts of intentional damage to ship com-
ponents—a grave threat to the highly technological, capital-
intensive Navy.

One of the first publicly disclosed acts of sabotage during
the Vietnam period occurred on May 26, 1970, aboard the
destroyer U.S.S. *Anderson*, in San Diego. As the ship was preparing to steam into the Pacific for Vietnam, it suffered a
major breakdown, resulting in some two hundred thousand
dollars worth of property damage and a delay of several weeks.
An investigation disclosed that someone had dropped nuts,
bolts, and chains down the main gear shaft. Three sailors were
charged for willful destruction and sabotage, but because of
a lack of evidence the case had to be dismissed. A similar
incident occurred in November of 1971, when naval reservist
James Field caused one hundred thousand dollars damage to
the U.S.S. *Chilton* while the ship was docked at Norfolk.

The level of sabotage grew steadily during 1972 with the
escalation of naval involvement in Indochina. The situation
suddenly reached crisis proportions in July of 1972, however,
when, within the space of just three weeks, two of the Navy's
aircraft carriers were put out of commission by attacks from
within. On July 10, 1972, a massive fire broke out on the
carrier U.S.S. *Forrestal* at Norfolk. The blaze swept through
the admiral's quarters and extensively damaged the ship's radar center, resulting in over $7 million damage. The incident

was the largest single act of sabotage in naval history, and it delayed the ship's deployment for over two months. A nineteen-year-old seaman apprentice, Jeffrey Allison, was apprehended soon afterward and charged with arson and sabotage, as well as possession of LSD. On December 7, 1972, a military court found Allison guilty and sentenced him to five years in prison. In late July, another major act of sabotage shook the carrier U.S.S. *Ranger*, docked at Alameda, California. Just days before the ship's scheduled departure for Vietnam, a paint scraper and two twelve-inch bolts were inserted into the number-four-engine reduction gears, causing nearly $1 million damage and forcing a three-and-a-half-month delay in operations for extensive repairs. Pat Chenoweth, a soft-spoken young sailor from a broken home, was arrested and accused of the attack. Although military commanders for years refused to legally define the Vietnam intervention as a war, Chenoweth was in fact charged with the grave offense of "sabotage in time of war"—a crime punishable by thirty-five years in prison. After a lengthy legal battle and over ten months in pretrial confinement, Chenoweth was acquitted, in June of 1973. In their efforts to exonerate Chenoweth, defense lawyers pointed out that numerous other sabotage incidents had occurred on the *Ranger* during 1972 and that it was common for sailors to brag about or claim credit for such acts. They documented over two dozen instances of willful destruction during May and June alone, including cut fire hoses, bomb threats, a plugged fire main, fuel in the fresh-water supply, a flooded compartment, and assorted damage to generators and oil pumps.

Evidence from various other sources indicates that sabotage became an increasingly severe problem throughout the Navy during the air war. One indication of the extent of the problem comes in figures supplied to the House Internal Security Committee by the Navy Department in late 1971. The Navy listed 488 "investigations on damage or attempted damage" during fiscal year 1971, including 191 for sabotage, 135 for arson, and 162 for "wrongful destruction"; the figures showed a considerable increase over earlier years. Captain Ward of the *Constellation* told a press conference in November of 1972 that "saboteurs were at work" during the period of unrest aboard his ship. He admitted that bomb and ordnance handling machinery had been damaged and that various other types of equipment had disappeared over the side. The problem became so serious that the Navy initiated a program of monitoring sensitive machinery aboard ships with television cameras. Top Navy officials have spoken openly of the trouble. At his retirement as Commander in Chief of the Atlantic Fleet in October of 1972, Admiral Charles K. Duncan termed the increase in sabotage a "grave liability" to naval operations. Flanked by Admiral Zumwalt at a ceremony aboard the carrier U.S.S. *Kennedy* in Norfolk, Admiral Duncan referred to "about a dozen" incidents during the previous months and urged the immediate expulsion of those responsible for such acts. In its report on Navy disciplinary problems, the House Armed Services Committee also disclosed "an alarming frequency of successful acts of sabotage and apparent sabotage on a wide variety of ships and stations. . . ." The Committee reported receiving "a list of literally hundreds of instances of damage to naval property wherein sabotage is suspected."

The House Committee's report also contained a startling admission of how resistance among sailors actually undermined naval combat operations during the bombing campaign in 1972. The investigators found that the uprising aboard the *Kitty Hawk* in October was closely related to disruption of normal fleet rotation due to sabotage. It will be remembered that the sudden and unexpected order to the *Kitty Hawk* to return to combat duty provided the spark in an already tense situation that led to violence. In the Committee's words: "This rescheduling apparently was due to the incidents of sabotage aboard her sister ships *U.S.S. Ranger* and *U.S.S. Forrestal.*" With two of the Navy's principal carriers out of commission due to sabotage, the *Kitty Hawk* was forced to cancel its scheduled return to the States and sail once again for the Tonkin Gulf. Thus sabotage and black resistance combined in the fall of 1972 to physically impede the Navy's ability to carry out its mission. The House Armed Services Committee summed up this crisis in the fleet in alarming terms:

> The U. S. Navy is now confronted with pressures . . . which if not controlled, will surely destroy its enviable tradition of discipline. Recent instances of sabotage, riot, willful disobedience of orders, and contempt for authority, instances which have occurred with increased frequency, are clear-cut symptoms of a dangerous deterioration of discipline.

In late December 1972, the Pentagon finally responded to this new rebellion in the ranks, again resorting to the expedient of mass discharges. Three thousand sailors were immediately handed administrative discharges, many of them less than honorable, and an additional three thousand men were identified for release in the following months. The mass-discharge policy, along with the demobilization of the fleet after the January peace accords, eased the pressure within the Navy and effectively lowered the level of enlisted resistance. The changes by no means ended the movement among sailors, however. Black uprisings and political organizing have continued into the cease-fire period and still constitute a serious challenge to the status quo within the Navy.

2.   "Airmancipation"

The Air Force has always enjoyed a special position among the branches of the military. It is generally viewed as the most desirable service and, even in the midst of crippling manpower shortages elsewhere, has had no difficulty meeting enlistment quotas. Similarly, resistance among airmen never has been as militant or pervasive as in the Army, Navy, and Marine Corps. Part of the reason for this is the comparative lack of oppression within the Air Force. The training is less dehumanizing, the work is more technical and interesting, and base conditions are generally more comfortable than in the other branches. Also important is the abstract nature of technological warfare. Only a minority of airmen are ever actually embroiled in combat operations, and even for these, daily activities involve routine technical tasks of maintenance and aircraft preparation. The actual bombings and their victims are never encountered. The airman is not forced to endure the extreme hardships experienced by infantrymen and sailors at sea. Despite these circumstances, however, the GI movement did take root within the Air Force, steadily growing in strength in direct relation to the service's role in the air war. Indeed, resistance in the Air Force came to be a major restraint on American bombardment in Indochina, ultimately forcing the Pentagon to limit air operations in the final stage of U.S. intervention.

I

First appearing in 1969 and 1970, the movement in the Air Force initially comprised only a handful of organizations, and, as far as is generally known, involved very little mass action. Two of the earliest groups were "United Servicemen's Action for Freedom" at Wright-Patterson AFB in Ohio, and "GIs United Against the War," publishers of *Aerospaced* at Grissom AFB in Indiana. Organizing also emerged in 1969 at Chanute AFB in Illinois, where airmen and students of the University of Illinois founded *Harass the Brass* (later changed to *A Four Year Bummer*) and opened the first coffeehouse for airmen, the "Red Herring." On Armed Forces Day 1970, the group sponsored a "trial of the military" at the local Champaign campus, attended by several hundred airmen and students. Armed Forces Day actions also occurred in 1970 at two other air bases: Grand Forks AFB in North Dakota, with a May 16 rally of one thousand civilians and GIs; and Barksdale AFB in Louisiana, where a peace festival attracted approximately one hundred fifty airmen. Various other anti-war groups existed within the Air Force prior to 1971, but their activities were generally quite limited and received little notice or civilian assistance. Most support of the GI movement continued to focus on the Army, with little recognition of the potential for resistance within the Air Force.

Perhaps the first mass political organizing within the Air Force appeared during the summer of 1970 in England, where actress Vanessa Redgrave and other British activists helped inspire an important resistance movement among American airmen. The effort began with a June 7, 1970, anti-war gathering in London's Lyceum Ballroom, at which five active-duty leaders of the resistance in Europe spoke of their personal struggles and of the growing GI movement in Germany. A number of airmen attending the event later met with the soldiers and, with support from the British civilians, founded the newspaper and organization *People Emerging Against Corrupt Establishments* (P.E.A.C.E.). The group soon became self-sustaining and grew into one of the most successful organizations of the GI movement, encompassing all eight Air Force bases in England (with an identified local representative at each post) and reaching out to a large percentage of the twenty-two thousand airmen stationed in the country. With a widely circulated, professionally edited newspaper and a very open, almost legalistic approach, the group enjoyed a massive following. Their major political action, one of the largest in the history of the Air Force movement, came on May 31, 1971, when some three hundred airmen gathered in London's Hyde Park to present an anti-war petition to the U.S. embassy. To circumvent the Pentagon's prohibition against overseas demonstrations, the servicemen and their families walked in groups of five to the embassy, where they presented the names of over one thousand active-duty supporters of the petition. Embarrassed commanders reacted to the action by singling out Captain Tom Culver, a Vietnam veteran and, ironically, the group's legal counsel, court-martialing him for illegally demonstrating in a foreign country. In response, one hundred GIs defiantly gathered at the London embassy on August 1 and presented petitions demanding an end to regulations against overseas assembly. P.E.A.C.E. remained active for several more months and published fourteen issues of its newspaper. The group folded in the fall of 1971, however, when almost all its active members were summarily discharged.

Situated close to Indochina and deeply immersed in the war effort, the vast American Air Force network in Asia also witnessed important GI resistance. The very first overseas organization in the Air Force, *Hair* ("Human Activities in Retrospect"), appeared in August of 1969 at Misawa AFB in northern Japan. The usual problems of cadre turnover and repression initially overwhelmed the fledgling group, but by the summer of 1970 it achieved a more stable footing, thanks to support from Beheiren and the opening of the first GI coffeehouse in Asia, the "Owl." Political action also surfaced in 1971 at Yokota AFB near Tokyo, where airmen and civilians from the Pacific Counseling Service and Beheiren launched the paper *First Amendment*. On July 18, 1971, a rock and peace festival sponsored by the group attracted over two hundred servicemen. Clark AFB in the Philippines was a principal staging area for American operations during the Vietnam War (despite official U.S.-Philippine agreements to the contrary) and was, as well, a major center of enlisted resistance. The first group at the base, publishing *The Whig*, emerged in the summer of 1970, while another organization, aided by activists from the National Lawyers Guild, appeared in the fall of 1971 with the journal *Cry Out*. Operating out of a military counseling center in the village of Santa Maria, this second effort played an important role in mobilizing opposition to the air war. The center was attacked three separate times by Philippine policemen and was closed down completely in October of 1972, following the Marcos Government's declaration of martial law. Organizing also occurred at Kadena AFB in Okinawa, where black airmen in late 1970 founded the paper *Demand for Freedom*. Openly supporting Okinawan demands for removal of U.S. bases, the brothers at Kadena adopted a strongly anti-imperialist program. When "Zengunro," the Okinawan base-workers' union, staged a violent anti-American strike in December of 1970, thirty black airmen issued a public statement endorsing the union's aims.

II

As in the other services, black airmen were the most militant and politically active resisters in the Air Force. Faced with the prejudices common to all minority servicemen—unequal job assignment, a greater proportion of disciplinary punishments, the suppression of non-white culture—blacks in the Air Force were forced to defend their own interests through independent black organizations (so-called black study groups) and occasionally in open rebellion. At the end of 1970, *Air Force Times* noted the existence of some twenty-five black culture groups, many of them actively engaged in struggle against discrimination and repression. One such organization, affiliated with the American Servicemen's Union, was the "Black Discussion Group," active during 1971 at Plattsburgh AFB in New York. Another group at work in 1971 was "Concerned Black Airmen," which made its debut at Chanute AFB on May 17 with an on-base memorial service for Malcolm X. The group carried on an extensive campaign to improve the plight of minority servicemen but received little co-operation from base authorities. After months of unanswered appeals and mounting frustration, violence flared at Chanute during the evenings of August 7 through 9, leaving the base exchange, theater, and gas station damaged and resulting in injury to several airmen. Blaming the up-

rising on command intransigence, approximately eighty concerned airmen a few weeks later picketed a high-level meeting
of the Air Training Command to press home their continuing
demands for full black equality.

Violence erupted at other air bases during the course of the
war—but never as extensively as at Travis AFB in May of
1971. From May 22 through 25, this primary Vietnam
transfer point in northern California was crippled by the largest mass rebellion in the history of the Air Force. A whole
book could be devoted to just the Travis story, for in many
ways it epitomized the racism and black revolt eroding the
American armed forces. The roots of the conflict, as in so
many previous examples, lay in command repression, growing
black restiveness, and a general crisis in morale—with a fracas
at an enlisted men's club providing the spark for a generalized uprising throughout the base. Fighting apparently began
on Saturday afternoon between black enlisted men and
women and military policemen and continued in scattered
clashes through the entire weekend. The minority barracks
area was cordoned off, and a number of black airmen were
arrested. The main clash came on Monday evening, the
twenty-fourth, when over two hundred enlisted people, some
whites included, attempted to free the imprisoned brothers
and were met by three hundred MPs and nearly eighty civilian police called in from surrounding communities. In the
ensuing battle, over six hundred airmen were drawn into the
brawl, an officers' club was burned to the ground, several
dozen people were injured, and 135 servicepeople, most of
them black, were arrested. Fighting continued into the next
day, with armed guards patrolling the base and all incoming
traffic searched at the gate. For a few incredible days, Travis
was in a virtual state of siege, with nearly all base activities
abandoned in a frantic attempt to restore order.

In the wake of the Travis uprising, the Pentagon hurriedly
dispatched special race-relations advisers to the base in a
highly publicized effort to prevent further resistance. Indeed,
as black militance increased during 1971 and 1972, the Air
Force inaugurated an extensive "human relations" program
not just at Travis but throughout the service, establishing
racial-harmony councils and minority-affairs officers at nearly
every major base in the world. The new reforms had little
impact, though, for they did nothing to alter the roots of

racism. In fact, they seemed aimed more at channeling grievances into controllable outlets than effecting real change.
Many blacks thus dismissed the race-relations program as
mere cosmetics—instead, continuing to build their own independent political organizations. At McChord AFB in Washington, for example, seventy-five black airmen, including
many who had been transferred to the base following the
Travis riot, established the "Coramantee Brothers Council"
and during the summer of 1971 launched a series of programs
to combat discrimination. Among the Council's activities were
the investigation of off-base housing, legal-rights counseling
for enlisted people, and greater black participation in on-base
cultural and educational activities. The brothers were powerful enough to gain official recognition at the base, and on
one occasion even sponsored a visit by a representative of the
Black Panther Party. Blacks continued to organize at many
other bases and, mindful of the Travis rebellion, confronted
racism with a new sense of determination and collective
strength.

III

Resistance in the Air Force reached its peak during the
Indochina air war. As in the Navy, the huge increase in American bombing in the latter stages of the war produced a major
upsurge in internal political opposition. In early 1971, as
few as ten GI papers circulated within the Air Force, but by
the spring of 1972 the number jumped to more than thirty.
Dissent among airmen thus grew in direct relation to the enlarged role of air power in the Indochina intervention. In an
early-1972 analysis of trends in the GI movement, the House
Internal Security Committee recognized this pattern clearly:
"The trend towards organizing among U. S. Air Force personnel, in line with U.S. continued air activities in Indochina, is
quite obvious."

A major factor in this development was a recognition
among civilian radicals of the Air Force's crucial new role in
the war, with a consequent increase in support projects at air
bases. Vietnam veterans and other political activists linked
with the growing number of resisters in the Air Force, and,
often with the aid of USSF, established newspapers and
organizing centers at numerous bases. At Travis AFB, for ex-

ample, a 1971 Armed Forces Day gathering of some one hundred servicepeople occasioned discussions on the need for on-going work at the base and led to the opening of a permanent organizing project. One of the most successful Air Force groups emerged in a similar manner at Mountain Home AFB in Idaho. The project grew out of a meeting between attorney-author Mark Lane and several Mountain Home airmen at an April 24 peace rally in Boise. The airmen felt that many at Mountain Home shared their goals of peace and greater GI rights and that the time was ripe to launch an organization and paper at the base. Lane, agreeing to act as legal counsel and assistant to the project, promptly moved to Mountain Home, where he worked with the airmen for several years. An old theater became the "Covered Wagon" coffeehouse and meeting hall, and the articulate, well-produced journal *Helping Hand* soon began appearing regularly. According to the masthead of the first issue, the paper's editorial staff consisted of sixteen enlisted men and four officers. The organization quickly attracted a substantial following among first-termers at the base, drawing as many as one hundred fifty active-duty men and women to its early meetings. As so often during the GI movement, though, the project's successes made it the target of violence: On November 21, the Covered Wagon and all its belongings were destroyed in a suspected arson attack. The assault failed to deter the group, and it continued to enjoy the support of local airmen.

Surging opposition to the war within the Air Force became dramatically evident in a series of protests in October of 1971, many at bases with no previous history of dissent. The first of these took place during the anti-war Moratorium on Wednesday, October 13. At Mountain Home, fifty airmen and civilians conducted a noon-hour vigil on the base at the BX cafeteria, and later that evening seventy-five people attended a rally at the Covered Wagon. The Moratorium was observed in San Antonio as well, where a large number of airmen from Lackland AFB participated in an evening rally sponsored by the GI Co-ordinating Committee. A week later, one hundred fifty airmen and civilians joined in an October 19 anti-war gathering near Minot AFB in North Dakota. On Veterans Day, October 25, demonstrations occurred at yet three other bases: At Westover AFB in Massachusetts, airmen and civilians with the newly established "Off the Runway" coffeehouse sponsored an anti-war rally outside the base gate. At Lowry AFB near Denver, fifty airmen and one hundred civilians gathered for a rally sponsored by the new paper *Getting Together*. In Arizona, the formerly all-soldier newspaper *Where Are We?* published at Fort Huachuca, was strengthened by the growing participation of airmen from nearby Davis-Monthan AFB. Fifty of the new activists marched in a Veterans Day peace rally in Tucson.

By 1972, the changing nature of the Indochina war significantly transformed the GI movement, shifting activity from the ground forces to the Air Force and the Navy. Indeed, during the first half of the year, the number of organizing projects within these forces actually surpassed those in the Army and the Marine Corps. New political groups appeared at many major air bases previously unaffected by the movement: Forbes AFB in Kansas, Lackbourne AFB in Ohio, Richards-Gebaur AFB in Missouri, MacDill AFB in Florida, Kirtland AFB in New Mexico, Fairchild AFB in Washington, and others. Along with an increasing volume of disciplinary infractions, accelerating AWOL and desertion rates, and expanding drug use, the growing political opposition movement marked the period as the most turbulent in Air Force history. At each new escalation of the bombing in Vietnam, airmen responded with a clamor of protest. The Nixon administration's intensification of air attacks during Christmas of 1971, for example, led to co-ordinated demonstrations at three major bases on January 8. At Fairborn, Ohio, approximately one hundred airmen joined with several hundred other people for a march to the gates of Wright-Patterson AFB. At Mountain Home, one hundred servicemen and civilians gathered on base for another demonstration at the BX cafeteria. And at Travis AFB, two hundred servicepeople and civilians staged a protest vigil outside the main gate.

The government's massive bombing campaign during the 1972 Easter offensive in Vietnam sparked the most intensive wave of protests, with demonstrations and rallies occurring almost daily at dozens of bases throughout the world. On April 7, two hundred fifty people turned out on one day's notice for a rally outside Westover AFB. On the eighth, seventy-five airmen and WAFs at Mountain Home conducted an anti-war vigil outside the base gate, an action they repeated on following weekends for more than a month. On April 10, GIs publishing the paper *Special Weapons* at Kirtland AFB demonstrated against a military recruiting center in downtown Albuquerque. On April 13, airmen from McGuire AFB in New Jersey formed a picket line at the gate of the base, obtaining more than one hundred active-duty signatures on a petition against American intervention. Anti-war activity even surfaced during this time at the headquarters of the Strategic Air Command at Offutt AFB, Nebraska. Airmen and local civilians formed the "Omaha Military Project" and began publishing the paper *Offul Times*; on May 11, they sponsored an anti-war demonstration outside the gates of the base attended by more than two hundred people. The upsurge in Air Force resistance also carried over into Armed Forces Day with a May 13 teach-in at Mountain Home attended by some five hundred airmen and civilians, as well as smaller May 20 rallies near Travis, March, Lackbourne, Pease, and Westover AFBs.

Opposition to the April escalation also surfaced among airmen in Asia. On April 22, nine GI-movement activists, including representatives from Yokota and Misawa AFBs, held a joint press conference in Tokyo to condemn the air war and all U.S. foreign intervention. The most dramatic GI response came in the Philippines, where the actions of two American airmen precipitated a minor political crisis in that country. On May 17, Sergeants Tom Andric and Wayne Evans, both active with the *Cry Out* group at Clark AFB, held a press conference at the National Press Club in Manila to denounce the U.S. escalation and expose the use of American bases as "forward staging areas" in that effort (a violation of the official Bases Agreement). After making their disclosure to the press, the airmen were contacted by Senator Benigno Aquino and invited to present their testimony before a closed session of the Philippine Congress. The story received extensive press coverage throughout the country and prompted a storm of criticism against the Marcos government and the United States, including a violent anti-Vietnam demonstration outside the American embassy on May 20. Marcos himself was forced to call a press conference on May 18 to deny the GIs' charges and a few days later announced that all existing U.S.-Philippine treaties would be renegotiated. The two airmen, meanwhile, were confined to Clark AFB and then shipped back to Travis AFB on May 22.

The swell of resistance within the Air Force continued into

the summer of 1972 but then gradually diminished with the reduction of Indochina air operations and the advent of peace negotiations. The decline in protest activity was temporarily reversed in December of 1972, however, by the Nixon administration's bombing blitz against North Vietnamese population centers, which prompted renewed cries for an end to American intervention. At Offutt AFB, for example, one hundred GIs and civilians held an anti-war rally outside the gates of the base on Christmas Eve.

The most important opposition to the December bombing, though, came from men involved in actual hostilities in Thailand. In a development unparalleled in the history of the Air Force, two combat pilots refused to fly bombing missions, in opposition to U.S. policy. On December 18, at the very outset of the renewed attack, twenty-six-year-old Captain Dwight Evans, pilot of an F-4 Phantom in the 34th Tactical Fighter Squadron, balked when ordered to strike North Vietnam and stated he could no longer participate in the war. Nine days later, Captain Michael Heck, a B-52 bomber pilot stationed at U Tapao, decided, as he said later, "that a man has to answer to himself first" and also refused to fly. A veteran of seven years in the Air Force and more than two hundred previous combat missions, Heck became increasingly uncertain of U.S. policies in Vietnam throughout the 1972 escalation. The Administration's sudden reversal of policy in December and the realization that his targets were now hospitals and civilian sectors, however, left Heck in what he termed "moral shock." When, after a one-day pause for Christmas, his name came up for flight duty on the twenty-sixth, Heck decided he could no longer comply with his orders. He later explained his action by evoking the Nuremberg principle and the serviceman's fundamental allegiance to the standards of morality:

> . . . no man has the moral right to completely surrender his conscience to any authority military or civilian. A man has not only a right, but an obligation to disobey an order that is conscientiously objectionable.

Not just Heck and Evans but hundreds and perhaps thousands of airmen in Thailand and Guam resisted the American bombardment of Indochina. This crucial segment of the movement largely escaped public attention, though, primarily because of a blackout on press coverage of Air Force combat bases. The struggle in Thailand and Guam apparently never acquired a strong organizational base, but through sabotage and a general air of defiance and inefficiency, GI obstruction had a major impact on U.S. operations. Morale within the Southeast Asia command deteriorated sharply throughout the 1972 escalation, and during the bombing of Cambodia in the first half of 1973 plunged to crisis levels. One clue to the growing frustrations of enlisted men stationed in Thailand was a sharp increase in heroin use. Prior to the 1972 build-up, the positive detection rate in urinalysis testing was only 0.5 per cent. In the first part of fiscal year 1973, however, the rate of detected heroin use at the six Air Force bases in Thailand jumped to 2.5 per cent. Given the ease with which the tests could be circumvented, the real rate of use probably was twice as high. (Similar testing in Vietnam, for example, indicated a 5 per cent addiction rate at the same time that surveys showed the actual rate to be 10 to 20 per cent.) In addition, GIs from the Marine air base in Thailand reported frequent sabotage, or "fodding" (foreign-object damage), and it's likely that the Air Force, too, encountered numerous incidents of intentionally damaged engines, particularly during 1973.

A dramatic indication of the growing unrest in Thailand and Guam came in May of 1973, when Senators Fulbright and Kennedy published a series of letters received from men in the combat zone. One man wrote:

This is the first time I have felt it necessary to write a Congressman, but I am soliciting your support to get us B-52 crew members back home. . . .

Another exclaimed:

I for one, sir, do not wish to die as a mercenary for a foreign dictator.

And a third airman warned:

Ground crews no longer care whether or not their planes are safe and operational. Flights of crews do not wish to fly wasted missions and consequently abort when given the opportunity. . . . Prisoners of Guam—Don't let them be forgotten!

In May, four of these "prisoners of Guam" boldly defied

military authority and joined with Congresswoman Elizabeth Holtzman in a historic legal suit challenging the constitutionality of the Cambodian bombing. Captain James Strain, a B-52 pilot and veteran of 230 previous combat missions, Captain Michael Flugger, a co-pilot, and Lieutenant Arthur Watson, an electronic-warfare crewman, were immediately removed from flight operations because of their action. In June, a fourth officer associated with the suit, Captain Donald E. Dawson, further shocked the Air Force by refusing to pilot a B-52 mission. Dawson decided against participating in the bombing because, as he stated, "I began to think of what had happened on the ground after a mission." On June 19, he informed commanders of his intent to submit an application for conscientious objection.

Ultimately, resistance to the Cambodian raids undermined American military capabilities and forced the Air Force to curtail combat operations. At the end of May, 1973, the Pentagon announced that B-52 missions over Cambodia were being reduced by 40 per cent. Military spokesmen claimed that the cuts were intended primarily to save money, but veteran Washington *Post* correspondent Michael Getter reported that Defense Department officials seemed more concerned with "an increasing morale problem among B-52 bomber crews." According to Getter, the restiveness of the men in Asia apparently played a major role in the decision to limit flights:

> Despite the official assertions there are indications that the Air Force is facing a deepening morale crisis among pilots and especially among crews of the B-52s. . . . High ranking Defense Department sources say the morale situation at Guam has been poor for some time now. . . . These sources say the morale problem at U Tapao Air Base in Thailand is also growing worse daily.

The Vietnam intervention ended, therefore, with the Pentagon unable to rely on even the "highly trained specialists" of its elite service. Just as resistance within the Navy disrupted the routine of the Seventh Fleet and hobbled naval war activities, the opposition of airmen helped curb the fury of the air war in Cambodia.

CHAPTER 7

THE CONTINUING CRISIS

Many assumed that withdrawal from Vietnam and signing of the Paris peace agreements would eliminate political opposition within the ranks. Despite the cease-fire, however, resistance and organizing activity not only survived but in some places actually increased during 1973. Low-ranking enlisted people, both blacks and whites, have continued to challenge authorities and demand radical changes in the purpose and nature of military service. But many projects, sapped by discharges and plummeting enlisted-manpower levels and unable to adapt to shifting circumstances, lost mass support and were forced to close. The total number of active organizations and newspapers dropped from nearly one hundred in 1971 to approximately thirty in mid-1973. Along with the decline in numbers, the GI movement also experienced a change in political emphasis. No longer facing active combat abroad, GIs naturally have shown more interest in concrete issues of daily life than in matters of foreign policy. As a result, organizations have responded to the basic grievances of enlisted life and sought to improve day-to-day conditions within the ranks. Repression, racism, and the military justice system, always important concerns of GI activists, are now the principal focus of continuing resistance. The oppression of enlisted service insures that the GI movement will remain a permanent feature of the American military.

I

In early 1972, the Fort Lewis-McChord AFB GI Alliance became one of the first groups to express this altered emphasis, by inaugurating a campaign to improve off-base housing. At Fort Lewis, as at other major bases, low-ranking enlisted people and their families often live in tenement developments, where, because of their transient status, they are easy prey for negligent or exploitive owners. Responding to complaints of local GIs, Alliance members conducted an investigation into GI housing in the town of Tillicum and pressured landlords and the Fort Lewis housing referral office to make improvements. Through the action, the Alliance gained increased recognition on base and attracted renewed GI support. Other Army projects, groping for new directions in the wake of troop withdrawals, quickly followed suit. The GI Union at Fort Bragg, after a period of frustration in the early months of 1972, recognized the need to deal with the basic issues of service life and launched a similar drive to improve local living conditions. Conducting a survey of soldier apartments in the small town of Spring Lake, they found that a large percentage of the residences had faulty plumbing and heating and that complaints to landlords frequently were ignored. Lists were compiled of area landlords, and enlisted men and their families were counseled on housing-code regulations and small-claims-court procedures. The effort provided valuable assistance to military families and acquainted many new servicemen with the Fort Bragg GI movement. The Ft. Hood United Front also initiated a housing campaign in the first half of 1972. Information about housing and landlords was distributed and a tenants' council was established in the Simonsville section of Killeen. A petition to improve GI housing was signed by over three hundred people and presented to the area Board of Realtors. None of these projects produced spectacular results or attracted massive support, but they were important indications of a crucial new turn in the GI movement and showed that political activity could be sustained in a "peacetime," volunteer Army.

The same kind of concern over daily living conditions appeared within the Navy. We have already seen how resistance during the bombing campaign of 1972 was sparked by unsafe and oppressive conditions aboard ships; the same problems led to further unrest after the signing of the Vietnam peace agreements. The first and most striking example of this occurred on the helicopter landing ship U.S.S. *Ogden* during minesweeping operations off the coast of North Vietnam. On March 30, 1973, twenty-three of the twenty-five men in the ship's Air Operations division refused to work in protest over equipment hazards and harassment from superiors. The men presented a petition to the commanding officer charging that the ship was unsafe and that supervisory officers ignored requests for improvements. The captain ignored the sailors' grievances, however, and threatened to jail the entire group. Ten of the men gave in, but thirteen defied the command and refused to return to duty. The rebels were transferred immediately to Subic Bay and were court-martialed for willful disobedience. Meanwhile the *Ogden*'s sister ship, the U.S.S. *Duluth*, encountered similar difficulties as it prepared to sail from San Diego. Fed up with unsafe conditions and the harassment and overwork imposed by the ship's zealous new commander, crew members in April formed their own organization, and, with the help of the Center for Servicemen's Rights, published several issues of the *Free Duluth*. Few changes were made, however, and when the *Duluth* left for Southeast Asia, on June 4, 1973, thirteen men, including a chief petty officer, went AWOL.

Oppressive conditions prompted the same kind of resistance at two other Navy bases in the first half of 1973. In Long Beach, sailors from the U.S.S. *Okinawa* organized an "Enlisted Men's Rights and Grievances Committee" and circulated a petition against improper shipboard conditions and rigid personnel restrictions. They also blasted military recruiters for misrepresenting the true nature of military service. When the petition was presented to the ship commander, however, the organizers were punished with extra work assignments. At Portsmouth, New Hampshire, restrictive hair regulations, command harassment, and inadequate food service led, in April 1973, to a two-week mess-hall strike by inmates of the Portsmouth Naval Prison. Beginning on April 19, the strike produced a two thirds drop in attendance at meals and at times was supported by as many as three hundred fifty of the four hundred men in the brig. The effort apparently was initiated by blacks, but men of both races participated and supported the drive to improve local conditions. Unfortunately, black-white unity crumbled a few weeks later, and frustrations from the command's refusal to meet their demands resulted in bitter racial fighting.

II

The brawl at Portsmouth, which reportedly sent seventeen men to the hospital, was only one of several racial conflicts within the Navy during the cease-fire period. The mounting influx of black recruits, coupled with persistent institutional discrimination, resulted in continued black revolt throughout 1973. Additional outbursts occurred in January aboard the amphibious assault ship U.S.S. *Inchon* and in July aboard the carrier U.S.S. *Franklin D. Roosevelt*. At the end of May, black and white sailors from the U.S.S. *Coral Sea* clashed for several nights at the Japanese port city of Sasebo. A special human-relations committee and a meeting between the commander and a delegation of blacks had failed to halt worsening racial tensions during the carrier's West Pacific cruise, and when the ship pulled in for shore leave on May 26, fights broke out at local bars for three consecutive nights. (The situation was seriously aggravated by the command's liberal use of the white Shore Patrol and an armed Marine detachment.) The ship was forced to leave Sasebo on May 30, two days ahead of schedule; eight black and Puerto Rican sailors were arrested for their role in the incidents.

At many bases, minority servicemen formed political organizations to defend themselves against repression and fight for equal opportunity. The Black Servicemen's Caucus, founded in San Diego in 1972 and active in the *Kitty Hawk* and *Constellation* rebellions, expanded its operations and by early 1973 opened additional offices in Orange County, California, and in New Orleans. In Norfolk, black sailors joined with local civilians to form an organization known as the "Tidewater Africans." At Camp Lejeune, black Marines attempting to organize against discrimination narrowly escaped serious injury at the hands of white supremacists. On May 2, 1973, the "United We Stand" bookstore and organizing center in Jacksonville was destroyed by a bomb explosion. Approximately twenty black Marines had been meeting at the center with a representative of the National Black Draft Counselors, and the attack came in apparent anticipation of a third meeting. Usually, assaults on GI-movement offices end up in the "unsolved crime" category, but in this instance Leroy Gibson, leader of "Rights for White People," was arrested and charged for the act. One of the most successful examples of black organizing occurred in 1973 at Walter Reed Army Medical Center, where black enlisted men joined with civilian base workers in forming "United Blacks Against Discrimination" (UBAD). With support from a number of senior black NCOs, the group created pressure for improved conditions at the hospital and successfully defended active-duty members against command repression. Numerous other black groups—often informal in nature and unrecorded by the press—were formed on bases and ships throughout the services. As in earlier years, black servicemen have remained the most active and highly organized sector of the GI movement.

While blacks have normally stood alone in resisting racial abuses, the post-Vietnam GI movement, with its greater emphasis on daily grievances, witnessed an increasing number of instances of common black-white struggle. One example of this unity was the defense of black airman Frederick Stubbs within Lowry AFB's 3320th Retraining Group—a controversial "rehabilitation" center notorious for oppressive and discriminatory practices. In the early-morning hours of March 1, 1973, Stubbs was beaten by white military policemen, charged with assault and resisting arrest, and, despite extensive injuries, placed in solitary confinement. In response, white activists publishing the newspaper *Blue Screw* joined with blacks in mobilizing support for Stubbs throughout the base. Approximately sixty GIs and civilians attended the first day of his June court-martial, including several white airmen from the elite student pilot school at Lowry and over twenty men from the retraining group. Black and white GIs continued to attend the sessions in the following days, in some cases going AWOL to do so. The incident set an important precedent for black-white unity at the base and showed that racial divisions could be overcome through political action.

The predominately white Vietnam Veterans Against the War organization at Fort Lewis, Washington, also worked with blacks to combat racism. A special pamphlet was written and distributed on the base to inform GIs of the root causes of discrimination within the military. During the winter of 1973, the group picketed the offices of Washington Congressman Floyd Hicks to protest the biased findings of the House Armed Services subcommittee on disciplinary problems, which Hicks chaired. The group's most successful practice, though, came within individual units at the base. On March 20, 1973, for example, twenty-five black, brown, and white GIs from the 864th Engineers Battalion confronted their commanding officer with demands for more respect from their superiors, the immediate removal of NCOs using racist slurs, better job assignments, greater schooling opportunities, and time off after field exercises. Interestingly enough, these demands came up a few months later in hearings before the House Armed Service Committee and were generally endorsed by Army Secretary Robert Froehlke. A third example of growing enlisted unity involved defense of the "Camp Allen 13," the black sailors court-martialed for participating in the November 26, 1972, rebellion at the Norfolk Naval Correctional Facility. The Tidewater Africans were joined by white civilians and GIs calling themselves the "Defense Committee." In the first half of 1973, the two groups worked together effectively to mobilize support for the black prisoners.

III

As the GI movement turned inward, the military justice system and abuses of command authority inevitably sparked increased criticism. Attracted to the ranks by visions of a new, professional military, voluntary recruits found instead archaic and repressive disciplinary methods and a harsh and unresponsive bureaucracy; the result was an enlarged struggle for GI rights. One of the first groups to articulate this growing concern was the Defense Committee, in Norfolk. Formed during the *Forrestal* sabotage trial of seaman Jeffrey Allison in late 1972, the Defense Committee focused primarily on providing legal assistance to servicemen and mobilizing pressure against hazardous working conditions. Through the newspaper *Grapes of Wrath* (with a circulation of approximately nine thousand), the Committee established local chapters in individual units and ships throughout the Tidewater area. During 1973, the Defense Committee concept spread to other East Coast bases, and by the end of the year, similar committees existed at Portsmouth, Newport, Philadelphia, Jacksonville, and Charleston.

Nowhere has the problem of GI rights and military repression generated more turmoil than in Germany. Determined to root out the troubles of the Vietnam era, Seventh Army commanders in early 1973 launched a massive campaign to suppress internal opposition and eliminate drug use. In January, several leading GI activists with the papers *FighT bAck* and *FTA with Pride* were suddenly ordered back to the United States. In July, a "summer counterintelligence offensive" was mounted against enlisted organizers and their civilian supporters. On a more general level, a crude and blatantly unconstitutional campaign was launched against "known or suspected drug abusers." In the 71st Maintenance Battalion, in Nellingen, for example, soldiers were notified in late 1972 that even if *suspected* of drug use, their pass and driving rights would be revoked, civilian clothes would be forbidden, all non-military furnishings would be taken from the barracks, and, incredibly, doors of private rooms would be removed. In September of 1973, General Michael Davison issued USAREUR Circular 600-85 authorizing such practices as strip-down searches of "soldier body cavities," unannounced day or night drug inspections, the use of dogs in no-knock room searches, and the banning of anti-establishment or drug-related songs and posters.

Not surprisingly, such policies backfired and led to a resurgence of GI resistance. On February 10, 1973, fifty soldiers and civilians, aided by civilian attorneys from the newly opened Heidelberg office of the Lawyers Military Defense Committee (LMDC), gathered in the town of Butzbach to establish the "Committee for GI Rights." Initially headed by Specialists Ted Strickland and Stephen Sands, the Committee organized significant political opposition to the Army's campaign, and in the spring of 1973 filed a historic legal suit against General Davison's anti-drug policies. Prepared by attorney Robert Rivkin and ably argued before Washington Federal District Court by LMDC Director David Addlestone, the case resulted in a major GI victory: In February 1974, Judge Gerhard Gesell declared that Circular 600-85 was an unconstitutional violation of servicemen's rights and ordered that most of the program be terminated. (The Justice Department has since appealed the case, and the decision is now under higher-court review.) Other reactions to the mounting repression in Europe included a January 22 demonstration at McNair barracks in Berlin and, in September, the founding of the "Council on Rights and Equality" and the newspaper *Write On* at Bitburg AFB. The attempted crackdown also resulted in a series of sabotage and arson attacks. Several hundred thousand dollars' worth of damage was caused by fires at Baumholder, Bad Kreuznach, and Bitburg. On March 16, three Molotov cocktails exploded inside the headquarters building of the 1st Squadron, 1st

U. S. Cavalry, in Schwabach, causing extensive damage. In Neu Ulm, thirty-eight trucks and seven rocket-launcher platforms of the 1st Battalion/81st Artillery were damaged by GI saboteurs on May 1. The Army's repressive policies, far from reducing unrest, helped account for a major increase in resistance among soldiers in Germany during 1973.

The most widely supported organizing effort of the post-Vietnam GI movement involved Article 15 of the UCMJ. Seeing non-judicial punishment as the most inequitable and detested feature of military discipline, the Ft. Hood United Front began a campaign in the summer of 1972 to alter the system and democratize military justice. The group drew up a petition to Congress demanding that the right to impose summary punishments be transferred from the commanding officer to a board of three enlisted men, grades E-1 through E-9, to be chosen every ninety days in company-wide elections. Their statement concluded that "a democratically elected board would change the present system of intimidation and harassment to one of fairness and justice." The campaign met with immediate success, gaining over eight hundred signatures in less than two weeks. As other organizing projects heard of the idea, they quickly adopted it themselves: over one hundred fifty soldiers and airmen signed a similar petition drawn up by the Fort Lewis-McChord AFB GI Alliance, and airmen at Mountain Home AFB likewise joined the effort. With GI groups growing more concerned with military justice during 1973, Article-15 petitions circulated at more that twenty bases in the United States and overseas. On October 12, 1973, two servicemen, one from Travis AFB and the other from Okinawa, presented the names of over one thousand active-duty supporters of the petition to black House Armed Services Committee member Ron Dellums (D-Calif.), who pledged to work for a complete overhaul of the UCMJ. The Article-15 campaign has attracted the support of thousands of low-ranking enlisted people, and continues today as a vital struggle of the GI movement.

IV

The GI movement first developed in response to the Vietnam War, and throughout its history displayed a consistent anti-imperialist focus. While other concerns have assumed greater immediate importance in the post-Vietnam environment, opposition to overseas intervention remains widespread within the ranks and represents a constant undercurrent threatening future Vietnam-type operations. Nowhere is this more evident than in the West Pacific, where more than two hundred thousand American servicemen are poised for possible counterinsurgency missions. GI organizing remains vigorous in the area, with five full-time GI centers in Okinawa and Japan and numerous informal GI groups within ships and individual units throughout the region. In 1972, two important new servicemen's organizations were established in Okinawa: the "People's House" and *Omega Press* near Koza, and the "United Front" and *Han Sen Free Press* near Marine camps Schwab and Hansen at Kin. In March 1973, active-duty servicemen and Vietnam veterans from Kin joined a mass civilian rally to support demands for Okinawan independence and removal of all U.S. bases. On May 25 and 26, three Camp Hansen GIs were arrested by Marine officials for distributing the *Free Press* and soliciting signatures on a petition to Congress. On June 9, 1973, nearly fifteen hundred GIs, dependents, and Okinawan civilians attended a "soul/rock/folk" festival sponsored by VVAW in Koza. The gathering gave a major boost to the GI projects on the island, including the newly opened Women's House in Koza, and helped forge greater black-white unity.

In Japan, *Semper Fi* and the Vietnam veterans' organization at Iwakuni have remained active throughout the postwar period. The most serious unrest among Iwakuni Marines, though, surfaced not in Japan but at the remote Marine air base at Nam Phong, Thailand, to which hundreds of local troops were assigned (on "temporary duty") in 1972 and early 1973. Opposition to the continued bombing of Indochina and oppressive duty conditions at the post generated substantial resistance. *Semper Fi* was mailed to key contacts and distributed regularly at the base, and a number of protest meetings and sabotage incidents occurred. The main organizing center at Iwakuni also remained active during 1973 but was hampered by command repression. The "Hobbit" coffeehouse was declared "off-limits," and on July 4 six Marines were arrested at the base for distributing "unauthorized literature"—the Declaration of Independence. The Iwakuni project survived, though, and in the second half of the year gained increased support from returning veterans of Nam Phong. At Yokosuka Naval Base, near Tokyo, sailors with the "New People's Center," in the spring of 1973, launched a campaign against Pentagon plans to homeport the U.S.S. *Midway* at the station. Recognizing that the move would create hardships for their families and would be a step toward facilitating military interventions, men aboard the carrier initiated a petition against homeporting and all U.S. military expansion in Asia. Approximately two hundred crew members and dependents signed the petition before it was suppressed by ship commanders. These protest activities in Japan and Okinawa demonstrate the critical importance of civilian support. National Lawyers Guild and Pacific Counseling Service workers are active at each location, and the legal aid and support they provide play a crucial role in sustaining GI resistance. Their experience again proves the value of military support projects.

In October of 1973, American servicemen suddenly found themselves facing potential combat action in the Middle East. As Arab and Israeli forces battled to a tenuous standoff at the Suez Canal, the carrier U.S.S. *Independence* and other elements of the Sixth Fleet were rushed to the area from Norfolk, and the 3rd Battalion/6th Marine Regiment at Camp Lejeune was deployed to the Mediterranean a month ahead of schedule. The 82nd Airborne at Fort Bragg and other Marine units at Camp Lejeune were placed on standby for possible immediate overseas shipment. In response to the prospects of American intervention in the Middle East, twenty active-duty GIs and civilian activists gathered in Jacksonville, North Carolina, on October 13 to demonstrate against U.S. involvement. The assembled representatives of Fort Bragg, Charleston, Norfolk, and Camp Lejeune circulated a petition urging Senator Fulbright "to immediately introduce legislation forbidding the introduction of U.S. forces into the current Mideast hostilities." Nearly three hundred Marines and military dependents quickly signed the petition—before the effort was temporarily halted by the arrest of three of the participating servicemen. Scott Miller, stationed at Fort Bragg, and Randy Thompson and Mark Ratlin, of Little Creek Amphibious Base in Norfolk, were apprehended by Jacksonville police and turned over to local MPs. No charges were filed, though, and the men were subsequently released.

The harassment failed to deter the petitioning, however, and the drive continued at East Coast bases for several weeks. On November 2, a delegation of GIs and civilians traveled to Washington to present Senator Fulbright's office with the names of three thousand supporters of the petition, many of them active-duty servicemen. The swell of opposition to the short-lived Middle East mobilization suggests that future American interventions are likely to encounter a resurgence of internal resistance. The continuing GI movement thus stands as a potential democratic constraint on military adventurism—an essential check on the intrusion of imperial power into Third World nations.

V

The continuing resistance of the postwar era adds vital new dimensions to the GI movement—and compounds the task of summing up and assessing its meaning. Obviously, dissent cannot be dismissed as a temporary aberration of the Vietnam War. Nor can the widespread upheaval of recent years be blamed on permissiveness, or subsumed under the simplistic heading of "race and drugs." Indeed, GI resistance and the military manpower crisis have created massive difficulty and internal disruption throughout the services. The unique and truly unprecedented character of recent events can perhaps best be seen by comparing the contemporary situation with earlier periods in American history. Vietnam was not the only modern war to witness dissent among enlisted men; each major military action of the century encountered at least some degree of rank-and-file unrest. A look at the circumstances and extent of these historical precedents will provide a better understanding of the GI movement and broaden our knowledge of its root causes.

The most consistent form of enlisted resistance through the years has been the struggle of black servicemen against racism. In every major American war, minority troops have attempted to win for themselves a share of the democratic rights they were sent into battle to protect; the result has been a long history of confrontation and rebellion, with uprisings occurring frequently in each of the world wars and in Korea. Hundreds of thousands of blacks served with distinction during World War I, but despite their sacrifices were unable to secure justice within their own country, particularly in the South. In September 1917, blacks of the 24th Infantry Regiment engaged in a bloody battle with white residents of Houston, Texas, killing seventeen townspeople. Afterward, thirteen black soldiers were convicted of murder and mutiny and were immediately hanged, while forty-one others were sentenced to life imprisonment. In another dispute, a month later, black soldiers of the New York 15th Infantry were transferred en masse to the European front after they stormed a hotel in Spartanburg, South Carolina. Numerous other racial rebellions occurred in the ranks during the war and within civilian communities in the years immediately following, as black Americans made a major bid for freedom. During World War II, nearly one million blacks served in the ranks but again suffered segregation and slave-like oppression. In one incident in 1940, blacks of the 94th Engineers Battalion, in Gurdon, Arkansas, were so harassed by local citizens and members of the Arkansas State Police that they were forced to desert their bivouac area and return to their home base in Michigan. The largest black uprisings of the war took place at Fort Bragg, Camp Robinson, Camp Davis, Camp Lee, and Fort Dix. Opposition to menial and unsafe working conditions also prompted mass mutinies at Marbry Field, Florida, and Port Chicago, California. According to John Hope Franklin, "innumerable" additional clashes occurred on and off base throughout the course of the war. In 1948, President Truman officially ordered the end of segregation within the armed services. His act did very little to change the conditions of service life, however, and severe discrimination persisted (as documented in a classic study by then Special Counsel to the NAACP Thurgood Marshall). De facto segregation continued to plague minority servicemen during the Korean War and led to numerous enlisted rebellions—one of the largest a mutiny by an all-Puerto Rican unit of the 65th Infantry. The widespread black resistance of the Vietnam era, therefore, can be seen as an extension, indeed an intensification, of the historic fight of minority servicemen for their rightful portion of the freedoms they have defended.

Apart from the efforts of non-whites, the largest and most important example of previous soldier dissent is what one historian has called "The Army Mutiny of 1946," what was known at the time as the "Bring Em Home" movement. After the long and bitter world war, American troops eagerly awaited a speedy return to the States. The War Department had other ideas, however, and not only delayed demobilization but transferred troops from Europe to the Pacific, ostensibly for occupation duty. Many troops suspected that their real mission was to protect American interests in China and in other Asian countries, and they quickly became angry at this unwanted burden. The first hint of growing unrest came in a protest telegram sent to the White House on August 21 from 580 members of the 95th Division stationed at Camp Shelby, Mississippi. In September, troops of the same division harassed and openly booed General Harry Lewis Twaddle when he attempted to explain why troops were needed overseas. Throughout the fall of 1945, the campaign gained momentum, as soldiers around the world deluged congressmen with letters and telegrams, and families of the servicemen formed over two hundred "bring back daddy" clubs. By December, resentment among troops began to reach explosive proportions. On Christmas Day 1945, the day by which many had expected to be home, four thousand troops marched to the 21st Replacement Depot headquarters in Manila carrying banners with the message "We Want Ships."

The movement suddenly burst into feverish activity when the War Department announced, on January 4, 1946, that Pacific demobilizations would be cut from eight hundred thousand to three hundred thousand per month. Seldom has a military announcement created so much furor. On January 6, thousands of active-duty demonstrators in Manila attempted to storm the headquarters of Lieutenant General Styer. The next day, twenty-five hundred men continued the march and brought their complaints before the command's attention. That evening, twelve thousand troops (some reports say as many as twenty thousand) jammed into the Philippine Hall of Congress to continue the protest and listen to speeches denouncing American plans in East Asia. The upsurge quickly spread throughout the world. On January 7, two thousand GIs rallied at Camp Foster, France. On January 8, more than five thousand soldiers sent telegrams from Saipan; thirty-five hundred men on Guam staged a hunger strike; fifteen hundred soldiers rallied in Reims, France; and one thousand men marched in a torchlight parade down the Champs Élysées in Paris. On January 9, eighteen thousand men took part in two giant protest meetings on Guam; five thousand soldiers demonstrated in Frankfurt; fifteen thousand protested in Honolulu; and five thousand staged a rally in Calcutta. Protests also erupted within the United States, when one thousand soldiers and WACs at Camp Andrews, Maryland, booed their commanding officer as he attempted to explain the delay in discharges. After this wave of initial outrage, the GIs established ongoing organizations to continue their campaign, frequently led by men with trade-union experience. On January 10, the Manila Soldiers Committee held its first meeting, with 156 elected delegates representing some 140,000 soldiers. (One of those elected to the organization's eight-man central committee was then-Sergeant Emil Mazey, now Secretary-Treasurer of the United Auto Workers Union.) As the struggle continued and became more organized, its political perspective broadened to include demands for enlisted men's rights. On January 13, five hundred GIs in Paris met and adopted a set of demands that became known as the "Enlisted Man's Magna Carta." The program called for the abolition of all officer privilege, proposed that officers serve at least one year as enlisted men, and urged that court-martial boards be composed of enlisted men.

Faced with a growing rebellion within the ranks and fearful of its increasing political sophistication, the War Department finally gave in. Troop ships were quickly dispatched to Asia, and all plans for possible Asian intervention were dropped. In a very real sense, the "Bring Em Home" movement was a major restraint on American postwar foreign policy, undermining the capability to suppress revolutionary upheavals in China and Southeast Asia. The movement also played a role, albeit less successfully, in subsequent efforts to reform enlisted life. In response to a flood of complaints over the abuses of officer privilege and the injustices of military law, the War Department appointed the Doolittle Board as a special commission to suggest new policies. The Board recommended a number of far-reaching proposals to reduce the distinctions between officers and enlisted men and improve conditions within the ranks, but its advice was largely ignored. Instead, Congress in 1950 approved the UCMJ, authorizing some slight improvements in court-martial practice but leaving enlisted life basically unchanged.

Less extensive but important internal opposition also developed during the Korean conflict, particularly during the political stalemate in the war's latter stages. From 1951 to 1953, the desertion rate showed a sharp upswing, jumping from 10.1 to 29.6 per thousand in the Marine Corps and from 14.3 to 22 per thousand in the Army. The biggest scandal of the war, though, was the conduct of American prisoners of war held in North Korea. In June 1952, ninety-four American and British POWs sent a letter through the UN condemning their governments' war policies. When the conflict ended, thirty-eight American GIs reportedly chose to remain in North Korea; as many as two hundred soldiers were suspected of collaboration with the enemy. A public uproar followed these revelations, fanned by alarmist accounts such as Eugene Kinkead's *In Every War but One,* and as a result the Pentagon introduced the Armed Forces Code of Conduct to remind servicemen of their patriotic duties.

The post-World War II protests were by far the largest of these historical precedents and represent the only example comparable in scale to the GI movement. While the We Want Ships upsurge was a pervasive and widespread phenomenon, however, it appeared for only a short time in response to specific demands for demobilization. By contrast, the GI movement has existed continuously since 1967, comprising a total of more than three hundred servicemen's newspapers and organizations and reaching out to hundreds of thousands of GI supporters. The movement remained at a relatively mass level for four years, from 1969 through 1972. As many as one thousand servicemen participated in demonstrations at Fort Hood, Fort Bragg, Fort Bliss, Camp Pendleton, Heidelberg, and San Diego; tens of thousands more joined in countless additional rallies and protest actions at bases throughout the world. The GI movement also has encompassed a profound cultural and generational gulf within the ranks—marked by widespread drug use and breakdown of the vital NCO-GI nexus—as well as an extensive wave of disruption and direct resistance—evident in sabotage, violent uprisings, and the like. Such sustained, pervasive resistance is clearly without parallel in American military history.

Today's dissent is also unique in the depth of its political expression. While the Bring Em Home movement was motivated partly by anti-interventionism and demands for soldiers' rights, the overriding concern was postwar demobilization. By contrast, the GI movement has projected an articulate, highly developed program opposing all American involvement in Southeast Asia and advocating greater human dignity and democracy within the ranks. The demand to end the Indochina war has been on the agenda of nearly every GI group and has been at the heart of the resistance movement from its very inception. This anti-war emphasis includes more than mere opposition to the Vietnam intervention, however. Many groups have developed a more thorough, radical opposition to all counterinsurgency operations abroad. Nearly all the overseas GI groups, most black organizations, the various chapters of MDM, and many other servicemen's groups have called for the end of all foreign intrusion in the affairs of Third World peoples. For many GI radicals, withdrawal from Vietnam is only the first step toward the larger goal of self-determination for all underdeveloped societies and demilitarization in America. The GI movement has also focused on the demand for greater servicemen's rights. Whether seeking First Amendment liberties, an end to racial discrimination, reform of the military justice system, or an end to repressive administrative practices, GI groups have relentlessly fought for a more humane and democratic military. In pursuing greater individual freedom and the rights of citizenship, GI activists have embraced the Nuremberg principle, asserting that servicemen have not only the right but the responsibility to oppose unconscionable military policies. Never has such an overtly political movement developed within the ranks.

The most striking feature of the current upheaval has been its impact on military operations. Disaffection peaked not in the aftermath of war but in the very heat of combat. Fraggings and combat refusals in Vietnam, sabotage and riots within the Seventh Fleet, and the collapse of morale in Thailand all came during active military hostilities and were important factors in limiting U.S. military options. Indeed, at least in the case of the infantry in Vietnam, GI resistance substantially limited American combat capabilities and played a key role in the decision to withdraw U.S. forces. Moreover, as we shall examine in Chapters 8 and 9, the manpower and morale difficulties of the Vietnam era also were an important consideration in fundamental alterations of American military strategy and in the sweeping personnel-policy changes associated with the all-volunteer force. Reaching into every major military installation on the globe and influencing virtually every aspect of service life, the GI movement is without question the most serious internal challenge ever faced by the American armed forces.

VI

Our study would be incomplete without attempting to explain the reasons for dissent. Clearly, a major factor has been the Vietnam War. The movement emerged directly from that conflict and closely followed its evolution—shifting from one service to another as the nature of the attack changed, and periodically surging in response to specific military decisions. Indeed, the most militant and committed activists were precisely those men with direct combat experience. Of course, it would only be expected that the longest and most bitterly disputed war in American history should result in questioning within the ranks. The resistance movement surged, though, not merely because of the conflict's unpopularity but because of the particular type of war fought in Vietnam—because of the very nature of counterinsurgency warfare. The American intervention hopelessly attempted to defeat a successful rural-based revolution. The introduction of conventionally equipped expeditionary forces and the application of massive firepower could not destroy popular support for the insurgents and indeed only increased anti-Americanism. As population control and forced urbanization emerged as the dominant policies, the American mission degenerated into an orgy of indiscriminate destruction. Young servicemen sent to protect America from the Communist menace found not John Wayne heroics but free-fire zones, "recon by fire," body counts, My Lai, the bombing of population centers—the long and dismal array of atrocities that constituted American policy in Vietnam. The immersion of credulous GIs in this dehumanizing experience was a fundamental cause of the upheaval within the armed forces.

Another major factor in the development of GI resistance has been the nature of military service itself. The oppressive conditions of enlisted duty have repeatedly sparked defiance and internal opposition. Racial discrimination, the most pervasive and damaging of these grievances, has caused particularly widespread unrest among black servicemen. Given the large and steadily mounting percentage of non-whites within the ranks, discriminatory conditions have inevitably led to frequent black rebellion. The stifling rigidity of military discipline has also contributed to GI unrest. Maintenance of officer privilege and of a repressive penal code are constant irritants to enlisted people and have often led to resistance. The GI movement also has been influenced directly by specific policies and administrative acts. The "early out" discharges of 1971 and 1972, for example, decimated many political protest groups and reduced internal unrest. On the other hand, major acts of repression, such as the Army's crackdown on dissent and drugs in Germany during 1973, have often increased internal opposition. The current military crisis thus is clearly related to the conditions and policies of the services.

It can be argued, though, that these circumstances existed in the past (that military service was in fact a great deal more difficult in earlier times than now), without causing the kind of disruption evident today. Indeed, the continuation of resistance in recent years—despite the end of Indochina hostilities and the introduction of extensive liberal reforms—raises profound questions on the causes of the military crisis and forces us to seek other explanations. The point is that, apart from the specific purpose and nature of military service, there have to be other reasons for the unprecedented difficulty now facing the military—that the roots of the crisis lie within civilian society. Military manpower shortages, for example, while partly related to conditions on the inside, seem to reflect primarily a generalized disdain for military service among young people. Similarly, the prevalence of drug use in the ranks is largely the result of a spreading drug culture throughout the society. The general upsurge of radical politics in recent years has also been a major factor, helping to foster a more critical view of the military among many young people and providing invaluable direct support to GI organizations. Black resistance is also obviously related to emerging black nationalism, with the services now a major arena of the black power revolution. Indeed, while Detroit, Watts, and other cities quieted down in the late 1960s, Camp Lejeune, Travis, Mannheim, Long Binh, the *Kitty Hawk*, and countless other military bases exploded in black rebellion.

There is little doubt that the decline of the armed forces is intimately tied to changes in American society.

All these points are important, but they do not convey the crux of the matter: many young people today simply do not find the military relevant to their basic needs. There is something in the nature of contemporary society that weakens the warrior ethic, some characteristic of our affluent, technological civilization that seems incompatible with the military. According to Max Watts, journalist and long-time supporter of the GI movement in Germany, the same kind of difficulties experienced within the American military exist within the armed forces of nearly all the advanced industrial nations. Watts has studied internal resistance and unrest in the German, French, Italian, Dutch, Japanese, Austrian, and numerous other armies and concludes that the present military crisis in the United States is directly related to similar developments elsewhere. His intriguing hypothesis is that the evolution of industrial society is leading to a generalized decline in the armed forces of all developed countries, that a high degree of capital accumulation and the life-style changes this entails result in a marked change of attitude toward the military. It is a fascinating and potentially historic finding (Watts may soon publish a book on the subject)—one that I think best explains the ultimate basis of the decline of the military. There seems to be an inherent trend in the ascent of industrial society antithetical to military institutions. The development of civilization may be reaching the point envisioned by Marcuse where the repressive structures upon which it was built are becoming obsolete. The authoritarianism and rigidity of military hierarchies are ill suited to a consumerist, gratification-oriented society; nor do they fit the emergence of countercultures and "liberation" life styles. The austerity of garrison life and the narrow, nationalistic pursuits of armies are increasingly irrelevant to the youth of advanced industrial society.

PART II

CHAPTER 8

GETTING BY WITH LESS

Resistance to the military has had a profound impact on defense and foreign policy. While the Pentagon clings to a strategy of global dominance, the manpower resources for such a mission are no longer available. Popular political pressures and unrest in the ranks have resulted in declining force levels, reduced military readiness, and, as we observed in Indochina, diminished combat effectiveness. Out of the crisis has emerged a sweeping re-evaluation of the role of the armed forces and the development of a new military strategy for maintaining foreign imperial interests without the large-scale commitment of forces.

I

For the Pentagon, perhaps the chief lesson of Vietnam has been that sustained counterinsurgency warfare is no longer a realistic option, that the commitment of a huge expeditionary force is politically and militarily disastrous and threatens the very survival of the armed forces. Maxwell Taylor, whose *The Uncertain Trumpet* heralded the strategy of "flexible response," was one of the first to recognize the limitations of this doctrine in Vietnam. In a speech before the National War College (reported in *Fortune* in 1970), General Taylor warned that "limited war" was no longer possible and that future foreign operations would have to involve "declared war of clearly defined objectives," fought "without conscripts or reservists." Similarly, Colonel Zeb Bradford, assessing the Vietnam experience in a 1972 issue of *Military Review*, envisioned a "very circumscribed role" for the postwar Army, asserting that the political and military inflexibility of ground forces and the "potential political constraints" of new manpower policies would confine conventional forces to a "narrower range of likely contingencies."

The strategy of using massive ground forces for counterrevolutionary warfare has been abandoned. Under new tactical arrangements now being developed, foot soldiers are to be replaced by machines and advanced electronic devices, in a system of technological warfare characterized by General Ellis Williamson as "firepower, not manpower." A crucial element of this is the "electronic battlefield," first publicly announced by General Westmoreland in a historic address to the Association of the United States Army in 1969. "We are on the threshold of an entirely new battlefield concept," the general intoned, one that will "replace wherever possible the man with the machine."

> On the battlefield of the future enemy forces will be located, tracked and targeted almost instantaneously through the use of data links, computer-assisted intelligence evaluation and automated fire control. With first round kill probabilities approaching certainty, and with surveillance devices that can continually track the enemy, the need for large forces to fix the opposition physically will be less important.

The heart of this system consists of the use of electronic sensing devices that can detect the presence of enemy forces by distinguishing them from the surrounding environment.* Another advanced surveillance invention designed to replace soldiers is the sensor-equipped remotely piloted vehicle, or RPV. These drones, now being developed by the Army at Fort Monmouth, would be fitted with television cameras and infrared sensors to monitor and target enemy positions. To complement these innovations, the Army is developing elaborate new machine weapons—including newer, more mobile tanks; faster, more maneuverable helicopters; and extremely accurate bombs and missiles (the so-called "smart bombs," designed to lock on targets through infrared or electromagnetic sensors, or through laser beams).

While the infantry has been replaced by electronic sensors and machines, the role of the Air Force and the Navy in U.S.

* See Mike Klare, *War Without End* (New York: Alfred A. Knopf, 1972), Chapter VII, for a detailed examination of these weapons systems.

military planning has been enlarged. American forces will maintain and in fact increase their level of applicable fire-power, despite reduced force levels, through greater use of tactical air support and other forms of bombardment. For-wardly stationed Air Force bases, such as those maintained in Thailand, the Philippines, Turkey, and elsewhere throughout the globe, will insure that Air Force jets are ready for combat. In addition, the Air Force's new "bare base" concept, with fully operational tactical air bases established in remote re-gions in just three days, will further allow U.S. planes to inter-vene rapidly anywhere in the world. The most striking fea-ture of U.S. machine warfare plans is the new role now reserved for naval forces. According to Admiral Zumwalt,

> it has become increasingly clear that future U.S. mili-tary involvement overseas will call first for the high-technology, capital-intensive services—air and naval forces —to support the indigenous armies of threatened allies. So, as I understand the Nixon doctrine, the Navy's future con-tribution will be even greater than in the past.

Forwardly deployed aircraft-carrier groups, literally within hours of an emergency, can deploy fully equipped, combat-ready Marine detachments, backed up with immediate tacti-cal air support. Thus withdrawing American ground forces will be replaced, as we have seen in Indochina, with a massive tactical air armada from Air Force bases and Navy carriers.

Another crucial component of the new American military alignment is the development and support of mercenary armies in client states strategically located throughout the world. While the United States will concentrate on technol-ogy and machine-delivered firepower, the manpower for still-necessary ground operations is expected to come from those states whose military establishments have been and continue to be the special focus of U.S. training and financing. As stated by President Nixon, "we shall look to the nation di-rectly threatened to assume the primary responsibility of pro-viding the manpower for its defense." This American policy, reverting to the classic colonial policies of earlier imperial powers, involves lavish U.S. economic and military assistance to regional military powers (such as Iran, South Korea, and Brazil), which will be expected to provide the ground forces necessary to suppress insurgents in their areas. The Iranian intervention in Oman is a clear example of this strategy in actual operation. Substitution of foreign troops for Americans has many advantages to Washington's war planners, reducing the cost of American foreign operations and diminishing the visibility, and thus the unpopularity, of U.S. imperial violence. Most importantly for our analysis, though, by relying on the armies of foreign military dictatorships, the United States can continue its interventionist policies despite insufficient manpower resources.

Within this new configuration of American military power, the reduced active forces will have a crucial function. Describing a "striking strategic consensus" among top Pentagon policy planners, Morris Janowitz estimated a likely future active force of 1.7 million men, deployed as follows: 100,000 Marine Corps; 450,000 Navy; 450,000 Air Force; and 700,000 Army. Many of the units now stationed overseas will be returned to the United States, subject to rapid potential redeployment through use of the C-5A Galaxy aircraft. European forces are likely to be reduced to near 150,000, while the bulk of the forces now stationed in Asia, including the Army's divisions in Korea, will be withdrawn, leaving only advisers and technical support units. While the ground forces as a whole will be drastically reduced, the Army will maintain two mobile reserve divisions for rapid deployment in emergency situations: the 82nd Airborne at Fort Bragg and either the new Tri-Cap Division at Fort Hood or the 101st Airmobile at Fort Campbell. The Marine Corps likewise will maintain a reserve of active forces for use in "sub-theater or localized warfare"; in fact, the Corps has actually increased the number of troops assigned to combat specialties. At the same time, a large number of U.S. servicemen will serve in what Mike Klare has described as "the mercenary support infrastructure," i.e., the vast establishment required to provide logistics, communications, and air support to U.S.-client armies. Particularly in Asia, American servicemen will be required to perform many highly specialized technical functions necessary to assist U.S.-financed mercenaries and provide backup for U.S. firepower. Thus, the United States is seeking to carve out new tactical patterns in the wake of the battlefield stalemate in Vietnam and the crisis evolving out of that conflict. Although manpower resources have diminished sharply, the Pentagon hopes to maintain America's global commitments through the use of mercenaries and advanced technology.

II

An integral part of the new military strategy is an increase in the readiness of the nation's 900,000 standby-reserve forces. The Pentagon has abandoned the disastrous Vietnam-era policy of increasing draft calls and expanding the size of the active forces to meet an emergency, and in the future will rely instead on a smaller force backed up by combat-ready reserves. Secretary Laird defined this "Total Force" concept as follows: "The Reserves and Guard will be the initial and primary sources for augmentation of the active forces in any future emergency." The increased emphasis on weekend warriors is quite clearly the result of the reduced strengths and capabilities of the active forces. As the 1971 Army Greenbook candidly explained: "If the active structure continues to decline, while strategy requirements remain the same, then Reserve divisions will have to be mobilized for any major commitments."

Unprecedented budgetary outlays for the reserves confirm the seriousness of these plans. Pentagon spending for reserve forces has increased from $2.2 billion in fiscal year 1969 to $4.4 billion in fiscal 1974 and $4.8 billion in 1975. Reserve expenditures have increased as a percentage of the total defense budget from 2.9 per cent in 1968 to 5.2 per cent in fiscal 1974. Moreover, these figures do not include the costs of huge stockpiles of equipment now being issued to reserve units, including such items as M-16 rifles and UH-1 helicopters. In fiscal 1970, Army standby forces received $300 million worth of new combat equipment, but in 1971 that figure jumped to $725 million and in 1972 rose to $1 billion. The annual value of equipment transfers has hovered near the $1 billion mark since and, according to a 1974 Brookings Institution study, is expected to remain at that level through 1977. A similar build-up has occurred within the Navy, and, although precise statistics are unavailable, the Brookings study estimates that cost figures, if known, "might be more impressive than those of the Army." Depending on how the value of this equipment is measured, the annual outlay for reserve forces now totals between $5 billion and $7 billion.

The most important feature of this new role for the reserves is the development of an active combat capability. While standby units have been and will continue to be used frequently in civil disturbances (the National Guard was called up 260 times between January 1965 and October 1971), the greatest emphasis in the Total Force plan is on achieving an "ever-increasing combat readiness" for potential use in foreign intervention. This is being accomplished through the "associate unit" or "round out" concept, whereby reserve units complement and train with similar active-duty forces. The 72nd Mechanized Infantry Brigade in Texas was one of the first outfits to begin joint training exercises, participating in maneuvers with the 1st Cavalry Division at Fort Hood during 1971. Since then, major elements of the active forces have devoted an ever-increasing amount of time to co-operation with reserve units. A striking example of these combat preparations occurred in Southern California in the summer of 1973, when four thousand Marine reservists and five thousand regular Marines participated in Operation "Alkali Canyon," the largest desert-warfare exercise for Marine reserves in forty years and a clear signal of possible involvement in the Middle East. With the increased importance of naval forces in U.S. interventionist planning, the Navy reserve also is being prepared for an unprecedented role in the combat fleet. In 1971, Secretary Laird announced that naval reservists might soon be given responsibility for operating two aircraft carriers, the first time in history that ships of this size would be manned by the reserves. Other aspects of the reserve build-up include the substitution of National Guard for active forces in Nike Hercules Air Defense facilities, increased pilot training and airlift responsibility for the Air National Guard and Air Force Reserve, and conversion of Naval air reserve units from the F-8 to the more modern F-4. The Pentagon thus seems fully committed to molding the reserve forces into a major component of American military strength. Indeed in September of 1974 Manpower Secretary Brehm made the shocking proposal that the President or Secretary of Defense be allowed to mobilize fifty thousand reservists for up to ninety days without prior congressional approval or declaration of national emergency. The once-safe haven of the reserve forces is being prepared for the serious business of war.

Implementation of this new role for the reserves has not

been an easy matter, however, and there are many who seriously doubt that the stand-by forces will ever achieve the degree of readiness desired by the Pentagon. The most immediate challenge to these plans is the enlisted-manpower crisis, which, as noted in Chapter 1, has had a severe impact within the reserves. The end of the draft and continued aversion to military service among young people have resulted in steadily falling reserve force levels. By the end of fiscal 1973, total reserve shortages exceeded sixty thousand—nearly 7 per cent below the mandated strength of 976,000. The recruitment situation finally became so bleak that the Pentagon was forced to reduce its reserve manpower objectives for fiscal year 1974 to 910,000. The following passage from the House Armed Services Committee Report on the 1974 Defense bill offers a revealing glimpse into the military's manpower difficulties:

> This request represents a reduction of 66,544 from levels authorized for FY 1973. Rather than fully reflecting actual requirements, the request represented in part the best estimates of what the Services will be able to recruit and retain in FY 1974. The committee is not particularly pleased with this approach to defense planning. Nevertheless, it is recognized that there is a severe manpower shortage in the Reserves today, and that it would be futile to mandate an average strength requirement which is beyond attainment.

These shortages clearly jeopardize plans to rely more heavily on the reserves—at least as they are currently organized. The impact of the deficiencies may be mitigated, however, by the Brookings Institution's determination that 310,000 people could be trimmed from reserve rolls without appreciably affecting military capabilities. Indeed Secretary Schlesinger strongly suggested in his 1975 Defense Report that the Pentagon might very well go along with such suggestions and implement a major reorganization of the reserves, thus eliminating the problem of recruitment failures.

Even if manpower difficulties can be resolved, though, increased use of the reserves faces the more fundamental challenge of enlisted morale problems. Reserve units are notorious for their laxity, particularly during unpopular assignments such as the 1970 New York postal workers' strike, and any large-scale mobilization for overseas intervention undoubtedly would create widespread internal disruption. The resistance of weekend warriors thus could become a vital factor in helping to limit military adventurism. Indeed, reservists have spoken out frequently in recent years and have played an active role in the GI movement.

The major organizational vehicle for reservist activity during the Vietnam era was the "Reservists Committee to Stop the War" (RCSW), founded in Berkeley in early 1970 by Adam Hochschild. Through a newsletter entitled *Redline*, the Reservists Committee grew rapidly and within a year comprised some fourteen hundred members in a dozen local chapters. One of the most active affiliates was "Reservists Against the War" (RAW), which appeared in the Boston area in the summer of 1970, with contacts in some twenty-five local reserve units. The first major RCSW action was a historic legal suit filed in Washington in May of 1970 challenging the right of 122 congressmen and senators to hold commissions in the reserve forces. The Committee contended that the practice was not only a dangerous extension of military influence within Congress but a direct violation of the Constitution's prohibition against simultaneously occupying legislative and executive office. (Both the Washington, D.C., District Court and Court of Appeals ruled in favor of the Committee, but the Supreme Court denied the suit in 1974.) In 1970, the Committee also obtained more than twenty-two hundred reservist signatures on a petition demanding immediate American withdrawal from Vietnam and other overseas bases. In 1971, in response to the increasing use of stand-by units against student protests within the United States, nearly five hundred reservists also signed a "no more Kent States" petition, pledging to oppose the use of arms against fellow Americans. With approximately three thousand members, mostly among reservists in the Army and the Marine Corps, RCSW and its local affiliates remained actively opposed to the Indochina intervention throughout 1971 and 1972.

As in the active forces, the winding down of the Vietnam War altered the nature of dissent within the reserves and led to increased emphasis on the injustices of military service and the struggle for democratic rights. In early 1973, for example, seventy-six guardsmen in Madison, Wisconsin, formed the "National Guardsmen's Betterment Association" to attack some of the inequalities of the reserve system, focusing on such issues as hair length, lack of group health insurance, etc. Several organizations have concentrated primarily on demands for longer hair, the most prominent of these a group named BALD ("Brothers Against Legalized Degradation") in Norfolk, Virginia. Perhaps the most progressive new reserve organization has been the "Reserve and National Guard Organizing Committee," formed in Chicago in the summer of 1972. The Committee grew out of a dispute in the 928th TAG Airlift Group at O'Hare Airport in which two hundred fifty reservists signed a petition against restrictive haircut regulations. The group quickly broadened its political focus, however, and through a newsletter entitled *The Rag*, developed contacts in numerous other Chicago-area units. The Committee has been active in providing legal counseling, publishing a "Summer Camp Survival Kit" during the 1973 training season, and, most recently, mobilizing reservists to support the January 1974 independent truckers' strike. Similar organizations have appeared in other parts of the country in recent years as well. Indeed, the renamed Reservists Committee to Stop War still operates in Boston, occasionally publishing *Redline* and continuing to provide a forum for political activity. The presence of these groups is a clear signal to the military that enlisted reservists are not likely to be enthusiastic about call-ups for unpopular causes.

III

Of all the new policies resulting from the decline of military service, none is more striking than the Pentagon's decision to increase the number of women in the military. For the first time in American history, women are assuming a major role in the armed forces and will soon constitute an important share of the nation's military strength. The percentage of women on active duty is expected to jump from approximately 2 per cent in 1973 to over 5 per cent by 1978. Figure 9 illustrates this dramatic increase.

Not only are women being brought into the military in increasing numbers, they are being assigned to an expanded range of duties. Previously restricted to only a small percentage of available jobs, women may now legally hold nearly 75 per cent of the occupations in the military. Except for combat

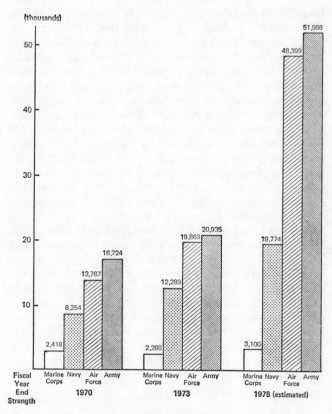

Figure 9
Women in the military.

duty, they are being welcomed into every area of service life.
While some have interpreted these changes as a victory for
the feminist movement, in fact the Pentagon has been motivated not by the advances of women's liberation but by insufficient enlistments among men. As early as 1972, Secretary
Laird saw increased female enlistments as a key means of
avoiding threatened manpower shortages and reducing the requirement for male enlistments. In 1973, both the General
Accounting Office and the Brookings Institution saw greater
female recruitment as essential to meeting defense manpower
needs. The use of women in the military thus is primarily

a means of maintaining huge armed forces despite declining enlistments.

Much has been made of the new opportunities available in the military, but, while many service positions are now open in principle, servicewomen still face serious discrimination in promotions and job assignments. As in the larger society, women in the military are excluded from positions of authority and are disproportionately assigned to low-skill, service occupations. In 1972 a House Armed Services subcommittee published a report on the utilization of military manpower, accusing the Defense Department of "mere tokenism" in its policies toward women. The subcommittee found that enlisted women are promoted much more slowly than men and are overwhelmingly concentrated in the lower grades. In the Army, for example, 1972 statistics show that the percentage of all enlisted people in grades E-1 to E-3 is 26 per cent, but that 51 per cent of the women are concentrated in the bottom three positions, nearly double the service average. Air Force figures show an even greater disparity, with 27 per cent of all enlisted people assigned to the lower grades, compared to 64 per cent for women only. In the Navy, the percentage of women in grades E-1 to E-3 is an incredible 71 per cent. The Committee hearings also disclosed that the women services are discriminated against in command assignments, with only half the expected proportion of officers. In 1971, the officer/enlisted ratio for the entire Army was 1:4.9 but within the Women's Army Corps was 1:9.2. In the Air Force, one in every fifty-five enlisted persons is a woman, but among officers only one out of a hundred is a woman. Job assignments for women also are extremely limited. Even though female recruits score higher on aptitude tests and are more likely to be high-school graduates than men, they are predominately placed in secretarial positions. According to the manpower-utilization report, nearly 70 per cent of all the women in the military perform administrative or clerical tasks. Thus women are being recruited not to serve equally with males but to fill non-skill clerk positions and free men for more important military jobs.

The subjugation of women in the ranks is closely tied to the sexism of military life. Military psychology is a murky and seldom-mentioned topic, but I think we must hazard some thoughts on the subject to understand the role of women. Machismo, the attitude of assertive male superiority, is an essential element of military culture and plays a key role in conditioning hostility and insensitivity among servicemen. In basic training and throughout my Army tour, I frequently sensed an alien, almost violent orientation toward sex. Isolated from sexual contacts and vulnerable to peer-group pressures, the soldier tends to develop a fantasized view of woman and sexual relations and to equate masculinity with belligerence. In the all-male garrison environment, sexual adequacy is demonstrated by physical endurance and aggressiveness. Military training practices consciously foster these associations, with those who fail branded "pussy" or "queer" and those who are suitably warlike designated "men." Ultimately, the soldier's weapon becomes a phallic symbol, with shooting from the hip a sign of unquestioned virility. I remember vividly the young buck sergeant in my basic-training company who frequently displayed his prowess with the M-16 by firing with the rifle butt lodged near his groin. In such a world, female relationships are typically superficial and exploitive, with a woman seen not as another feeling person but as a weak, less capable "object." The pervasiveness of prostitution near major bases reinforces this view of women and helps to maintain the illusion of male superiority. Thus, the discrimination encountered by servicewomen seems rooted in sexist prejudices at the very foundation of military life.

Given these conditions, the surge of female recruits now entering the services may kindle renewed internal resistance. As glossy recruitment promises fade and women find themselves in oppressive circumstances, the GI and feminist movements are likely to converge, with explosive consequences. Already, GI projects and military-counseling organizations are devoting considerable energy to the problems of servicewomen, and as their numbers grow, so will the prospects for political action. In August of 1973, for example, corpswave Andrea Sternberg, stationed at the Portsmouth (Virginia) Naval Hospital, set a precedent that may be followed with increasing frequency in the future: She resigned from the service because of unfair working conditions for women. With assistance from the Norfolk Defense Committee and a hurriedly prepared support petition signed by ninety other active-duty men and women, Andrea forced the local command to accept her resignation and managed to obtain an honorable discharge. In a press release hailing Andrea's release, the Defense Committee saw her victory as "an important step in the fight to win better working conditions and a just and democratic military for all enlisted people." Indeed, the struggles of women in the military will add powerful new pressures to the campaign for GI rights and a more responsive military.

CHAPTER 9

THE ARMY THAT WANTS TO JOIN YOU

The internal problems that gave rise to changes in tactical deployment were also responsible for one of the most important developments in the history of the American military, the shift to an all-volunteer force. Since 1970, the services have spent literally billions of dollars and instituted countless new programs in an unprecedented attempt to alter the basis of military service. Through sweeping pay increases and a vast array of internal reforms, the Pentagon has constructed a new professional force designed to maintain world-wide commitments without the social upheaval resulting from conscription.

I

One of the first acts of the Nixon administration was the appointment of the President's Commission on the All-Volunteer Force, to recommend proposals for eliminating the draft. The Gates Commission completed its work quickly, issuing its report in February of 1970, and soon afterward the signs of change began appearing. In May, the Army announced that appearance regulations would be revised to allow slightly longer hair. A month later, in a dramatic signal of the new emphasis on personnel problems, the Pentagon shocked the Navy establishment by appointing Admiral Elmo Zumwalt Chief of Naval Operations. Zumwalt was promoted over thirty-three other admirals and assigned the special mission of improving service life and bolstering sagging re-enlistment rates. The liberal innovator immediately began shaking up Navy traditions, ordering numerous changes through a series of highly publicized personal messages to the fleet, so-called "Z-grams." Among the measures announced during Zumwalt's first four months were relaxed uniform regulations, beer in the barracks, the opening of hard rock clubs, allowance of beards and longer hair, a ban on "panic painting" and other forms of unnecessary harassment, and liberalized leave policies. In December, Army Chief Westmoreland followed suit with a major directive altering the traditions of Army life—among other things, eliminating morning reveille, easing pass restrictions, and introducing beer in the mess hall. On January 28, 1971, President Nixon delivered a major address offering legislative recommendations for further volunteer reforms. Among the President's proposals were a huge jump in entry-level pay and a $500 million annual increase in allowances for quarters and dependents' assistance. In addition to greater compensation, the President recommended increased expenditures for barracks improvement, to provide more privacy and comfort in Army and Marine Corps barracks; for the upgrading of ROTC programs, to offer increased scholarships and subsistence allowances to college ROTC students; and for recruiting.

In that same month, the Army launched a comprehensive Volunteer Army (VOLAR) experiment designed to test its new liberal policies, focusing on the 197th Infantry Brigade at Fort Benning, the 3rd Armored Cavalry at Fort Lewis, and the 192nd Infantry Brigade at Fort Knox. An example of the program was the Fort Benning Plan, which comprised some 106 proposed administrative actions for improving Army life, including such measures as greater variety of food in mess halls, reduction of work schedules to five days a week, replacement of soldier KPs with civilians, scheduling of additional dances at post service clubs, and the improvement of barracks lounge areas. In addition, the Army conducted an experimental volunteer Army training program for basic trainees at Fort Ord. The program for the first time eliminated the requirement for shaved heads and called for a change in the traditionally abusive manner of drill sergeants. The experiment also removed such practices as infiltration-course training, midnight inspections, and excessively long working hours. All these innovations apparently were considered successful, and in the early part of 1972 many of the liberal policies and training improvements were adopted throughout the Army as official policy.

These were by no means the only changes accompanying the all-volunteer force. Indeed, one could completely fill a book of this size just listing the hundreds of policy initiatives and experiments designed to attract volunteers and reduce internal unrest. We shall look at only a few of the more important and controversial programs, though, particularly those policies aimed directly at the military's major political and social problems. The rise of black nationalism has been one of the Pentagon's gravest internal difficulties, and it is thus not surprising that a great deal of effort has gone into race-relations policies. Unfortunately, most of the changes have been ineffective and have done little to alter the basic roots of military racism. Recruits are now given special instruction on racial affairs; black GIs are allowed to wear modified afro haircuts; and ethnic products have been introduced into base PX stores. But the more fundamental injustices faced by minority servicepeople—excessive pretrial confinement, discriminatory job assignments, etc.—have not been altered.

One potentially important change, though, has been the development of human-relations councils and of a program of equal-opportunity officers within the command structure. Nearly every sizable unit within the armed forces now has a human-relations council, usually consisting primarily of low-ranking enlisted people, which meets regularly to suggest means of improving racial harmony and, during periods of black-white friction, becomes a center of crisis intervention. In addition, the services also appoint within each command a specially designated "equal opportunity officer" or "special assistant for minority affairs," who often has more contact with personnel affairs than the commanding officer. Neither the councils nor the special officers enjoy any real independence, though, and their ability to ameliorate racial tensions is thus quite limited. In fact, the councils seem primarily designed to co-opt and dissipate black militance by channeling demands for reform into administratively controlled outlets. In a tactic frequently employed by industrial management in its struggles with trade unionists, the most articulate and effective GI spokesmen are offered leading positions in these councils and thus are brought under command scrutiny.

Another critical social dilemma for the armed forces is drug abuse, and here again a major series of new personnel policies have been introduced to deal with the situation. In the fall of 1970, the Army instituted the controversial "amnesty" program, whereby soldiers with drug problems were encouraged to enter rehabilitation programs, with the promise that no punitive action would be taken against them (the name "amnesty" apparently caused distress among certain officials, and the program was consequently renamed "exemption"). Rehabilitation centers were set up at Army commands throughout the world; eleven such centers existed in Vietnam alone. The Navy and Marine Corps joined the program in 1971, with two major rehabilitation centers—at Jacksonville, Florida, and Miramar, California—and numerous smaller centers throughout the United States and in Asia. As part of this program, numerous military posts established so-called "rap houses" or "halfway centers," often staffed by enlisted men, at which drug abusers could obtain counseling. While it appears that some of these programs were successful in helping servicemen, in many cases the military's excessive emphasis on returning the soldier to duty and inability to provide the kind of positive reorientation often needed to overcome addiction have resulted in many failures. Moreover, as Senator Harold Hughes and other critics have pointed out, the rehabilitation program offers no guarantee of confidentiality, and the information obtained thus frequently becomes the basis for court-martial or punitive-discharge proceedings.

No base in the country developed a more far-reaching program of internal reform than Fort Carson. Recognizing the failure of traditional methods to cope with the turbulence among young servicemen, Major General Bernard Rogers introduced some of the most comprehensive personnel-policy changes of the entire all-volunteer project. In early 1970, well before the Army began its main experiments, General Rogers acted to make life at Fort Carson less onerous—by eliminating reveille and morning formations, ending such harassments as late-night work parties and Saturday inspections, and allowing soldiers to decorate their living quarters in whatever manner they wished. The general was also one of the first to introduce a racial-harmony council and a drug-therapy center. The most far-reaching of General Rogers' new policies, however, was an extraordinary attempt to introduce a measure of enlisted men's participation, of military democracy, into personnel policies. An "Enlisted Assistant to the General" office was established, with direct access to the post commander, to function as a top-level representative of low-ranking GIs and to investigate the complaints of enlisted people. The office, first manned by Sp/5 William Rosendahl, was provided with a secretary, telephone, and staff car, and effectively served as an ombudsman service for first-term soldiers. In another policy initiative, one very obviously aimed at the local GI dissent organization, the general opened an on-post coffeehouse, the "Inscape," complete with psychedelic decorations and a program of guitarists and folk singers. Of all these reforms, perhaps the most remarkable was the formation of an elected Enlisted Men's Council. Each company at the fort elected representatives to sit on the post-wide council. The chairman of the central council, a position first held by Sp/4 Scott Gray, was exempt from military duties and, with the Enlisted Assistant to the General, was the primary enlisted representative before the Fort Carson command. As with all the volunteer projects, however, none of these measures conferred any real power on enlisted men or altered the basic abuses of military justice and command influence. Nonetheless, certain Project Volunteer innovations, particularly the pioneering efforts of General Rogers, establish an important precedent for real reform. If extended, such programs as servicemen's councils, special enlisted assistants, and minority representatives could be a step toward achieving a more humane and democratic military.

II

The all-volunteer force has been an immensely expensive proposition. The cost of attracting enlisted volunteers has drastically altered the nature of the defense budget and led to huge increases in military spending. The largest portion of this advance has resulted from boosts in the salaries of servicemen, which from 1968 to 1974 increased an average 113 per cent. Part of this gain was caused by the Rivers Amendment, passed in 1967, which provides servicemen annual cost-of-living pay increases equivalent to those granted civil service workers. The bulk of the increase, however, came in November of 1971, when, in response to the Gates Commission recommendation that higher initial salary levels would be necessary to draw sufficient recruits, Congress enacted a sweeping $1.8 billion pay raise; nearly all of this volunteer increase went to enlisted people with less than two years service, resulting in an immediate 55 per cent jump in recruit pay. Entry-level salaries rose from $134 per month in January 1971 to $329 a month in January 1974. According to Defense Department statistics, the incremental cost of volunteer-force pay increases in fiscal year 1974 was $2.3 billion.

Another, more controversial aspect of the pay costs associated with the all-volunteer force is the combat-arms enlistment bonus. The 1971 Pay Increase Act contained a provision authorizing the Defense Department for the first time in modern history to offer a bounty of up to three thousand dollars for enlisting in the infantry. The reason for this new program, first tried with a limited, fifteen-hundred-dollar payment in June 1972, was the disastrously low level of combat volunteers during 1970 and 1971. Figure 10 shows that, during the worst period of the manpower crisis, the Pentagon was signing up a mere 5 per cent of the five thousand men required for combat duty every month.

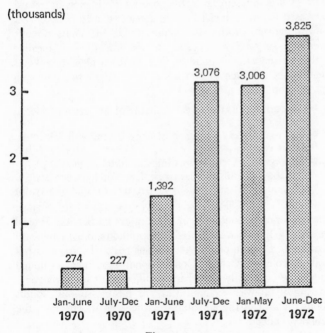

Figure 10
Army combat enlistments—monthly average.

Although enlistments initially increased in response to the bonus offer, the number of volunteers began dropping rapidly again in early 1973. In April, Army combat enlistments fell below one thousand, and as a result, the Pentagon, in May, extended the duration of the program and increased the payment to twenty-five hundred dollars. Despite these unprecedented efforts and the expenditure of an estimated $68 million in fiscal 1974, however, the Army has been unable to attract the volunteers it needs. Secretary Howard Callaway reported in February of 1974 that the Army obtained only 63 per cent of its requirement for combat enlistments during 1973.

The combat-bonus program has been the subject of heated controversy ever since it was first proposed. During the Senate debate of 1971, Senator Edward Kennedy called the bonus "neither wise, nor just, nor fair." He decried it as reflective of "the underlying philosophy of any mercenary army." Despite such doubts, however, the government is moving toward increased use of financial lures to attract volunteers. Even before the advent of the all-volunteer force, the Pentagon was spending an average of $200 million annually on so-called variable re-enlistment bonuses. The Defense Department has since requested even greater authority to grant the following special bonuses:

- ► $3,000 for a three-year enlistment in certain special skills
- ► up to $15,000 for re-enlistment during critical retention years
- ► $4,000 for extension of duty by certain officers
- ► $2,200 for enlistment or re-enlistment by reservists
- ► $15,000 per year and $350 per month special pay for medical officers

These proposals, contained in the Uniformed Services Special Pay Act, will cost an estimated $400 million annually by fiscal year 1976. Because of the tremendous costs, the requests initially encountered some Congressional resistance, although they were eventually passed in modified form in April 1973. Soaring manpower expenditures are raising serious doubts about the cost of the all-volunteer force and its effect on the military budget.

In the 1970s, for the first time in American history, military spending increased at the conclusion of a major war.

While part of this gain is the result of inflation and a continued arms race, the principal reason for the increase is a huge jump in manpower costs—reflected in a dramatic shift in the share of the budget devoted to personnel. From 1968 to 1975, total manpower outlays rose from $32.6 billion to $47.5 billion, i.e., from 42 per cent to 56 per cent of the military budget. These increases have taken place even as total manpower levels have dropped sharply: for a military establishment with 1.3 million fewer under arms, we are paying $14.7 billion more in personnel costs. Even the figure of 56 per cent of the defense budget is too low, according to Mississippi Senator John Stennis. The chairman of the Senate Armed Services Committee estimated in 1972 that if housing, recruiting, and other, similar items were included in manpower cost accounting, the figure for actual total personnel spending would approach 67 per cent—two of every three defense dollars! By contrast, the Soviet Union spends only 35 per cent of its military budget on such costs. Manpower costs have grown so exorbitant, in fact, that they are squeezing other sectors of the defense budget. In 1971, the Senate Armed Services Committee warned that "disturbingly high" personnel expenditures were draining resources away from research and modernization projects and that because of soaring manpower costs the United States might "face serious difficulties in having sufficient quantities of weaponry."

Defense Department officials have labored prodigiously in recent years to defend the high cost of military manpower, arguing that only a small portion of these increases are the result of ending the draft and implementing the all-volunteer force. Pentagon statistics for fiscal year 1974, for example, place total additional volunteer-force outlays—including pay raises, special bonuses, scholarships, and extra recruiting expenditures—at $3.1 billion. These figures are open to question, however, for they seriously understate total volunteer costs. The General Accounting Office's May 1973 report on the volunteer force estimated that volunteer-related reforms not requiring legislative enactment would add an additional $1 billion to these figures. The Congressional watchdog agency also pointed out that in Fiscal Year 1974 the Army budgeted some $2 billion, apart from Project Volunteer funding, for so-called "soldier oriented" programs, many of which were closely associated with volunteer policies. One of those who has chal-

lenged Pentagon figures vigorously is former Defense Department official and aide to President Johnson, Joseph Califano.
During a heated exchange with Congressman William Steiger
(R-Wisc.) and Manpower Secretary Roger Kelley, in the
spring of 1973, Califano emphasized that the total cost of
the all-volunteer force was far above the Pentagon's estimates,
amounting to as much as $5.6 billion. Whatever the exact
numbers, it would seem that when all the associated expenditures of the volunteer force are included, the program costs
considerably more than official Pentagon figures would indicate, and must be considered a primary reason for soaring
manpower spending.

The intent of all this is not to disparage the concept of
voluntary service or to intimate I would prefer conscription,
but, rather, to point up the tremendous sacrifices and expenses
involved in attempting to achieve an all-volunteer force—at
least the kind of massive Army presumed to be necessary for
the United States. Despite the optimism of the Gates Commission and glowing reports from the Pentagon, eliminating
the draft has been an extremely arduous process, requiring
the outlay of bewildering sums of money. Defense experts and
previous government study commissions recognized these
problems during earlier discussions of the volunteer force and
rejected the proposal as too disruptive. For example, the
House Armed Services Committee's 1967 Civilian Advisory
Panel on Military Manpower Procurement turned down completely voluntary military force as "exorbitantly expensive"
and "creating the concept of defense of the nation by mercenaries." Why was the all-volunteer force unacceptable then
but welcomed four years later? Why, given the colossal costs
and uncertainties involved, has the government been so in-
sistent on implementing the program?

III

The all-volunteer force was introduced and accepted, in my
view, primarily because of the political and social pressures
caused by resistance to the military. In 1973 hearings before
the House Armed Services Committee, Army Secretary Robert Froehlke tried to explain the reasons for ending conscription to a skeptical Chairman Hebert: "The Volunteer Army
was politically very popular when the decision was made in

1968 . . . because of a very unpopular war, and an unpopular draft." One element of the political argument for a volunteer force was the unprecedented wave of popular opposition and civil disobedience encountered by the Selective Service System. A careful reading of the official Gates Commission report in fact lends support to this view. The Commission reported that the greatest cost of the draft was the social divisiveness caused by "efforts to escape conscription"—involving direct draft defiance for some and purposely distorted careers for others. The panel reasoned that the efforts of prospective inductees to escape conscription imposed heavy financial losses on the society, what they termed "the cost of collecting the implicit tax." The assessed dollar value of such evasion was put at $3 billion, by far the highest cost of the system, according to the Commission's estimates. The report also expressed concern over the direct political effects of conscription. Recognizing the widespread disenchantment with military and government policy, the Commission warned that the draft "weakens the political fabric of our society and threatens the delicate web of shared values that alone enables a free society to exist." They predicted that such difficulties would be "completely avoided by an all-volunteer force."

The volunteer force also was accepted as a means of alleviating social pressures within the military itself and of eliminating the morale and disciplinary problems thought to arise from use of the draft. In a September 1971 article in the New York *Times*, R. Drummond Ayers reported the assessment of many leading Army commanders that resistance occurred only among draftees or draft-induced volunteers, and that ending conscription would "increase the number of true volunteers . . . and thus eliminate many troublemakers." The Gates Commission shared this view and, again belying its political motivations, argued that voluntary service would remove the threat of internal resistance:

> The draft creates unnecessary problems for the military. Selection by lottery compels some to serve who have neither a talent nor a taste for military life. . . . These men present morale and disciplinary problems which otherwise would not arise. Some spend much of their military service in confinement, because it is so difficult for them to adjust to military service. Dissent within the military presents particularly ticklish problems for the armed forces of

a free nation. The problems raised by the forced military service of those who are unwilling or unable to adjust to military life will be largely overcome by voluntary recruiting.

Seeing the GI movement and low morale as primarily caused by draftees and reluctant volunteers, the Pentagon embraced the all-volunteer force as a means of changing the social base of the military and thus eliminating unrest.

Of course, the end of conscription did not halt the GI resistance movement. The assumption that a professional military would be free of dissension, that volunteers would be more docile and acquiescent than draftees, proved wrong. In fact, the GI movement had always been primarily a movement of enlistees, and filling the ranks with volunteers thus actually increased the likelihood of internal dissent. Indeed, the volunteer armed forces have encountered record peacetime levels of AWOL and desertion and are still troubled by widespread political opposition and black unrest. The volunteer force has faltered in other respects as well. It has created an unprecedented crisis in the defense budget and has contributed to severe manpower difficulties in the reserves. On a more fundamental level, it has failed to attract a sufficient volume of recruits to maintain force strengths. The days of volunteer recruitment may be numbered.

IV

From the very beginning, the all-volunteer force was viewed as a risky and uncertain enterprise. Many leading figures within the defense Establishment were opposed to the program initially and have remained unconvinced since. In "Army in Anguish," Washington *Post* reporters Johnson and Wilson found that "almost every senior officer we interviewed for this series had grave private reservations about going volunteer." None of the influential veterans' organizations and reserve officers' groups have ever favored the project. Many of those within the armed services committees in Congress, including Senator Stennis and Representative Hebert, also have expressed doubts. The views of many of these people were captured in Congressman Hebert's remark, "the only way you get a volunteer army is by drafting."

Recent recruitment figures seem to bear out these apprehensions. On January 27, 1973, Secretary Laird announced that the Pentagon was ending its use of the draft. Enlistment rates dropped almost immediately. The Army failed to meet its recruitment quota in February and for the next eight months in a row. Enlistment goals were met in November and December but only because of a drop in recruit quality, evidenced in an increase in the percentage of high school dropouts accepted. Indeed, throughout 1973 there seemed to be an inverse relation between quality and quantity, what Secretary Callaway referred to as "trade-offs." In the spring, for example, the Army concentrated on enlisting at least 70 per cent high school graduates, but in the process fell nearly 25 per cent short of its total requirements. The Navy and Marine Corps also experienced recruitment shortfalls during 1973, as evidenced in Figure 11.

The Army recruited 24,000 fewer men than expected during 1973 and as a result fell ten thousand below its desired strength of 775,000. Enlistments were also deficient for the first four months of 1974, meaning that Volunteer Army recruiting goals were met in only two of the first fifteen months of operation.

Partly because of these failings, many within the defense Establishment seem to have given up on volunteerism and reform, anticipating a return to conscription. An increasing number of reports have come into GI projects of commanders reintroducing the harsh methods of the "old Army." In many units, the liberal experiments of recent years are giving way to more traditional military standards of rigid discipline and strict uniformity. Enlisted-men's councils and similar innovations pioneered at Fort Carson have been abandoned. Servicemen stationed overseas have encountered a particularly sharp reversal of performance standards. In Germany, for example, Army commanders in early 1973 launched an intensive crackdown on drug use and dissent, resulting in almost total curtailment of civilian privileges for those even suspected of such behavior (see Chapter 7). Similar repression has surfaced in Okinawa and Japan. There is also evidence that certain military officials have purposely allowed the recruitment effort to falter, hoping to hasten the return of the draft. At his departure from the Defense Department in June of 1973, retiring Manpower Assistant Secretary Roger Kelley described adver-

		January-March	April-June	July-September	October-December	1973 Total
ARMY	Total Enlistments	35,700	25,600	41,500	37,800	140,600
	Percent of Goal	(92.2%)	(76.4%)	(79.7%)	(93.1%)	(96.3%)
NAVY	Total Enlistments	14,300	16,300	23,700	13,700	68,000
	Percent of Goal	(102.2%)	(71.2%)	(96.7%)	(100.7%)	(83.7%)
MARINE CORPS	Total Enlistments	11,400	11,300	13,700	9,800	46,100
	Percent of Goal	(96.6%)	(103.7%)	(85.6%)	(89.1%)	(87.8%)
AIR FORCE	Total Enlistment	20,000	19,100	18,700	14,000	71,800
	Percent of Goal	(100%)	(100%)	(101%)	(100.7%)	(95.2%)
ALL SERVICES	Total Enlistments	81,400	72,300	97,600	75,300	326,500
	Percent of Goal	(96.3%)	(83.7%)	(87.8%)	(95.2%)	(90.4%)

Figure 11
Non-prior-service male enlistments, 1973.

saries of the volunteer force as "bolder and more frequent in their acts of sabotage against the system." The man chiefly responsible for the program claimed that foes of the volunteer project could "demonstrate a need for the draft by letting failures occur."

Advocates of a return to the old methods found a powerful spokesman during 1973 in General William Westmoreland. The general stated to New York *Times* reporter Ben Franklin in June that while he recognized its "political appeal" he had "uncertainties as to the wisdom of the program." A short while later, on August 17, the former Army Chief of Staff signed an editorial in the New York *Times* strongly attacking the all-volunteer force and calling for renewed but modified use of the lottery, a system in which "draft quotas would be issued if and when required . . . to make up for the shortfall in enlistment in both the regular and reserve forces." The idea of drafting reservists also has been raised by other officials, most notably former Defense Secretary Laird. In his final report before leaving the Defense Department, the Secretary warned that if Congress failed to enact additional bonus legislation it should be prepared to "grant induction authority . . . to provide men and women for Reserve forces duty." Given the already exorbitant level of manpower spending, Congress is not likely to favor additional volunteer expenditures. If reserve and active-duty enlistments continue to fall, appeals for renewing conscription will grow louder.

The failure of the all-volunteer force is rooted in the fundamental contradictions of America's armed forces. The plan was doomed from the very beginning, despite the tremendous efforts involved, for it attempted to reconcile an outdated, aggressive mission with a youth "market" unwilling to cooperate. Despite the end of the Vietnam War, the military remains a discredited, authoritarian institution with a purpose irrelevant to the material concerns of the nation's youth. The volunteer force will not succeed, nor will young people want to join the service, unless a more humane, truly professional environment exists within the ranks—i.e., unless the injustices and discrimination encountered by enlisted people are eliminated. Similarly, the armed forces will not attract sufficient volunteers, at least not at a reasonable cost, unless manpower

levels and overseas troop strengths are lowered. Voluntary recruitment is superior to conscription, but it can work only
in a greatly reduced, democratically structured armed force
confined to realistic national defense.

CHAPTER 10

THE RECRUITMENT RACKET

I

An integral part of the volunteer-force effort has been the creation of an immense recruitment apparatus reaching out to ever larger numbers of young people and widening the military's influence in society. During recent years, recruitment forces have been significantly increased: There are now over twelve thousand military field recruiters, backed up by thousands of additional administrative support personnel. The largest gain has been for the Army, which from 1971 to 1973 increased its total number of recruiters from 2,350 to 4,725 and expanded the number of recruitment stations from 982 to 1,628. Total recruiting costs for all services have jumped sharply: In fiscal year 1975 expenditures for all active and reserve recruitment amounted to an astounding $590 million. Figure 12 summarizes this growth in recruitment resources.

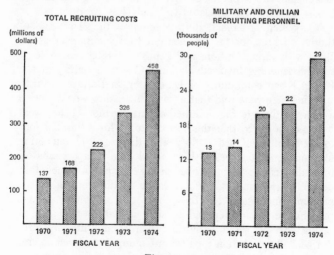

Figure 12
Defense recruiting resources.

The expansion of recruitment is spreading a system notorious for its lack of honesty. Utilizing special-access information such as lists of those ordered for preinduction physicals or of graduating high school seniors, many recruiters employ questionable, high-pressure methods. An example of such tactics was exposed by Congressman John J. Rooney of New York in February of 1972. Rooney complained to the Federal Trade Commission of "huckstering and double talk" from recruiters who sent letters to young men in his district deceiving them into thinking they had mandatory appointments at the recruitment office. Similar practices were uncovered by the Central Committee for Conscientious Objectors (CCCO) during 1972 at Plymouth High School in Plymouth, Michigan. Local recruiters had sent letters to prospective graduates in the spring implying that it was part of their draft obligation to return enclosed forms requesting additional information about military service. Included in the letter were misleading remarks that enlistment would be preferable to "waiting for the draft and serving for a period of two years which includes two additional years of active reserve and an additional two years of inactive status upon completion of active duty." Of course, the letter failed to mention that this obligation is standard for all draftees and for some who enlist as well, nor did it point out that the reserve status is in fact totally inactive and unrelated to Ready Reserve duty.

Many recruiters make alluring promises they have no authority to keep, or fail to mention the conditions that go along with various options and bonuses. A recent example of such dissembling involved National Guard recruiting in the Puerto Rican community of Dorchester, in Boston. Spanish-speaking men were told that as guardsmen they would receive a salary of three to four hundred dollars per month; they were not told, however, that this was true only for the initial four to six months of active duty and that for the remaining five and one half years they would receive approximately forty dollars per month. The men were also informed that dependent allotments would increase as the number of dependents increased, that they could quit anytime after six months, and that they had to sign up within two days of taking entrance examinations. When community organizer Art Melville, of Action for Boston Community Development, heard of the incident, he sought the help of the military support office in the area. The Legal In-Service Project promptly sent two counselors to talk with the men; after hearing of the real conditions of guard service, seven of the eight involved decided not to join. Even the hawkish House Armed Services Committee admitted, in 1973, that some recruiters "present an unrealistic picture" and that "recruiting advertising appears to promise more than the Navy is able to deliver." In its Report on Disciplinary Problems in the U. S. Navy, the Committee stated that the disillusionment resulting from such deception, especially among black recruits, was an important factor behind rank-and-file unrest.

Apparently the pressure on recruiters is so intense and the resulting fraud so pervasive that the Pentagon itself has been forced to acknowledge the problem and apply pressures for reform. On June 13, 1973, the Army announced that a nationwide investigation by its Criminal Investigation Division had uncovered numerous examples of deceit and had led to the reassignment of 107 recruiters in a seven-month period. The inquiry, extending into thirty-seven states, encountered reports of particularly widespread abuses in Syracuse, New York; Kansas City, Missouri; and San Antonio, Texas. Among the examples of recruiter malpractice cited by the Pentagon were manufacturing false high school diplomas, providing "crib" sheets to recruits about to take qualification tests, overlooking police records that might disqualify potential enlistees, accepting physically unfit men, and falsifying residency requirements. The Army Audit Agency, in a report dated April 13, 1973, found similar evidence of improper enlistment practices. In a detailed examination of recruitment during fiscal year 1972, the agency disclosed that thousands of ineligible applicants had been accepted for service and many recruits were given "unauthorized pre-enlistment training." As a result, nearly five thousand had to be discharged later for improper enlistment, at a cost of over $8 million.

One of the most shocking critiques of military recruitment appeared in an NBC Television News Special broadcast on November 11, 1973. Reporting on the Army's recruitment command in Jacksonville, Florida, newsman Bob Rogers documented an extraordinary series of illegal tactics forced upon recruiters by excessive pressures. One enlistee reported that his arrest record was concealed when he entered the Armed Forces Entrance and Examination Station and that a recruiter had given him a phony high school diploma. Another recruit, Private Carl Bradford, confided that his recruiter sent someone else to take an entrance examination for him. In his inquiry, Rogers also uncovered extensive fraud in enlistment qualification tests, resulting in the acceptance of numerous unqualified recruits. In the summer of 1973, for example, after a new test had been in use for some time, test scores increased dramatically, the average jumping from 21 to 44. On September 24, after several months of these unusual results, the Jacksonville station gave a surprise verification test. Instead of paralleling the original results, about 30 per cent of the verification-test scores showed a significant drop, with some scores off by as much as 40 points. When asked if he thought this was an indication of cheating, an official conceded, "there had been some prior exposure in some cases to the test, yes." Fraud and deceit of this kind have transformed the recruitment system into a national scandal.

Not only are young people often unfairly enticed into the military in the first place, but once in the service they have no means of legal redress against false promises. The enlistment contract and various "statements of understanding" which recruits must sign contain numerous loopholes; item 54 of DD Form 4, the so-called merger clause, voids the oral promises of recruiters and makes a claim of false inducement nearly impossible to sustain. The Harvard-based Committee on Military Justice (formerly the Committee for Legal Research on the Draft and the Military) has described the enlistment contract as an "extremely one-sided document, specifically designed in advance to make its terms easily avoidable by the military but strictly binding on the soldier." The agreement is coercive in nature and lacks mutuality and thus, according to the Committee, "should in no wise be considered contractual." Despite the new attention being given to recruitment, this unjust system is being expanded without change.

An integral part of recruitment is advertising. Figure 13 shows the increase in promotional spending among all the services in recent years. The 1974 figures break down to $34.9 million for the Army (chief agency: N. W. Ayer), $30.1 million for the Navy (Grey), $7.4 million for the Marine Corps (J. Walter Thompson), and $17.1 for the Air Force (D'Arcy-MacManus). In addition to these paid advertisements, the Pentagon takes ample advantage of the FCC's public-service

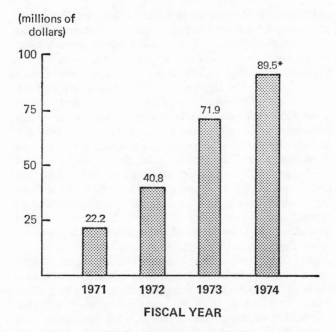

(millions of dollars)

*Does not include an additional $8 million requested for "all-inclusive Dept. of Defense recruiting advertising."

Figure 13
Department of Defense recruiting advertising.

regulations to obtain free broadcasting time. Hundreds of television and radio stations daily broadcast without charge tapes provided by the services. The 1972 value of these "public service" ads amounted to over $32 million. The Pentagon's massive advertising operation now ranks the armed forces among the nation's largest advertisers.

II

A closer examination of the reasons why young people enlist will provide better insight into the basis of the recruitment pitch. The available evidence indicates that most volunteers join the military to escape limited personal and economic opportunities. Roger Kelley, recently retired Assistant Secretary

of Defense for Manpower and Reserve Affairs, testified before
the House Armed Services Subcommittee on Recruiting and
Retention in 1971 that the two reasons most frequently given
for enlisting were "to obtain a better opportunity for advanced
educational training" and "to acquire a skill or trade valuable
in civilian life." The University of Michigan's Youth in Transition study of over two thousand high school students corrob-
orates Kelley's statement. A 1969 sampling by the university's
Institute for Social Research found that the most frequently cited reasons for voluntary enlistment were, in order
of preference, "to learn a trade or skill that would be valuable
in civilian life," "to become more mature and self-reliant,"
and "opportunity for advanced education, professional training." Similarly, in a 1964 Department of Defense survey of
approximately eighty thousand enlisted people, nearly 47 per
cent of non-draft-motivated volunteers gave as their reason for
entry, "to learn a trade" or "to become more mature." As
might be expected, economic motivations are especially keen
among the less affluent. A 1955 Public Opinion Surveys, Inc.,
study of 1,031 civilian males aged sixteen to twenty years,
found the propensity to enlist highest among youth with little
chance for additional education. The survey showed that
those with the strongest positive attitude toward military service had the lowest educational goals and came from disadvantaged backgrounds. The previously mentioned Youth in
Transition 1969 study also found that those intending to
enter military service were below the mean in intelligence and
family socioeconomic level.

Perhaps the best indication of the socioeconomic basis of
military service is the link between enlistment and unemployment. In the words of former Manpower Assistant Secretary
Harold Wool, "studies of enlisted trends have shown . . .
that enlistment rates have been positively correlated with fluc-
tuations of youth unemployment." A 1967 Pentagon contract
study by economists S. H. Altman and A. E. Fechter found
that "a given percentage change in the unemployment rate
for male youth was associated with a similar percentage
change in Army enlistment rate." More recent studies, however, indicate that the unemployment-enlistment nexus may
not be as direct as these remarks suggest. In 1973, Brookings
Institution scholars Martin Binkin and John Johnston conducted a state-by-state cross-sectional analysis that they said

"fails to demonstrate a strong relation." Another study by the University of Michigan's Survey Research Center found that, while unemployment is not generally linked to enlistment, "there are certain circumstances under which it can play a part." The study found a strong relationship when the local unemployment rate exceeded 6 per cent, i.e., when the young person faced "very severe difficulties in finding a job." While the correlation between unemployment and initial enlistment is problematic, the influence of civilian unemployment on the decision to re-enlist is certain. As Secretary Kelley has stated: "There is a very accurate and historic relationship between high unemployment and high re-enlistment."

The armed services very consciously exploit these economic factors. Recruitment posters and enlistment slogans are specifically aimed at the occupational needs of high-school-age people: learn a trade—We'll Pay You $300 a Month to Learn a New Skill; interesting work?—If Your Job Puts You to Sleep, Try One of Ours; steady work?—We've Got Over 300 Good, Steady Jobs; etc. At school "career days," in unsolicited mailings, through targeted advertising, the recent high school graduate and others are exposed to the recruitment pitch. Emphasizing the uncertainties of the civilian economy and the supposed employment value of military duty, recruiters hope to persuade young people to join. Technically this is called volunteering. Although the overt compulsion of the draft may be absent, it is hardly "voluntary" for sixteen-to-nineteen-year-olds, facing a 13.4 per cent unemployment rate, to reluctantly succumb to intensive enlistment pressures.

Predictably, the current recruitment system is attracting a disproportionate share of youth from working-class and lower-income backgrounds. Data on educational level and mental standards indicate that the social quality of the enlisted force has declined since the advent of the all-volunteer force. From fiscal year 1972 to the first half of fiscal 1973, the percentage of recruits with high school diplomas dropped from 76 per cent to 68 per cent in the Navy and from 70 per cent to 52 per cent in the Army. The portion of enlistees in "above average" mental categories also has declined in recent years. (Recruits are assigned to categories I through IV according to results on written intelligence tests, with Categories I and II above average, Category III average, and Category IV below average.) The service-wide trend shows a decrease in Categories I and II and an increase in Category III. The Navy has witnessed a particularly steep decline; the percentage of new recruits in Categories I and II dropped from nearly 50 per cent in January 1970 to below 30 per cent in June 1972. Alarm over these trends caused Congress, in the fall of 1973, to attach a provision to the annual defense bill requiring each service to accept no more than 45 per cent high school dropouts and 18 per cent Category IV personnel. Secretary Schlesinger has promised to meet these standards, but he conceded they could "cause recruiting difficulties for the Army and Marine Corps." Indeed, the recruiting experience of 1973 suggests that the services are unable to meet quality standards without falling short of numerical quotas.

III

Given the importance of the notion that military service is a valuable means of learning a trade, we should examine the question more closely. Despite its widespread acceptance, the Pentagon's own data show that such a view is unfounded. Detailed studies by Harold Wool describe a marked contrast between the types of jobs in the military and those in the civilian economy. In Wool's technical language, the "frequency of various specific occupations within the military structure differs sharply from that of similar occupations in the civilian economy": 13.4 per cent of enlisted jobs (i.e., infantry and other combat positions) have no civilian counterpart; 38 per cent of enlisted jobs (i.e., weapons and ship mechanics, etc.) account for only 1.5 per cent of civilian jobs; while 29 per cent of servicemen's jobs account for another 9.6 per cent of civilian occupations; overall, 80 per cent of military jobs are in areas that account for only 10 per cent of civilian jobs.

A look at specific occupations indicates just how extensive the problem is. Using 1960 figures, 10.6 per cent of all enlisted people work as aircraft mechanics, while only 0.3 per cent of the civilian labor force is so occupied. In absolute terms, 194,000 enlisted men work as aviation mechanics, compared with only 117,000 such in the entire civilian economy. Moreover, in the military there is a very high turnover rate and thus a large volume of men rotating through these positions, while, in the civilian sector, many of these slots are unionized and relatively secure. The same figures show that 13 per cent of enlisted positions are in electronics operation or maintenance, compared to only 0.5 per cent of civilian jobs. Again in absolute terms, there are nearly thirty thousand more positions in the armed forces than in the civilian sector, thus insuring a surfeit of potential veteran applicants. Even where broad functional similarities do exist, the actual skills and knowledge required may differ markedly. For example, electronics technicians for missile guidance would hardly be prepared for work as civilian radio and television repairmen.

Further study, based on social data, shows that the people most likely to enlist for purposes of economic advancement, i.e., those with the lowest socioeconomic and educational backgrounds, end up in precisely those positions with no value for civilian employment. This is most obvious in the combat arms, the least transferable military skill. The 1964 National Opinion Research Center (NORC) survey found that the lower an enlistee's educational level the higher his chances of combat assignment. Harold Wool found similar results based on mental-group classification. Servicemen in the lowest division, Category IV, constitute nearly 40 per cent of those in artillery and infantry positions.

These data demonstrate the impossibility of training lower-income youth through military service—and help unmask the controversial Pentagon program supposedly designed to perform just such a function: Project 100,000. Secretary of Defense Robert McNamara announced in 1966 that one hundred thousand previously disqualified men from the lowest mental groups would henceforth be accepted into the armed forces. (Over three hundred thousand have actually entered through the project, since renamed New Standards.) McNamara claimed that military service would provide the poor with an opportunity "to return to civilian life with skills and aptitudes which for them and their families will reverse the downward spiral of human decay." However, according to Army General Walter Kerwin, 41 per cent of the soldiers entering under the program were assigned to combat duty (thus confirming the suspicion that the project's real purpose was more to provide additional troops for Vietnam than to aid the needy). As with many who join the military to learn a trade, the Project 100,000 servicemen were victims of a cruel hoax. Former Assistant Secretary Wool, McNamara's own

manpower chief, candidly assessed such efforts as follows:
"Those enlisted personnel assigned to the ground combat specialties and other uniquely military duties could expect little
or no direct benefit from their military occupational training
in future civilian jobs."

Survey data from veterans on the usefulness of military
training for civilian employment corroborate these findings.
In the 1964 NORC survey cited above, veterans were asked
to evaluate their military training. Only 9.4 per cent said it
had been of "considerable use," 23.4 per cent termed it of
"some use," while 67 per cent said their training had been of
"no use." Within the group viewing military training favorably, however, were only 8.9 per cent of those who had served
as enlisted men; of those who had served in the combat arms,
only 4 per cent reported favorably. Another 1955 study, of
three thousand airmen, produced similar results. All the men
studied were from highly skilled fields, including five of the
most technical positions in the Air Force. Only 40 per cent
of the separating veterans attempted to find civilian jobs related to their Air Force training; of those who did try, fewer
than half were successful.

These points about the usefulness of military service for
civilian employment are confirmed in a 1961 study performed
for the Senate Armed Services Committee by sociologist Albert Biderman. The monograph showed that very few careerists secured employment in fields related to their military position. Nearly all the officers and senior enlisted men surveyed
were disappointed at the lack of utilization of their skills in
civilian jobs. As the report stated, "even in the military specialties where transfer appears most likely (such as medical
and dental specialists; electronic, electrical and mechanical
repairmen; and craftsmen) . . . no more than one-third to
one-half moved directly into comparable jobs." Biderman admitted that this was because "close relationships between
military and civilian occupational specialties apparently occur only in a minority of cases."

A 1972 report prepared for the Office of the Special Assistant for the Modern Volunteer Army found the same pattern.
Interviews with a large number of soldiers disclosed that "the
overriding complaint at the end of their tour is the lack of
career training." According to the study, most troops leaving
the service feel cheated by the Army and find themselves

without usable skills. "Relatively few end their first term with a belief that they have improved their civilian career potential via skills training."

This lack of job benefits is partly the result of chronic misutilization, i.e., the assignment of enlisted people to the wrong jobs. The Comptroller General reported to Congress in 1971 that 10.4 per cent of enlisted people at Army bases in the United States were assigned to duties other than those for which they were qualified. The same report stated that misutilization was even higher overseas, nearly 21 per cent in Korea. Besides often being assigned to the wrong jobs, servicemen also must spend much of their time performing non-occupational, make-work details. Although information on the subject is scanty, the few available studies give a startling indication of the extent of the problem. A 1958 study of missile crewmen quoted by Wool gave the average work week as: twenty-two hours in actual missile maintenance; sixteen hours for guard duty; and an incredible thirty-two hours in such wasteful duties as cleanup, KP, picking up cigarette butts, inspections, etc. Another 1961 study of Navy electronics technicians, showed that "time devoted to duties entirely outside the area of electronics accounted for about half the workday of personnel at the apprentice level and about one-fourth the work time of most senior technicians." Under chaotic conditions such as these, it is no wonder that military service cannot provide worthwhile occupational training.

IV

While the decision to end the draft is a welcome step toward reducing government intrusion in the lives of young people, the volunteer system replacing conscription offers no cause for joy. The recruitment system presents a distorted view of military service and consciously exploits the financial and social uncertainties of the less affluent. As we have seen, the entire approach is fraudulent, for it promises economic advancement that the armed forces are incapable of providing. (Nor should the military have such a domestic-welfare function in a healthy society.) Moreover, the system seems unable to attract a representative cross section of the population and, as early critics feared, imposes an unjust burden on the lower classes. Clearly, major reforms are needed if the volunteer force is to succeed. We must find a means of military recruitment that avoids phony job-training appeals and insures greater equity in military service. Such a goal may seem remote, but important new evidence from the University of Michigan's Survey Research Center suggests that a more desirable volunteer system can be established through a new approach to recruitment—one that shuns the current emphasis on financial lures and replaces promises of in-service training with a guarantee of paid civilian education.

As part of the previously mentioned Youth in Transition study, Jerome Johnston and Jerald Bachman questioned over one thousand prospective high school graduates on their reaction to a new type of enlistment appeal, a government pledge to finance four years of advanced educational training. Their proposal provided that recruits would be guaranteed four years of civilian instruction, either before or after service, in exchange for a four-year enlistment:

> The government agrees to assume the cost, including living expenses, for up to four years of schooling at a college or technical/vocational school to which you can get accepted. In return, you serve on active duty for four years. You must *enlist first*, but the schooling could come either before or after you serve.

The investigators found that this incentive was four times more likely to attract enlistments than the second-ranked inducement, higher military pay. Johnston and Bachman also discovered significant social differences between the groups choosing these two alternatives. Those responding positively to the schooling incentive had a relatively high family socioeconomic background and scored in above-average categories in mental aptitude tests. These young men rated considerably higher in socioeconomic background and mental abilities than those attracted by pay alone and in fact scored above those already serving in the ranks. The clear implication is that such an appeal might be an important step toward improving the quality of the volunteer force. The authors were sufficiently impressed with these findings to elaborate their schooling incentive in a specific "Four for Four" plan, included at the end of their volume on *Young Men and Military Service*. Although the Defense Department partly funded the investigations resulting in the plan, Pentagon officials have expressed little interest in it and apparently have no intention of pursuing the proposal. Nonetheless, the plan represents a major advance over current methods and would be a positive means of attracting more capable and socially representative people into the enlisted ranks.

A paid-schooling system would have other important advantages: Those willing to serve first and enter school afterward would insure that a sizable portion of those serving in the ranks were first-termers intent on returning to civilian life. All would agree, I think, that we must avoid filling the ranks with people who view themselves only as military professionals, with no ties to the civilian society. The schooling incentive would guarantee a continuation of the citizen-soldier tradition of servicemen whose primary commitments lie outside the military. On the other hand, those taking their schooling first would emerge from the experience considerably broadened and more mature; they would not only be more capable of performing technical tasks but would also be less impressionable and more critical of abuses of authority than the typical eighteen-year-old recruit. A new system of enlistment incentives would also allow for ending the current fraudulent and exploitive recruitment system, with its spurious promises of training through military jobs. In its place, a considerably scaled down (hence less expensive) and more honest program could be installed. Job training and educational services would remain in civilian institutions, where they belong.

Other changes are also necessary to reform the recruitment process. One major improvement would be a pre-enlistment orientation program providing recruits a three- or four-day trial introduction to military service. Such a program, successfully practiced in Great Britain for several years, would allow potential enlistees to learn about the armed forces, without obligation, before committing themselves to a full term of service. The Army experimented with the plan for a time during 1972 at Fort Jackson but abandoned the proposal before giving it a chance to succeed. The trial enlistment program should be resurrected and instituted throughout the services as a means of eliminating many recruiter abuses. Another step toward a more equitable recruitment system might be a change in the legal status of the enlistment agreement, guaranteeing servicemen the right to sue over breach of contract.

As important as these measures may be, however, the ultimate success of recruitment hinges not on the procedures of enlistment but on the very nature of the military. As long as the Pentagon attempts to maintain huge interventionist armed forces and continues to deny servicemen their basic human rights, recruitment efforts will encounter difficulty. In the final analysis, voluntary recruitment can succeed only if young people feel the military serves their interest.

CHAPTER 11

BLACK ON WHITE

In early debate over the all-volunteer force, a frequent criticism was that such a policy would lead to a largely black Army. The Gates Commission and opponents of the draft parried these challenges by offering assurances that the racial composition of the services would not be materially altered by the end of conscription and by arguing that military pay increases would attract middle-class youth more than the poor. As we have noted, however, the actual experience of the volunteer force is quite different. Persistent manpower shortages and continued anti-military feelings among young people have forced the services to reach deeper into the lower socioeconomic strata of society, causing a marked increase in the percentage of non-whites within the military. Lured by financial and job-training incentives and compelled by a desperate need for economic advancement, blacks have turned to the military with increasing frequency in recent years and as a result now constitute a major share of the enlisted ranks.

The percentage of blacks in the Army will probably continue to rise in the future, for their share among new recruits is even higher than within the service as a whole. From February through December of 1973, the first eleven months of completely voluntary recruitment, 27 per cent of all new Army recruits were black. If these trends continue, the enlisted ranks of the volunteer Army will soon be one quarter black (compared to the Gates Commission estimate of 18.8 per cent). Indeed, the Army's elite 82nd Airborne Division, the nation's most combat-ready unit, is already 26 per cent black.

In itself, the rising percentage of black recruits does not present a problem. Many Pentagon officials and leaders of the black community feel that non-whites should be allowed to enter the military as they wish, and most reject the notion

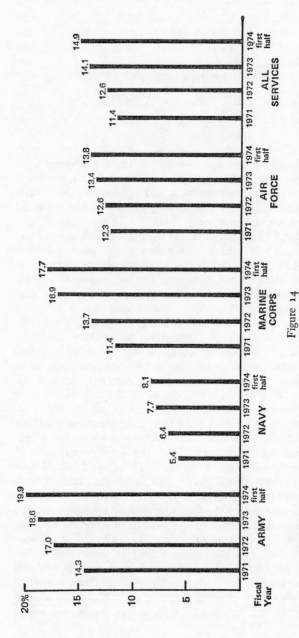

Figure 14

Blacks as a percentage of total enlisted strength (Note: Figures do not include Spanish-American and other minority servicemen, who comprise approximately 2 per cent of enlisted strength.).

that quotas or limits should be placed on black enlistments. More important than the number of blacks in the military is the question of what conditions these new recruits encounter once they are in the service. Many blacks are attracted to the ranks by the hope of improving their lives and escaping from the manacles of poverty and racism. Too often, however, their expectations are dashed by prejudices more severe than those they have fled. The frequent result is outrage and, as we have seen so often in recent years, confrontation and violence. If the services are not to be destroyed by the current increase in minority enlistments, the nature of enlisted service must be altered. The swell of black recruits demands that we address the problem of discrimination with renewed urgency.

I

Military racism has been the subject of heated controversy in recent years. The militance of black GIs and inquiries by leading black political organizations have focused growing public attention on the problems of discrimination and unequal opportunity for minority servicemen. Indeed the Congressional Black Caucus' first investigative hearing, conducted in November of 1971, dealt with precisely this issue, an indication of the deep concern over military racism within the black community. The most thorough exploration of the subject has been the Department of Defense's own four-volume *Report of the Task Force on the Administration of Military Justice,* issued in November of 1972. An examination of the Task Force's findings, as well as those of the NAACP and the Congressional Black Caucus, provides ample documentation of the overwhelming racism that pervades every aspect of service life.

The Negro soldier encounters bias as soon as he enters the service, in unequal job placement. Black servicemen are disproportionately assigned to so-called "soft core," or low-skill, occupations. Although constituting 12.1 per cent of all enlisted people, black servicemen in 1971 represented 16.3 per cent of those in combat specialties and 19.6 per cent of those in service and supply positions. Within frontline combat units, black participation is even higher. Many infantry units in Vietnam were more than twenty per cent black, with paratroop units in some cases approaching 50 per cent. By contrast, blacks held only 4.9 per cent of jobs in the electronics-equipment field. The basis of much of this kind of discrimination is the racial and cultural bias of military qualification tests. The placement of new recruits in particular occupational fields is determined primarily by written results on the Armed Forces Qualification Test (AFQT) and standard aptitude examinations taken upon entry. These so-called "pencil and paper tests" are inherently discriminatory, however, for they measure academic training and understanding of majority cultural norms rather than true intelligence and thus place the poorly educated at a disadvantage. Given the poverty and lack of educational opportunity in most black communities, such standards inevitably consign minority recruits to low-skill positions. Even within the same test-score bracket, however, blacks are more likely to serve in low-grade positions than whites. For example, in a survey of soldiers of the same pay grade, E-4, and the same, top-level mental-classification category, sociologist Charles Moskos found that 9.4 per cent of whites were assigned to combat compared to 15.5 per cent of blacks. Thus, black servicemen are not only subjected to biased qualification tests but suffer discriminatory assignment even when they achieve equal verbal standards.

In the area of promotions, the same pattern exists. Advancement opportunities are, in most cases, greater in skilled occupations than in the more menial positions in which blacks commonly find themselves. As a result, minority troops are promoted much more slowly than whites—a fact confirmed by military grade-distribution patterns. Blacks are disproportionately assigned to the lowest grades, E-1 and E-2, and to grade E-6 (the bottom rung for careerists), and they are underrepresented in grades E-4 and E-5 (the top first-term slots) and in the very highest positions, grades E-8 and E-9. In the Marine Corps, for example, figures for March of 1972 show that, although blacks constituted 13 per cent of total enlisted strength, they represented 17.9 per cent of those at E-1, 9.1 per cent of E-4's, 13.6 per cent of E-6's, and only 4.4 per cent of those at E-9. Nor can these results be explained solely by inadequate test scores, for even when they meet white standards, blacks are still likely to hold lower positions. The NAACP's 1971 study of the Seventh Army in Germany, *The*

Search for Military Justice, found that among non-high-school-graduate combat soldiers in the same test-score category, 30 per cent of the blacks were at pay grade E-3 or lower, while only 14 per cent of the white servicemen were at this low position. In the same group, fewer than 20 per cent of the blacks were at grade E-5 or higher, compared to 27 per cent of the whites. The exclusion of blacks is most pronounced in the officer corps, with the privileges of leadership and command overwhelmingly reserved for whites. The percentage of black officers, as of July 1974, was as follows: 4.2 per cent in the Army, 1.1 per cent in the Navy, 2.0 per cent in the Marine Corps, and 2.0 per cent in the Air Force.

Minority servicemen also suffer segregation in off-base housing. The NAACP report found that "black soldiers of all ranks mentioned discrimination in housing as a major grievance." Because of racist practices among civilian landlords, both in the United States and abroad, many blacks encounter extreme difficulties in securing adequate housing for their families and are often forced to live in undesirable developments far from their duty stations. Although military regulations forbid housing offices to list racist proprietors, in fact many landlords and rental agents registered with the military, particularly those in Europe and the Far East, regularly refuse to serve blacks. In Heidelberg, for example, the NAACP received affidavits alleging that over 85 per cent of the landlords listed with the military's Family Housing offices discriminated against non-whites. Base commanders not only ignore minority complaints, but, in the view of the Congressional Black Caucus, often conspire with local agents to circumvent open-housing regulations. By refusing to exert their considerable pressures against such practices, military authorities in effect sanction the segregation of GI housing.

Hemmed in by the barriers of prejudice and surrounded by a hostile military environment, many blacks cling to cultural and symbolic expressions as the last available means of asserting some form of personal identity. One of the most controversial symbols of black solidarity is the "dap," or "power greeting"—an elaborate series of hand slappings and finger snappings that can take as long as a minute to perform. Military commanders seem to have a special aversion to the practice and, at many bases, have issued regulations forbidding dapping. Ostensibly, such policies are intended to prevent slowing of lines at mess halls and PXs, but, as the DOD Task Force points out, by singling out the practice of a specific racial group rather than generally prohibiting all forms of obstruction, regulations against dapping are blatantly discriminatory. Blacks also express solidarity with one another through various forms of clothing and ornaments. Despite their merely symbolic nature, however, black power rings, slave bracelets, black liberation flags, carved black fists, and various other paraphernalia are often forbidden by commanders. The DOD Task Force disclosed other barriers to black self-expression as well. Black Muslims in some cases encounter difficulty practicing their religion; in one instance, the report noted that a group of stockade inmates had been denied access to the Holy Koran. The Task Force also criticized regulations at various bases prohibiting more than a specified number of persons from congregating at one place, a rule selectively enforced against non-whites. Yet another form of cultural discrimination involves entertainment policies at enlisted-men's clubs. Black servicemen often object that soul music and black performers are not included in base programs and that white career soldiers monopolize club entertainment with Country and Western music. Trivial as they might seem on the surface, disputes over cultural expression frequently lead to conflict and have sparked many of the black uprisings of recent years.

A related aspect of the problem of non-white culture is the military's almost total neglect of other minority groups—particularly those of Spanish-American descent. Indeed, according to statistical definitions, Puerto Rican and chicano servicemen do not even exist; they are subsumed under the classification "Caucasian," with no recognition whatsoever of their unique cultural and ethnic identity. Most of the deprivations they encounter relate to language. Because military entrance examinations and training programs are administered exclusively in English, many Spanish-speaking servicemen are automatically considered dull and consigned to the least desirable occupations. The result is the same kind of promotion and job-assignment prejudices encountered by blacks. The DOD Task Force also noted that some commanders actually forbid the use of any language other than English. A direct attack on the heritage and culture of Spanish-Americans, such regulations are, in the words of the Task Force, "an expres-

sion of intentional discrimination that should not be tol-
erated."

The system of military justice, notoriously harsh for all enlisted people, is most oppressive in dealing with minority
servicemen. Article-15 punishments, administered at the discretion of individual commanders, have resulted in particularly severe hardships. The Defense Department Task Force
disclosed that "a greater number of black enlisted men receive non-judicial punishment (25.5%) than their proportionate number at installations participating in this study."
Blacks receive punishments at double the white rate for such
arbitrary offenses as disrespect and provoking gestures, what
are termed "confrontation or status-type offenses." Often a
white can say or do the same thing with no consequences.
Courts-martial are also stacked against minority GIs, in a system described by the Congressional Black Caucus as "lily-
white justice." Blacks constitute less than 1 per cent of all
military lawyers. The NAACP report found only two blacks
among the forty-six military judges in Europe and none among
the 123 Judge Advocate General (JAG) captains. Not surprisingly, the Task Force reported that of the 1,471 servicemen tried by court-martial during its investigation, 34.3 per
cent were black, more than double their proportion of the
total enlisted population. Punishments administered to whites
and blacks were generally about equal, except for punitive
discharges. In general and special courts-martial studied by
the Task Force, 23.4 per cent of the blacks and only 16.9 per
cent of the whites received a punitive discharge as part of
their sentence.

Pretrial confinement, supposedly designed to detain only
serious offenders, is a key device by which commanders impose discretionary punishment and rid themselves of unde-
sirables. The informality of the procedures involved and a
lack of judicial guarantees invite frequent abuse and lead to
widespread racial discrimination. According to the Congressional Black Caucus, 50 per cent of the airmen held in pretrial confinement during 1971 were black. The NAACP likewise found a 50 per cent black percentage among soldiers
held in pretrial confinement in Europe. The DOD Task
Force disclosed that black detainees were confined an average
of five days longer than whites and that whites were twice as

likely as blacks to be released with no subsequent disciplinary or judicial action.

Predictably, military prisons contain a disproportionate number of blacks. According to 1971 Justice Department figures supplied to the House Armed Services Committee, blacks comprise 30 per cent of those in Army stockades and 53 per cent of those in Air Force prisons. In 1972, blacks represented 47 per cent of the prisoners at Fort Leavenworth, Kansas, and 43 per cent of the men in the 3320th Retraining Group at Lowry AFB, Colorado. Not only are blacks confined far in excess of their numbers, but, according to the DOD Task Force study at Fort Leavenworth, they receive significantly more severe punishments than whites. On the average, blacks are confined at hard labor a year longer than whites (2.9 years to 1.9 years) and are considerably more likely to be sentenced to total forfeiture of pay and dishonorable discharge.

The system of administrative discharge likewise works to the disadvantage of blacks, in this case transferring the punishment to civilian life. A less-than-honorable discharge results in a lifelong barrier to secure employment and in reduction of many vital benefits. Such a record, combined with already limited civilian opportunity, often condemns a black veteran to permanent exclusion from decent employment. The NAACP report claimed that in Europe blacks receive 45 per cent of all less-than-honorable punitive discharges. Figures provided to the Congressional Black Caucus for 1970 show that although blacks were only 11.7 per cent of total Air Force strength, they receive 28.9 per cent of less-than-honorable discharges. While not providing exact statistics, the DOD Task Force confirmed the discriminatory pattern of administrative discharges:

> In all services, blacks receive a lower proportion of honorable discharges and a higher proportion of general and undesirable discharges than whites with similar educational levels and aptitude. Thus the disparity cannot be explained by aptitude or lack of education.

The roots of military racism lie not only in the prejudices of the larger, civilian society, but in discernible conditions within the armed forces themselves—what might be called institutional bias. The DOD Task Force identified two types of racial discrimination, "intentional" and "systemic," the latter defined as "policies or practices which appear to be neutral in their effect on minority individuals or groups but have the effect of disproportionately impacting upon them in harmful or negative ways." The report rightly concluded that "systemic racial discrimination exists throughout the armed services and in the military justice system." Indeed, much of what might be considered "intentional" or purposive bias also can be traced to the structure of the military—particularly to the extraordinary discretionary authority placed in the hands of individual officers. By allowing commanders virtually arbitrary power over judicial and disciplinary proceedings, the services invite widespread abuse and, in effect, license discriminatory practices. Many officers retain deeply rooted prejudices, which, through excessive command influence, result in serious injury to minority servicemen.

Another important factor underlying racism in the ranks, a seldom acknowledged but crucial phenomenon at the very heart of the military establishment in America, is the social predominance of white Southerners. In a manner reminiscent of Prussian control over imperial Germany's military forces, the South has consistently dominated the commanding positions of the U.S. military. Throughout this century, the proportion of general officers born and raised in the South has averaged near 45 per cent. Morris Janowitz's definitive study of the officer corps, *The Professional Soldier*, found that "generals with southern affiliation were roughly twice overrepresented" and that consideration of other social data such as location of relatives and marriage into southern families "would further raise the figure." In addition to their ascendancy within the top circles of the Pentagon, white Southerners have firm control of the Congressional military establishment. The major military committees have been a virtual fiefdom of Southerners for many years and remain so today, as evidenced by their chairmen: House Armed Services, Hebert of Louisiana; Senate Armed Services, Stennis of Mississippi; House Defense Appropriations, Mahon of Texas; and Senate Defense Appropriations, McClellan of Arkansas. Add to these conditions the fact that most major military installations are situated in the South, and a picture of significant southern domination of the military establishment becomes clear. Of course, racial prejudice is by no means restricted to the South; but the disproportionate influence of the traditional South within the armed forces must certainly be considered an important determinant of military racism.

The result of cumulative injustices is that black servicemen often leave the service in worse condition than they enter. Far from being a model of successful integration, the armed services are thoroughly racist in nature, and, in fact, often sharpen racial divisions. A Pentagon committee set up to study unrest among Marines at Camp Lejeune in 1969 reported that "the [2nd] division and the Marine Corps are returning marines, both black and white, to civilian society with more deeply seated prejudices than were individually possessed upon entrance to service." A similar assessment was voiced by the DOD Task Force in describing the fate of many black GIs: "These men may return to their respective communities frustrated and even more crippled than when they entered the service." It should not be surprising, then, that minority servicemen have so frequently rebelled against military authority. Expecting personal advancement and some escape from racial oppression, black recruits instead encounter extensive discrimination in nearly every aspect of military life. The continuance of these racist conditions, at a time of increasing non-white enlistments, represents a serious challenge to the stability of the armed forces. The question of racism and black resistance is crucial to the future of an all-volunteer force, and indeed to the very survival of the American military.

II

The struggle of black servicemen has consistently been the most militant and progressive sector of the GI movement. As we observed in Part I, minority troops have been more active in opposing militarism than whites and have displayed remarkable political sophistication and group solidarity. Appearing in the Army and the Marine Corps in the late 1960s, spreading rapidly to the Air Force, and, in 1972, reaching into the Navy, the black resistance movement defiantly challenged discrimination and the ossified practices of military justice throughout the Vietnam era. Black political organizations and study groups surfaced at nearly every major base in the world; uprisings and mutinies erupted at dozens of locations: in Vietnam, at Fort Hood during the Chicago Democratic convention, within the Seventh Army in Europe, at Travis AFB, and aboard the *Kitty Hawk* and the *Constellation*. The struggle has continued into the current cease-fire period and, as the percentage of non-whites increases, is likely to intensify in the future. With the Pentagon unwilling to remedy the pervasive injustices of enlisted life, the proud young blacks now entering the ranks will have no choice but to continue the resistance and fight for their rightful share of the democratic freedoms they are supposedly defending. Two recent black actions seem to confirm this assessment and suggest a future of continued internal disruption. Disturbances in Korea and in the Mediterranean Sea in the fall of 1973 epitomize the contradictions of the all-volunteer force and graphically illustrate the bitter consequences of racism.

On Sunday, October 7, the Army's 2nd Infantry Division, stationed in the remote regions of northern South Korea, exploded in a massive outburst of black resistance. Mounting frustrations among minority soldiers, sharpened by widespread discrimination and months of excessive harassment, burst at the end of the Columbus Day weekend into simultaneous uprisings at three of the division's major bases. At Camp Stanley, a group of black soldiers confronted commanders over a local regulation prohibiting the black liberation flag as a "racially divisive symbol." The protest quickly got out of hand, however, and resulted in defiance of several officers and in a series of assaults. At approximately the same time, violence also flared near another 2nd Division post, Camp Pelham. A minor fracas at the Club Paradise in Sonnjuri village erupted into a huge racial brawl, spilling over into the streets and resulting in mobilization of the base MPs. When police arrived, most of the white troops left, but approximately seventy-five to one hundred black and Puerto Rican soldiers stood their ground and battled the MPs with rocks and bottles. Several MPs were injured, and the provost marshal in charge, a black lieutenant named Ronald Johnson, was felled by a blow from a cane. While these events were occurring, yet another disturbance took place near Camp Casey, the largest post in the division, situated approximately twenty miles south of the Korean DMZ. A crowd of some fifty to seventy-five blacks charged into several local clubs that allegedly discriminated against non-whites and forced them to close. Sporadic fighting broke out in the village of Tongdu Chong, and

MPs and off-duty company commanders were ordered into the town to restore order. In addition to these major incidents, smaller outbursts also occurred in the villages of Taegu and Pusan.

With defiance spreading throughout the northern sector, a division alert was sounded, and all troops were ordered to return to base immediately. As GIs began arriving at the camps, however, further violence erupted. When a sizable group of blacks from a segregated area known as "the crack" reached Camp Casey, they discovered that MPs were waiting to check their names as they entered. Apparently fearing they would be tapped as "agitators" responsible for the earlier disturbances, the brothers decided to rush the gate in an attempt to avoid detection. The MPs retaliated by firing tear gas, and a minor riot broke out at the base gate. Meanwhile, another group of blacks descended on the Camp Casey MP headquarters, demanding to know why non-whites were singled out as troublemakers. When the blacks were ordered into an overnight confinement cell for allegedly being too rowdy, violence flared again. Fighting broke out right inside the MP office, and the chief Provost Marshal, a Colonel Shannon, was struck on the head by a steel pot.

In the aftermath of the October 7 uprisings, the division went through a major shakedown. Numerous officers were removed from command or transferred. At Camp Pelham, for example, the battalion commander, an executive officer, and several battery commanders were immediately replaced. A 10 P.M. curfew was imposed, and for two weeks following the disturbances, soldiers were required to wear uniforms on and off post. Criminal charges were pressed against at least sixty-six soldiers, nearly all of them black or Puerto Rican. Only a handful of those charged ever came to trial, however, for when it was discovered that ACLU attorneys were inquiring into the case, the command quickly disposed of the matter by administratively discharging nearly all those involved.

The October outbursts occurred within fifteen minutes of one another at widely separated bases and involved a closely watched group of black activists known as the "heavy brothers." Because of this, some military officials attributed the revolt to a conspiracy by members of a so-called "Black Socialist Club." In fact, the violence resulted not from any conscious plot, but from an informal determination by minority troops to draw the line and resist further oppression. Blacks and Puerto Ricans in the division had been meeting on a regular basis for nearly a year, hoping to build an atmosphere of brotherhood and unity within a hostile military environment. The meetings were no doubt very political and black nationalist oriented and may well have included discussions of socialism. The main topic of concern for the brothers, however, was racism in Korea, particularly within the military-justice system. Statistics for the twelve thousand troops at Camp Casey for 1972, for example, indicate that while blacks constituted 17.2 per cent of enlisted strength they received 26 per cent of all Article 15's, 57 per cent of special courts-martial, and a startling 83 per cent of general courts-martial. Sixty-two per cent of those in pretrial confinement were non-white, and 62.5 per cent of all punitive discharges were administered to blacks. Indeed, two thirds of the sixty-six blacks arrested for the October 7 uprisings had a record of previous Article 15s, some with as many as five separate punishments. Conditions such as these, not an organized conspiracy, were the real cause of revolt.

Another factor underlying the disturbances in Korea was a controversial training program introduced by the division's new commander, Major General Henry Emerson. Naïvely assuming that "a busy soldier stays out of trouble" (as the New York *Times* put it), General Emerson instituted a wide range of new policies that he claimed would make military duty more relevant and challenging. Most of the soldiers in the division, however, probably found their new duties nothing more than a source of meaningless extra harassment. Everyone in the division was forced to run two and one half miles each morning at 6 A.M. All units spent two weeks out of every two months training at night under simulated battle conditions. Each man was required to attend eighteen hours of educational training per month. Special permission was needed to leave base, and only 25 per cent of the members of a unit could stay out on any given night. As the Army defense attorney for the black GIs remarked, "there is no doubt in my mind that the duty here put enormous stresses on NCOs and officers alike," resulting in a "harsh and intolerant" attitude toward subordinates. The general's reversion to "old Army" standards thus played a major role in the October 7 revolt. Intolerable harassment, extensive discrimination, and mounting black nationalism resulted in the largest Army uprising since the height of the Vietnam War.

Almost exactly one month later, racial disturbances again wracked the services, this time aboard the U.S.S. *Little Rock* in the Mediterranean Sea. Although less extensive than the Korean revolt, the November 8 events on the flagship of the Sixth Fleet were of major importance politically, for they occurred under conditions likely to prevail during future American military actions and may portend what could happen throughout the fleet in a period of extended operations. The pressures of mobilization, coupled with mounting tensions between young black crewmen and commanders, resulted in serious internal disruption and nearly led to a *Kitty Hawk*-type riot.

For months prior to November, most of the fifty blacks aboard the cruiser (with a crew of thirteen hundred men) attempted to improve ship conditions by submitting complaints and requests to their race-relations adviser, a senior enlisted man. The black chief petty officer relayed the messages of the young seamen several times but was told only that the command "would look into" the appeals. The blacks were demanding that their immediate supervisor, a white petty officer, be removed from his position for allegedly discriminating against non-whites. The brothers also charged that they were cheated out of liberty through juggling of duty rosters, that blacks on sick call could not receive medical excuses from duty as easily as whites, and that they were forced to perform most of the demeaning jobs on the mess deck. In August 1973, the race-relations adviser warned Captain Peter Cullins of growing unrest within the crew. In September, in another sign of rising tensions, most of the blacks gathered for a meeting on the fantail to discuss their grievances. A white officer was present and reported the substance of the crew members' complaints to the captain, but still no changes were made. Thus, by the time of the October Middle East mobilization, black-white relations were already severely strained.

The November 8 outburst began when Seaman Apprentice Eulie Jessie was struck on the head with a wrench by a white sailor. The second such assault in a matter of days, the incident enraged many of the black crewmen and created an extremely volatile situation. Captain Cullins quickly arrived at the scene and attempted to placate Jessie and the others, but his efforts had little impact. As a Lawyers Military Defense Committee statement aptly commented, "there were no reserves of good will for him to draw on"; even as the captain spoke, fights broke out in several parts of the ship. As violence spread and the situation aboard the cruiser deteriorated, a band of some one hundred fifty to two hundred whites gathered with knives, picks, and clubs to defend themselves from what they thought was a black riot. A full-scale melee almost ensued, but the captain quickly intervened and managed to calm the crowd down, thus averting certain bloodshed. All officers were then called up and ordered to remain at their duty stations during the night to keep the peace.

Following the November 8 disturbances, court-martial charges were pressed against twelve crewmen—ten black and two white. One of the whites was acquitted, and the other was quickly sentenced to forty-five days' confinement. The ten blacks obtained a delay in their trials, though, and secured legal assistance from William Schaap and Robert Rivkin of the Lawyers Military Defense Committee in Heidelberg, Germany. On February 13, 1974, the group held a press conference near the Naval Support Activity in Naples, Italy, to seek public support for their cause and condemn the pending courts-martial as unjust and illegal. The men contended they could not receive a fair trial because of prejudices aboard the *Little Rock* and improper actions on the part of the ship's commander. By acting as both accuser and convening authority in their courts-martial, the men charged, Captain Cullins violated a specific provision of the UCMJ supposedly designed to prevent this type of judicial conflict of interest. The sailors also expressed regret that violence had occurred aboard the ship, but they stressed that repeated efforts to present grievances through official channels had been frustrated by command intransigence. As nineteen-year-old Seaman Fred Crowder asserted, "racism in the Navy, at least on our ship, is not being dealt with in a satisfactory way." Another of the accused, Seaman Apprentice David Pryor, summed up what happened on the ship—and, indeed, captured the dynamic of black revolt throughout the services—with powerful eloquence:

Our problems went unsolved. Our questions remained

unanswered. . . . Aboard the U.S.S. *Little Rock* our hopes turned to hatred, dedication became disgust, eyes searching for acceptance turned inward, and our hands raised for help became clenched fists.

III

Clearly, the demands of black servicemen can no longer be ignored. As the percentage of non-whites increases, the services will be literally torn apart if the problems of racism are not addressed. The measures necessary to eliminate discrimination are well known and could be implemented without expense or disruption. The DOD Task Force, black organizations such as the NAACP and Congressional Black Caucus, and black GIs themselves have advanced hundreds of concrete proposals for improving the lives of minority servicemen. Nothing short of a major commitment to reform can restore the faith of minority servicemen and ensure harmony within the ranks. Continued denial of black aspirations can only lead to further unrest and violence.

The first step in altering the abuses of racism in the military must be a thorough overhaul of job-assignment and promotion policies. The use of culturally biased screening tests such as the AFQT (which the NAACP described as "a bonus for having grown up white") is not only unjust but may also be unlawful. In its 1971 *Griggs* v. *Duke Power* decision, the U. S. Supreme Court ruled that employment practices that exclude minorities and have no proven relation to job performance are in violation of the 1964 Civil Rights Act. Referring to this decision, the DOD Task Force asserted that current military testing procedures are not an adequate measure of likely job performance and thus may be illegal. The inequities of limited job assignment and promotion could be mitigated through the following actions:

► Aptitude tests should be reassessed to find a better means of accurately predicting job performance. Occupational assignment, school selection, and promotion should be based not on written tests alone but on indicated interest, previous development, and, as much as possible, actual on-the-job performance.
► The services should establish definite goals for minority representation in all major occupational specialties,

a program termed by the NAACP as an "armed forces 'Philadelphia Plan.'" To accomplish this, special efforts must be made to recruit non-whites into specialized skills. Many blacks already in the ranks must be offered "cross-training" and be reassigned to higher-level positions.

▶ Promotion boards ought to be restructured to include a percentage of minorities and women equivalent to their percentage in the service as a whole.

▶ Major efforts are needed to increase the proportion of minority officers and ensure that they are placed in responsible positions of command. The percentage of blacks accepted into ROTC programs and particularly the service academies should approximate their percentage within the ranks.

Significant changes are also necessary in the military's Equal Opportunity programs. The DOD Task Force found that the numerous policies instituted in recent years to achieve equality and racial harmony are "more rhetorical than real" and have not received adequate Pentagon support. One of the program's chief defects is that it places Equal Opportunity officers within the command structure and thus robs them of any independence in dealing with discrimination. A much more serious and expanded effort is required if "Equal Opportunity" is to have any real meaning:

▶ Officer fitness reports ought to include an evaluation of Equal Opportunity performance by the officers' own men. Such a program, similar to the rating of college professors by students, would allow promotion boards to judge effectiveness in dealing with minorities.

▶ The position of Deputy Assistant Secretary of Defense (Equal Opportunity) should be elevated to that of Assistant Secretary of Defense. The new office should have direct access to all Equal Opportunity officers and be empowered to conduct investigations without going through local commanders.

▶ All off-base housing policies and regulations should be administered by this new office. The Assistant Secretary of Defense (Equal Opportunity) should be authorized to negotiate with foreign governments, particularly those of Germany and Korea, for reform of overseas housing policies.

Change is most critically needed in the military justice

system. Disciplinary practices, both administrative and judicial, are perhaps the greatest single source of discrimination encountered by blacks. The question of transforming military justice, however, goes beyond the problem of racism; it is an essential step in the task of improving service life for all enlisted people. Eliminating discrimination in military justice requires sweeping democratization of the entire judicial process and must be considered as part of a thorough overhaul of all aspects of military discipline. The recommendations listed here are only those specifically relating to non-white servicemen; the many other necessary steps are discussed in the next chapter.

► The UCMJ should be amended to add a specific provision making discrimination a court-martial offense.
► The Pentagon should contract with civil-rights organizations to provide legal representation to black servicemen until the percentage of black military lawyers equals the percentage of blacks within the services. The military should provide incentives and educational opportunities to increase the number of black attorneys within the ranks.
► Court-martial boards should be restructured to insure proportionate representation of minorities and women.
► Administrative-discharge proceedings must embody greater judicial safeguards. The serviceman should be allowed access to counsel throughout the process, and at least one legally qualified officer should be required to sit on the review panel. Discharge boards should include minority membership.
► The services should implement an automatic monitoring procedure for Article-15 punishments. Whenever the black/white ratio of Article 15's exceeds by a stated amount that within a unit's enlisted population, all Article-15 cases should be immediately reviewed by higher authorities.

The services no longer have the luxury of deciding whether or not to end discriminatory practices. They have no other choice, for the continuing conflict over racism in the ranks poses a serious threat to the very survival of the military. Failure to act can only further inflame internal tensions and jeopardize military capabilities. In 1972, the Congressional Black Caucus warned that racial polarization "is rapidly approaching the point where the over-all effectiveness of the military as a fighting force will be seriously hampered, if not completely stalemated." The uprisings of October and November 1973 seem to confirm such a prognosis, for both occurred within key overseas units at the frontiers of potential military conflict. Indeed, the recent history of black resistance suggests that combat efficiency has already been substantially impaired. With the Army forced to take weapons from blacks in Vietnam and the Navy's largest ships encumbered by black unrest during bombing operations in the Tonkin Gulf and while on alert in the Mediterranean Sea, the military's ability to perform its mission is in grave doubt. Democratization and the elimination of racism are necessary to resolve the gnawing contradictions of military personnel policy and are, in fact, essential to the nation's security.

CHAPTER 12

SOLDIERS AND DEMOCRACY

Reform of the military is a difficult issue. In a sense, it's a misdirected effort which diverts attention from the more important question of what mission the armed forces perform. Global interventionism and the huge size of the military are at the very heart of the current crisis in the ranks, and they must be challenged if we are to regain control over the institutions of war. No internal changes can be meaningful unless force strengths are reduced and servicemen are returned to the United States, a task requiring long-term political struggle to eradicate the social roots of war. Commitment to this goal can't blind us to the immediate problems and needs of servicemen, though, and the possibilities of achieving greater democratic control and a more just and humane service now. We must press for a smaller, non-interventionist military, but we must do so in the context of conditions as they exist today.

I

No subject of armed-forces policy has generated more controversy than the question of the all-volunteer force, and it would thus seem the proper place to begin our discussion. Perhaps the central issue of the debate is whether or not an all-volunteer military increases or diminishes the likelihood of military adventurism. I think that such a force establishes limits on executive war-making powers and makes future Vietnam-type operations less likely. Without the easy option of expanding draft calls whenever additional manpower is desired, national security managers lose a crucial element of their ability to act unilaterally—a condition of considerable worry to many military planners. In rejecting recommendations for ending the draft in 1967, for example, President Johnson's Marshall Commission objected strenuously to the "inflexible nature" of a volunteer force, which they said would allow "no provision for the rapid procurement of larger numbers of men" in crisis situations. One suspects that such reservations are a principal reason why many Pentagon and Congressional military officials have been reluctant to support the all-volunteer force. The exorbitant manpower costs associated with the volunteer force add a powerful economic argument against excessive use of the armed forces. Recognizing that "the cost of manpower expansion would be tremendous," General Westmoreland complained in 1973 that "such realization could serve as a deterrent" to military planning. The volunteer force is also more open to popular control, because voluntary recruitment makes the size of the armed forces dependent on the participation of the nation's young people. General Westmoreland saw this point well: "In the final analysis the size of our forces will be determined by the numbers of men that can be recruited—not by security requirements," meaning that military capabilities will depend directly on the American people themselves, not on the fiat of Pentagon bureaucrats.

While an all-volunteer force possesses these advantages, and is obviously superior to the compulsive governmental intrusion of conscription, there remain widely held misgivings about the wisdom of a "professional" military. One of the most frequently heard arguments is that the all-volunteer force will lead to an Army composed exclusively of the poor, that, with the middle class exempt from military service, the majority of the population will have no interest in military affairs and hence little concern for restraining the use of the armed forces. This is an extremely important issue, for, as we saw during Vietnam, the prospect of being drafted played an important role in the student unrest that helped change the course of the war. It is also relevant because the present all-volunteer force is developing, as many feared, into an Army made up overwhelmingly of the lower classes. The questions, then, are these: Can the armed forces be made more socially representative of the national population, and will public criticism of the military disappear with the end of induction? The issues are of course closely interrelated, but for the sake of argument we shall look at each separately here, beginning first with the problem of whether or not dissent will continue in an all-volunteer environment.

Many have warned that an Army composed only of volunteers will no longer be subject to the healthy internal questioning evidenced during Vietnam. Inherent in this position is the view that the GI movement developed primarily because the military was forced to draft middle-class college students. While disgruntled ex-college students may have sparked some GI-movement activities, particularly certain of its more articulate expressions, the bulk of the GI resistance came not from draftees but from volunteers. The evidence available from an examination of the GI movement suggests that the majority of dissenters and organizers were volunteers from working-class backgrounds. While by no means conclusive, a number of small-scale surveys conducted in recent years confirm this. In March of 1970, the National Council to Repeal the Draft looked into the backgrounds of twenty-five members of GIs United Against the War at Fort Bragg. According to Tom Reeves of the Council, seventeen of the twenty-five activists had volunteered and sixteen of the group came from lower-middle-class families. In November of 1971, the United States Servicemen's Fund sponsored a GI-movement conference in Williams Bay, Wisconsin. Of the approximately fifty active-duty GIs and veterans attending from various organizing projects, the vast majority were volunteers, not draftees. At one meeting of active dissenters, an informal poll showed that eighteen of the twenty men present had volunteered. Additional evidence comes from an independent survey taken among members of Vietnam Veterans Against the War encamped on the Mall in Washington, D.C., on April 23, 1971. The results of 172 returned questionnaires showed that approximately two thirds of the veterans had enlisted in the service, while nearly 49 per cent listed their father's occupation as "labor." Further indication of the volunteer origins of GI dissent comes from the extensive history of protest within the Air Force and the Navy, neither of which uses conscripts, and the continuation of the GI movement beyond 1972, despite the end of the draft. These findings confirm the opinion of nearly every leading GI-movement figure with whom I had contact in writing this book. They also corroborate my own experience. At Fort Hamilton and Fort Bliss, most of the people involved in anti-war work were, like myself, volunteers from working-class families. To be sure, many had volunteered most reluctantly, and some had been to college, at least for a time; but very few were draftees. This should not really surprise us, given what we have seen of the oppression of enlisted service and the economic compulsion of volunteering. It seems certain that lower-middle-class enlistees will not shirk protest against policies and conditions they find intolerable. This was best summed up by Sp/5 Jim Goodman, former editor of the Baumholder *Gig Sheet* in Germany: "Draftees expect shit, get shit, aren't even disappointed. Volunteers expect something better, get the same shit, and have at least one more year to get mad about it."

Nonetheless, the question remains whether this dissent will continue into the future and whether military service can be more equitably shared by all sectors of the civilian population. Assuming that an all-volunteer force is desirable in other respects, is it possible to structure such a force to avoid an Army of only the poor and prevent isolation of the armed forces from society? As we noted in Chapter 10, investigators from the University of Michigan's Institute for Social Research have discovered evidence suggesting that this may indeed be possible, and they have proposed a plan for substituting financial lures with a widely appealing system of paid schooling guarantees. The Johnston and Bachman "Four for Four" plan (or any similar program based on a greatly expanded GI Bill) would be a crucial means of attracting a broader cross section of the population and would ensure that the services remain dependent on civilian society. Unfortunately, the Defense Department thus far has ignored such proposals and seems determined to continue the use of bonuses and other pecuniary incentives—a formula certain to jeopardize the volunteer effort. An all-volunteer force can be made to work and can attract a more representative cross section of the society, but it can do so only if we are willing to experiment with new approaches to recruitment.

II

In our analysis so far, we have assumed the desirability of attracting citizen-soldiers who will question abuses of military authority. Such a notion, of course, is not likely to generate much support within the defense Establishment. Guaranteeing the right to dissent would require extensive alterations in military justice and is certain to meet fierce opposition from Pentagon officials. Commanders can be expected to cling firmly to present methods and to warn of catastrophe from any weakening of command authority. A critical look at the nature of service discipline, however, finds little truth in the claims of military apologists.

Our first task is to probe the justifications for the traditionally accepted mode of military discipline. The basic explanation seems simple, at least on the surface: The organizational efficiency required on the battlefield demands total compliance with command decisions. It is assumed that men will not advance under fire without the impetus of inflexible authority, which must be instilled through rigid indoctrination and the threat of punishment. Colonel Heinl fervently argued this point in a recent attack on reform of military law: "Nothing save deeply inculcated discipline can drive soldiers or Marines to cross a fire-swept beach, storm a pill-box, or advance into the next house in street-fighting." In a similar vein, retired Army General Hamilton Howze argued in *Army* magazine in 1971 that traditional discipline must be maintained as the backbone of military efficiency: "In the last analysis it is the *authority of the commander* which gets the job done . . ." (emphasis in original). General Westmoreland repeated the same argument in describing the primary purpose of military justice: "Discipline is an attitude of respect for authority which is developed by leadership, precept and training . . . which leads to a willingness to obey an order no matter how unpleasant or dangerous. . . ."

Despite such claims, the available evidence casts considerable doubt on the value of military discipline. A number of scholarly studies suggest that men are not motivated in combat by command authority or training, but by simple personal concerns such as the desire to return home safely, mutual bonds with a buddy, and the basic drive of self-preservation. During World War II, Samuel Stouffer and a team of social scientists conducted a pioneering survey of the attitudes and experiences of enlisted men and officers, later published in the two-volume report *The American Soldier*. Concentrating on a veteran infantry unit that had fought through two Mediterranean campaigns, the scientists asked the men what motivated them under fire. They found a marked difference between officers and enlisted men in the value attached to military authority. When asked to select the factor "most important to you in making you want to keep going," enlisted men identified "leadership and discipline" least of all the incentives listed; only 1 per cent considered it their primary motivation. When officers were asked to name what they thought was most important to the troops, however, discipline was selected most frequently, by 19 per cent. The GIs were concerned not with military authority but with returning home safely and protecting their buddies. The research also indicated that the threat of punishment under military law had little impact on the battlefield, that men in the infantry were generally unmoved by potential disciplinary sanctions. Less thorough but similarly directed studies were conducted during Korea and Vietnam, with results confirming the seeming irrelevance of military discipline. Sociologist Roger Little observed Army units in Korea and concluded that solidarity among small groups was the most important factor in explaining the behavior of enlisted men in combat. Charles Moskos, studying GIs in Vietnam, saw combat troops as concerned only with their own personal survival. None of these studies found military discipline or authority important to combat motivation. The basic drive to return home safely and the intimacy of buddy groups seem sufficient to convince soldiers to co-operate and to sustain them under fire. There is no evidence that the strictures of military discipline contribute to combat effectiveness.

The rigidity of the present military code actually hinders morale and detracts from organizational efficiency. We have seen numerous examples in which not a lack of authority but its very excessiveness have increased dissension and unrest. Stern discipline has frequently only exacerbated internal difficulties and strengthened GI resistance. Servicemen rooted in a society increasingly skeptical of authority and established institutions must inevitably rebel against the arbitrary punitive methods of the military establishment. The present, medieval system is also fundamentally incompatible with the changed nature of modern military forces. The increasing pace of technological change and introduction of new and sophisticated military job specialties have changed the demands of military service, requiring greater abilities and more individual initiative on the part of each soldier. Military discipline and training, derived from times when armies had to be forced into open fire in mass infantry lines, can only impede the individual responsibility required in many modern military occupations. Moreover, an increasing number of servicemen work in a bureaucratic or technical environment similar to that found in many civilian jobs. Indeed, many now live off post and commute to their forty-hour-a-week military job very much in the manner of the average civilian. To claim that strict discipline is necessary for proper job performance under such conditions is absurd.

There are other reasons for overhauling military law and administration, perhaps the most basic being that people in the military simply deserve more humane treatment. The needless pain and suffering caused by the present system, often extending beyond service into civilian life, are obscene. Young servicemen must make many sacrifices just by the very nature of military duty, and there is no reason to impose further, unnecessary privation. Another argument for internal reform comes from the very nature of an all-volunteer force. Inherent in the move toward a more professional, voluntary organization is the principle of allowing greater individual responsibility. Military officials have defended liberal reforms such as the elimination of reveille, for example, in just such terms, stating that henceforth soldiers will be responsible themselves for showing up at work on time. As the all-volunteer force becomes more established, and as greater numbers of women enter the service, the impetus for expanding the scope of individual initiative will increase. Indeed, the volunteer force will be unable to fill its ranks unless it makes such concessions and convinces potential recruits they will be treated like professionals, not like pawns.

The final argument against the present system is that it fails to account for spontaneous motivation and the need for agreement with institutional objectives. Ultimately, rote discipline can never replace rank-and-file support for the larger mission of the organization. If enlisted people share such goals, they will perform efficiently; but if they are forced to act against their interests, no legal code will contain their objections. Men fought nobly during World War II, but when asked to remain abroad beyond their just due they howled mightily for ships. GIs fought well in Vietnam too, but rebelled when they sensed the hopelessness and immorality of their mission. The more an Army relies on spontaneous motivation in place of harsh discipline, the more unified and efficient it will be.

III

At the end of World War II, a shocked Western civilization reacted to the barbarities of fascism by seeking to establish safeguards against mass criminality—by appealing to the basic ideals of humanity and, at Nuremberg, adopting a code of individual moral responsibility. Asserting that the soldier's allegiance to the institution must not supersede his fundamental obligation to the standards of law and morality, the Allied powers, led by the United States, raised the principle of personal accountability as the ultimate defense against militarism. The final safeguard against an unresponsive and isolated military was to rest with the citizen-soldier. Guaranteeing his right to question ensured that the functioning of the military would be dependent on the willing support of its servicemen and on the society from which they were drawn.

This principle of military democracy found its most concrete application in the West German Bundeswehr, founded in 1955. At the end of World War II, the Allies determined that the Federal Republic should be completely demilitarized, without any type of military force. Within a few years, however, the pressures of the Cold War produced the inevitable decision to rearm. The lessons of World War II were not forgotten, though, and the Bundeswehr was deliberately and carefully structured to ensure firm civilian control and prevent separation of the military from society. Knowing well that the military could threaten as well as protect democracy, the founders of the Bundeswehr developed a system predicated on the notion that the individual soldier must be given not only the right but the responsibility to think and act independently.

The Soldier's Law, the basic internal code of the Bundeswehr, specifically embodies many of these principles. The soldier-superior relationship is very carefully defined to prevent coercive and unthinking submission to commanders. The superior's authority is said to derive solely from his specific military position, not from rank per se; an officer has no authority over his subordinates outside the military environment. Saluting and other forms of deference are thus voluntary, except during duty conditions. Through the Military Complaint Order, every serviceman is guaranteed the right to submit complaints of wrongdoing to higher officials. Such officers are obligated to process the complaint, and the petitioner retains the right of further appeal, including review by civilian courts. Under the Soldier's Law, the military penal code is radically transformed. Nearly all criminal and civil legal proceedings are the responsibility of civilian courts, with military defendants entitled to the same standards of impartiality and fairness accorded to civilians. The function of military courts is strictly limited; they retain jurisdiction over only a small number of purely military offenses, e.g., desertion, mutiny, misuse of authority, etc. Perhaps the most striking feature of the Soldier's Law is the soldier's representative, or *Vertrauensmann* (in English, "one who can be trusted"). Under this system, every company or corresponding small unit maintains an elected representative to speak for the enlisted men in dealings with the commander. No punishment or other type of personnel action may be taken unless the *Vertrauensmann* is consulted beforehand. Once elected, he serves in this position for one year and cannot be removed or punished by the commander. Although he possesses no direct control over military operations, the *Vertrauensmann* participates in all decisions relating to enlisted welfare and provides a direct voice for rank-and-file grievances. (This provision was first introduced by the Weimar Republic in 1921 but, significantly, was eliminated by Hitler in 1935.)

The Bundeswehr contains additional means of guaranteeing soldiers' rights. The special Military Commissioner of the Bundestag was established as an auxiliary organ of the legislature for controlling the military establishment. As an independent ombudsman responsible solely to the Bundestag, the Commissioner is specifically empowered to safeguard the constitutional liberties of servicemen; he may conduct an independent investigation of any soldier complaint and can inspect a military post at any time without advance notice. Soldiers are also specifically granted all the political rights of regular citizens. They may run for office and conduct political meetings; they may even join unions.

In an army of morally responsible soldiers, it is important that religious guidance and counseling come from an independent source. Thus, chaplains in the Bundeswehr have no military rank and are outside the regular command structure; their status is closer to that of a civil-service worker than a military officer. As only temporary chaplains, they remain members of their church and are regularly rotated back to civilian ministry. One of the most unique features of the Bundeswehr is the emphasis in military training on the concept of *Innere Führung,* or inner guidance. All forms of harassment and intimidation designed to break the continuity with civilian life and strip a recruit of his individuality have been eliminated. Instead, soldiers are identified and treated as "citizens in uniform" and are expected to retain responsibility for state policy. They enjoy the dignity and privileges of citizenship because, like true citizens, they must be guided by an inner sense of allegiance to the laws and morality of the society.

While the Bundeswehr is perhaps the clearest example of a democratic military force, numerous other countries also possess features of a more humane and libertarian service, which are instructive of the possibilities here. The Swedes pioneered the ombudsman system of protecting citizens from bureaucratic abuse, and for many years they have maintained a special military ombudsman to aid servicemen. In the Netherlands soldiers have won the right to form their own unions; the Canadian armed forces are also expected to be unionized within a few years. Canada further enjoys, along with Great Britain, New Zealand, and Australia, a system of civilian appeals boards that employ wide review powers over the decisions of military courts and thus protect servicemen from abuses of command authority. The Chinese Peoples Liberation Army (PLA) has devised particularly interesting egalitarian practices designed to deflate arrogance among officers. Under the 1958 "Officers to the Ranks" movement, all officer cadre, generals included, were obliged to spend at least one month a year in the ranks alongside enlisted men. Although this specific innovation has been dropped, new officers are still required to serve for a time as enlisted men. Indeed, the PLA retains an extraordinary degree of military democracy: enlisted men are encouraged to discuss and criticize command decisions, and all formal ranks, insignia, and caste distinctions between superiors and subordinates have been abolished.

IV

These examples provide a model for the type of reform needed within the American armed forces. In our search for greater democratic control over the military, we should follow the example of other nations in enlarging soldier liberties and attempt to institutionalize the principles established at Nuremberg. Numerous organizations and individuals already have proposed that we move in this direction, including the DOD Task Force on Military Justice, the ACLU, the Congressional Black Caucus, and numerous other organizations and individuals. The strongest voice for reform, though, has been that of the GIs themselves. In countless acts of resistance and protest, they have clamored for greater freedom and dignity and have pointed the directions reform must take. It's time we heed their cry and outline the steps necessary for creating a democratic military.

The UCMJ should be completely revised, with all but strictly military-related matters transferred to civilian jurisdiction and the vaguely worded catch-all offenses (Articles 133 and 134) eliminated. New provisions need to be added to carefully prescribe the duties and responsibilities of commanders and subordinates regarding potentially criminal acts. Articles 21 and 22 of the French Military Code offer an excellent example, the first denying the commander the right to order illegal acts, and the second requiring the soldier to object if such commands are issued. Acts that are contrary to the laws and customs of war, constitute a breach of the public peace, or violate the rights of citizens should be defined as unlawful, with legal penalties specified for those who order or carry out such policies. Such measures would establish a code of personal responsibility and make the Nuremberg principle a vital force within the military.

Change is also critically needed in military courts, where arbitrary command influence is at the root of widespread injustice. All court functions now belonging to the commander should be reserved to separate agencies: the investigating officer's report, similar to a Grand Jury decision, should be made binding on the convening authority; pretrial confinement should be limited and placed within strict judicial standards; military judges must be independent of the command struc-

ture and be granted full tenure; and the right of the commander to review court findings and change sentencing should
be abolished. In addition, the defense counsel must enjoy full
autonomy, independent of the pressures of command influence, and should be allotted greater courtroom powers. By far
the most important judicial reform, one that is indispensable
to military democracy, is the introduction of trial by jury of
peers. Command-appointed boards of officers and career
NCOs must be replaced by a jury of peers randomly selected
from those of the same rank as the accused. This provision
is crucial for insuring that citizen-soldiers will in fact exercise
their responsibilities to resist illegal commands. Servicemen
who would not risk a legal test before a jury of careerists
might be more willing to challenge questionable policies if
insured of a just hearing before their equals.

Another aspect of the penal code that must be altered is
non-judicial punishment. As noted earlier, Article 15 has created severe hardships for many low-ranking servicemen, particularly non-whites, and has been the subject of widespread
criticism. Thousands of troops have submitted petitions urging that the present system be abolished and that the power
to impose summary punishment be transferred to a board of
enlisted representatives equal in rank to the accused. This GI-
movement proposal should be adopted as an important step
toward alleviating the suffering engendered by current practices and as a means of checking the arbitrary power of commanders.

Not every GI is affected by service disciplinary policies, but
all enlisted men—careerists included—bristle at the indignities
and petty harassments of the military caste system. Officer
privilege has been the subject of rank-and-file hostility for
many years. Despite widespread public criticism, however, the
anachronistic social distinctions of military life remain intact:
enlisted men and officers have separate mess halls, separate
clubs, and separate latrines; commanders live in luxurious
homes, while GIs and NCOs live in row houses or family
apartments; officers may not perform manual labor; they are
"gentlemen" and their wives are "ladies"; etc. The degrading
rituals of "military courtesy" bear no relation to organizational
efficiency and in fact detract from enlisted morale by sowing
resentment and bitterness within the lower ranks. The galling
humiliations of officer privilege cannot be justified on the

basis of military requirements. The United States would do well to follow the example of the Chinese Army and abolish social divisions between officers and men.

One of the most controversial subjects of military reform is the administrative-discharge system. Nearly five hundred thousand Vietnam-era veterans have received less-than-honorable separations, often resulting in a lifelong barrier to GI benefits and decent employment. Since adaptability to the military has little or no relation to one's ability to function in civilian life, the permanent deprivations of a "bad" discharge constitute a vindictive and senseless form of oppression. While some have urged merely increasing judicial safeguards in the separation process, a growing number of organizations and individuals (including half the members of the Pentagon's own Task Force on the Administration of Military Justice) have called for a thorough overhaul of the entire procedure. The only just solution is to establish "one discharge for all": the current system of five separate discharge classifications should be completely abolished and replaced with a single, ungraded certificate denoting completion of service. Such a document, in the Congressional Black Caucus formulation, would indicate only the length of service, any special awards or decorations received, and a notification of whether it was based on medical reasons. The services could continue to discharge, but they could no longer mark a man for life or strip him of his rightful benefits.

The Vietnam Veterans Against the War organization has further demanded that such a reform be made retroactive, particularly to those veterans punitively discharged during the Vietnam era. Indeed, the question of upgrading the half million less-than-honorable separations among Vietnam veterans is a seldom mentioned but crucial element of the mounting public debate over amnesty. Given the frequency with which commanders resorted to discharges as a means of eliminating political opponents, many punitively released veterans must be counted among those who resisted the military and the Vietnam War. Similarly, the disproportionate number of blacks who received "bad" discharges were often leading activists in the GI movement and in many cases were victims of overt discrimination and repression. The question of amnesty, therefore, goes beyond the problem of draft resisters and deserters and must encompass the plight of hundreds of thousands of poor and working-class veterans who rebelled against the Vietnam-era military and were mangled by an oppressive administrative-discharge system.

V

Some may object that proposals for military democracy are hopelessly utopian, that military authorities will never yield to demands for GI rights. While the ultimate goals of the GI movement are admittedly distant, the resistance effort has not been without impact. Indeed, the pressures of continuous political struggle have resulted in important gains in recent years. Perhaps the clearest example of progress in the campaign for enlisted rights is the increasing influence of civilian federal courts in the affairs of military discipline—what might be termed "the civilianization of military law." In the past decade, servicemen have pushed relentlessly for Bill of Rights protections, and, through an unprecedented wave of GI court suits, have persuaded federal judges to assume jurisdiction over many crucial areas of military justice. The vaguely worded catch-alls, Articles 133 and 134, have been seriously challenged; court-martial defendants have won the right to individual counsel; various unjust and discriminatory regulations have been nullified; the right to on-post distribution of political literature has been granted; etc. The intrusion of civilian legal standards into the world of the military marks an important and potentially fundamental change in the nature of military law.

There have been literally hundreds of GI court cases, and it would be impossible for us to discuss even a fraction of them here. Rather, we shall review a few of the recent landmark decisions with greatest consequence. One of the most important of these involved two Fort Ord soldiers, Don Amick and Ken Stolte, who in 1968 distributed a leaflet urging fellow GIs to join an anti-war union. The two were court-martialed under Article 134 for "disloyal statements" and sentenced to three years in prison. In January 1973, however, Washington Federal District Judge Aubrey Robinson ruled that the Army had incorrectly interpreted the article in charging the two and threw out their convictions. The Robinson decision was extended two months later, when a Washington

Appeals Court declared that Article 134 was in fact unconstitutional because of vagueness and inadequate standards of guilt. The case involved Marine Pfc Mark Avrech, who had been convicted in Da Nang, during 1969, of anti-war activities. The Avrech decision was quickly followed by a historic order from the 3rd Circuit Court of Appeals on April 18, 1973: The Philadelphia court stated that Dr. Howard Levy, imprisoned in 1967 for refusing to train Green Beret medics, had been court-martialed illegally. The court not only concurred with the D.C. Appeals Panel in ruling Article 134 invalid, but also struck down Article 133, "conduct unbecoming an officer." Although the Levy decision was subsequently overturned by the Supreme Court and many of these gains were thus frustrated, the GI legal offensive has continued to advance on other fronts.

Civilian courts have expanded Bill of Rights protections by intervening in a number of key administrative cases. On October 31, 1972, the 2nd Circuit Court of New York ruled, in *Hagopian* v. *Knowlton*, that the West Point Military Academy could not dismiss a cadet for disciplinary reasons without a fair hearing. In a decision with important implications for service-wide discharge policies, the court stated that the Academy's procedures for expulsion did not provide adequate due-process guarantees. The courts have issued several judgments which for the first time permit the distribution of political literature within military installations. In November of 1972, the Supreme Court ruled that the conviction of anti-war activist Tom Flower for distributing literature at Fort Sam Houston was unconstitutional. In a sweeping First Amendment decision, the court declared that the military did not have the right to restrict access to parts of an installation generally open to the public. In a following case, *Jenness* v. *Forbes*, a Rhode Island district court decided that Socialist Workers Party candidate Linda Jenness could not be prevented from distributing political literature at Quonset NAS. Similarly, the 3rd Circuit Court of Appeals ruled on October 27, 1972, that Peoples Party candidate Benjamin Spock could not be barred from Fort Dix. Perhaps the most striking instance of civilian court intrusion in military administrative matters involved Judge Gerhard Gesell's February 1974 decision (discussed in Chapter 7) declaring General Michael Davison's drug-suppression program unconstitutional.

The growing influence of civilian legal standards has affected court-martial procedure as well, significantly expanding defendants' rights. In August of 1972, the district court of Hawaii granted habeas-corpus relief to a class of Navy and Marine inmates imprisoned by summary courts-martial at which they were not represented by counsel. Relying on the Supreme Court's historic Argersinger decision (which extended the right of counsel to all criminal proceedings resulting in imprisonment), the judge ruled that every defendant in summary courts-martial was entitled to qualified legal defense. In a following decision on April 13, 1973, Los Angeles Judge David Williams went further and decided that all Navy summary courts-martial were illegal; the judge ordered the release of over fifteen hundred sailors and Marines previously convicted and jailed without counsel. (Execution of the judge's extraordinary order was later stayed, pending further appeal.)

These are by no means the only examples of federal court action in recent years. Dozens of other important decisions have increased the rights of servicemen in a wide variety of areas, in some cases requiring the military to rewrite its regulations. As noted in Chapter 1, for example, the pressure of GI habeas-corpus suits has resulted in greatly liberalized treatment of in-service conscientious objectors. Similarly, reservists have succeeded in several cases in eliminating prohibitions against short-hair wigs. At some posts, servicemen's organizations have gained the right to distribute their newspapers on base. Thus, while progress in the struggle for GI rights has not been overwhelming, some slight improvements have been made in easing service disciplinary practices and enlarging First Amendment liberties. GI activists and their supporters have steadily chipped away at command prerogatives and have brought the once separate preserve of military law under increasing judicial review. The civilianization of military justice suggests that the GI movement has already had significant impact on the internal structure of the military and that democracy is slowly edging its way into service life. If these advances are to continue, though, the pressure of citizen action must be maintained.

VI

None of the proposals we have advanced can have any meaning without massive political support. The anti-war and military-resistance movements of the past decade have made strong beginnings toward achieving some of these goals, but much more is necessary if we are to sustain and expand the struggle for democratic control of the military. At the end of World War II, an upsurge in rank-and-file unrest similar to the GI movement swept through the services, creating widespread pressure for change; but Cold War repression and the Left's political weaknesses enabled the military establishment to withstand the challenge. Today the armed forces have been shaken by the GI movement, and, thanks to Watergate, the recent drift toward repression has been slowed. Thus the opportunities for change remain great, but we must not repeat the mistakes of the past and allow political pressures to subside.

The first task is to guard against the return of conscription. As active-duty force strengths continue to decline in the wake of the manpower crisis, reintroduction of the draft will become more and more likely. Youth and student groups should be particularly vigilant in this area, not only with lobbying activities but with preparation for a possible campaign of mass nonco-operation. The vast coalition of liberals, radicals, and conservatives that combined to lobby against conscription in recent years also must be alert to the possibilities of such a retreat. Libertarian and peace organizations should create a furor of protest at even the suggestion of a renewed draft. As the services claim that additional troops are necessary to prevent a military collapse, we must counter with the argument that overseas troop strengths can be reduced without damaging national security. As they lament the failure of voluntary enlistment, we should call for improvements in service life and reform of recruitment methods.

Even as we seek to preserve and improve the all-volunteer force, we must not be blind to its abuses, particularly the fraudulent methods of the recruitment system. Activists in various parts of the country have already launched counter-recruitment campaigns to provide young people a chance to judge more accurately the true nature of military service. Concentrating on the deceit of job-training promises and the repressive conditions of enlisted service, counterrecruiters have brought their message before a wide variety of forums. In Grand Rapids, peace workers from the Ammon Hennacy House distributed leaflets to high schools and debated recruiters before school forums. In Van Nuys, California, the Valley Peace Center has established a downtown "Counter Recruiting Office." At Fresno City College, counterrecruiters recently set up a table and display next to that of the Marine Corps and successfully persuaded many students to bypass the recruiters. The same group has posted anti-enlistment signs outside various public locations and applied to have its literature placed in local high school guidance centers. The American Friends Service Committee (AFSC) in Baltimore has been particularly diligent, speaking before students at some fifteen local high schools, publishing and distributing large amounts of counterrecruitment literature, and co-ordinating a February 1974 conference of over one hundred anti-military activists. The People's Coalition for Peace and Justice and the Fellowship for Reconciliation in New York have lobbied against plans to introduce Junior ROTC into state high schools. The Central Committee for Conscientious Objectors (CCCO) national office in Philadelphia now serves as a central clearinghouse for counterrecruiting ideas and has published several issues of an information-exchange newsletter, *Counter-Pentagon.*

For these and other groups organizing against the recruitment put-on, the most difficult problem is to meet the needs of young people for meaningful employment and economic security. As former Chicago Area Military Project activist George Schmidt has commented, "Counterrecruitment will never overcome an empty stomach." Unemployment (real and disguised) is a pervasive and inescapable fact of American economic life, and decent job opportunities simply do not exist for many working-class young people, particularly in the center cities and rural regions, from which so many recruits originate. Counterrecruiters from the Community for Nonviolent Action in Connecticut, for example, found that there are almost no job programs in their area and that the few that do operate are sponsored by large war industries. Also typical is the experience of AFSC chicano activists in San Antonio, who, given the oppressive circumstances of *barrio* life, are powerless to suggest alternatives to military service. Recognition of these cold realities need not deter counterrecruitment efforts, however. Even if a young person ultimately is forced to join, pre-enlistment counseling can prepare the recruit for the conditions he is likely to face and, most importantly, can acquaint him with the GI movement and military-support offices which can serve his needs.

The most important form of direct action is that which comes from soldiers themselves. The GI movement has been a major force in the decline of the armed forces. It has provided the primary impetus for many demands for change, and its continuation is essential to their chances of success. Since the decline of the Vietnam War, however, many former peace activists and supporters of GI projects have turned their attention elsewhere, assuming that internal dissent is finished. As our analysis has shown, however, the GI movement is still active: more than thirty GI organizing projects continue to operate at bases throughout the world. Moreover, given the strong possibilities of further American overseas intervention, the resistance may again swell to mass dimensions. Clearly, the GI movement is not dead, and the enlisted ranks remain fertile ground for political action.

One of the best prescriptions for the post-Vietnam GI movement was that offered early in 1973 by activists with the paper *FighT bAck* in Germany, based on four main points:

1. *Radicals must join the Army.* The role of radicals who purposely join the services to organize has been important throughout the GI movement and remains so today. Within the *FighT bAck* group, in the GI Alliance in Tacoma, and at numerous other projects, former civilian activists, some of whom gave up deferments to join, have been a vital force in sustaining GI dissent. The Progressive Labor Party has been particularly active in encouraging members to join the services. Other organizations should follow suit and send members into the enlisted ranks as an indispensable means of exerting direct pressure on the armed forces. The presence of even a few hundred committed activists could have great impact on the level of servicemen's dissent.

2. *Civilian support is crucial.* As we have seen throughout the history of the GI movement, such support has been a crucial ingredient of successful organizing. Civilian activists are most needed as political workers and counselors at local projects. Peace organizations should adopt programs for training civilians in military counseling and supporting them during a tour of duty working directly with servicemen at major

bases. The Pacific Counseling Service already has such a program for placing civilian staff, but additional work in this area is essential. Civilian aid is also needed in the form of funding, which can be channeled to the GI Project Alliance, PCS, or any of the still-active groups listed in Appendix B.

3. *The movement must deal with the basic grievances of the GI.* In the current "peacetime" environment, nearly all GI organizations have experimented with new political orientations aimed at dealing with the oppression of daily life. Of the many GI grievances that could form the basis for potential organizing, the two most important issues seem to be racism and military justice. With the growing number of minority recruits in the all-volunteer force, racial frictions have become acute, leading to greater concern on all levels with problems of discrimination. The GI movement should take the lead in calling for the judicial and administrative changes necessary to end racism and, wherever possible, should take direct action to expose specific racial abuses and practices. The Fort Lewis GI Alliance seems to have made considerable progress in this area, protesting individual racist commanders and creating pressure for better job assignments. A much more difficult task is to eliminate the racism that has plagued the GI movement itself and too often prevented low-ranking white and black GIs from uniting in common interest. In struggling against institutional bias, blacks and whites must also work to overcome their personal prejudices and realize the potential power of GI unity. The campaign against racism must include opposition to military justice as well. Continuation of military counseling and legal-defense work will help to relieve some of the hardship of enlisted life and provide aid to dissenters and others subjected to undue repression. Offensive actions, such as the widespread petition effort against Article 15, also should be pressed as an attack on the entire UCMJ. The foundations for sweeping reform of military justice are being laid now in the civilianization of military law. GIs and their supporters must continue to push for greater federal-court review and full Bill of Rights protection within the ranks.

4. *A newspaper or newsletter is necessary.* Nearly every servicemen's organization has coalesced around a newspaper as the best means available for communicating with other GIs. An important variation of this is unit newsletters, pioneered

at Fort Lewis, to expose abuses within individual units and mobilize political pressure at the local level. Unit newsletters appearing on a biweekly basis could then be supplemented by a monthly or bimonthly base-wide newspaper. This should be part of a general shift in the locus of GI action away from off-base coffeehouses, back to the barracks. Off-base locations are still needed for printing and counseling activities by civilian staffers, but GI activists should remain on base and work directly with people at their jobs and in the barracks.

To focus these organizing efforts and create an effective national voice for controlling the military, an unofficial, or "shadow," Ombudsman Office should be established, with the broad purposes of co-ordinating citizen activities at the local level, investigating GI grievances and the problems of military life, and lobbying with Congress and other government bodies on behalf of enlisted people. Such an agency, with a national office in Washington and regional centers in the South and in California, should be privately funded, ideally with monthly pledges from GIs themselves, and should adopt a program of broad popular appeal. The national functions of such an office might include publication of a service-wide GI-movement newspaper; establishment of closer liaison on military issues among the Congressional Black Caucus, the ACLU, and other groups pressing for changes in the armed forces; and adaption of lobbying strategy to actual organizing struggles. On the regional level, it could channel its informational resources to local groups, help with individual GI grievances, and provide funding and legal-defense aid. The plan is ambitious, attempting to combine the previous work of the GI Office, *Camp News*, and USSF in one organization, but some type of operation on this scale is essential. Such a "Servicemen's Ombudsman Commission" could succeed only if it encompassed a broad political base and appealed to masses of GIs as a viable means of improving their life within the military. Regardless of what form it takes, though, citizen action must continue. The massive wave of public opposition of recent years has been enormously important in restraining military adventurism. Continued work is necessary to establish democratic control over the institutions of war and to secure independence and dignity for people in the ranks.

VII

As mentioned at the outset, these reforms can come only in the context of reduced force strengths and a radically altered military mission. Maintaining a global interventionist capacity is the root cause of the current military crisis and must be challenged if we are to restore some measure of sanity to national affairs. U.S. force levels could be substantially reduced without hindering nuclear deterrent capabilities and without threatening national security. Strategic forces demand only minimal manpower commitments—currently about 115,000 servicemen—and the conventional forces required beyond this certainly need not total two million. For example, the Pentagon maintains over three hundred thousand military personnel in the European theater and earmarks an equivalent force within the United States for potential redeployment to that arena. However, given the increasingly obsolete assumptions underlying the NATO alliance and the lack of a matching commitment on the part of the allies we are supposedly defending, these forces could be significantly cut without impairing American security. Similarly, the United States supports over two hundred thousand servicemen in the West Pacific and reserves an even larger Asian contingency force within our own borders. Yet the dismal record of American involvement in eastern Asia and the lack of serious offensive capability on the part of the Chinese military suggests that these forces could be largely eliminated without negative consequence. A large portion of American forces are poised for counterinsurgency missions which provide no political or strategic benefit to the nation and in fact only heighten international tension. Even if one accepts the necessity of a strong national defense and an active American role in world affairs, the present U.S. defense establishment is excessive, unnecessary, and counterproductive.

The true test of national-security policy is how well it contributes to the well-being and stability of American society. By this measure we are very feeble, for we have ignored the wisdom of Eisenhower and others that national security cannot be obtained through weapons alone. Permanent mobilization and emergence of a garrison state have sapped the nation's internal strength and hastened social and political breakdown. Pandemic crime and urban decay, environmental ruin, rampant social and racial violence—all are signs that the American people are profoundly insecure. Indeed many urban residents are afraid to walk their streets at night. Neglect of the nation's acute domestic needs in favor of military commitments abroad can only undermine social cohesiveness and subvert real national security. The condition of society also directly determines the state of morale within the armed forces. Servicemen recruited from a society in turmoil are not likely to bring with them the sense of dedication and loyalty required by military organization. Racial tension, drug abuse, crime, a lack of unity and purpose—these and other signs of social disintegration show up in the military with devastating results. No level of military force can make a nation strong if critical social needs are ignored—if, as in America, the interests of government and of the people are no longer one.

In the final analysis the stationing of American forces abroad serves not the national interest but the class interest of the corporate and political elite. The maintenance of a massive, interventionist-oriented military establishment is based not on the nation's legitimate defense requirements but on the need to protect multinational investment and preserve regimes friendly to American capital. Imperialism is at the heart of the national-security system and is the force fundamentally responsible for the counterrevolutionary, repressive aims of U.S. policy. Only if we confront this reality and challenge it throughout society and within the ranks can we restore democratic control of the military.

Of course nothing can be accomplished without citizen involvement and active political struggle. During the Vietnam era enlisted servicemen created massive pressures for change, despite severe repression, and significantly altered the course of the war and subsequent military policy. To sustain and strengthen this challenge we must continue to build political opposition to interventionism and support those who defy military service. To this end the patriots who resisted the Indochina war should be granted universal and unconditional amnesty, as a sign of our agreement with their acts and as the first step toward restructuring the military and legitimatizing resistance to illegal war. The central lesson of the GI movement—and, I hope, of this book—is that people need not be helpless before the power of illegitimate authority, that by getting together and acting upon their convictions people can change society and, in effect, make their own history.

NOTES—REFERENCES

These pages serve as a reference for specific factual statements in the text and as a general bibliographical guide to further study. I have used the following abbreviations for frequently cited sources:

HASC — *Hearings Before the Committee on Armed Services, House of Representatives*—followed by numbers for the Congress, the Session, and the volume in that series of hearings.

SASC — *Hearings Before the Committee on Armed Services, U. S. Senate*—followed by numbers for Congress, Session, and volume.

HADS — *Hearings Before the Defense Subcommittee of the Committee on Appropriations, House of Representatives*—followed by numbers for Congress, Session, and volume.

SADS — *Hearings Before the Defense Subcommittee of the Committee on Appropriations, U. S. Senate*—followed by numbers for Congress, Session, and volume.

HISC — "Investigation of Attempts to Subvert the United States Armed Services," *Hearings Before the Committee on Internal Security, House of Representatives, 92nd Congress, 1st and 2nd Sessions*—followed by volume number (I, II, or III).

CN — *Camp News*, newsletter of the Chicago Area Military Project.

GINDB — *GI News and Discussion Bulletin*, journal of the United States Servicemen's Fund and the GI Project Alliance.

The reader will note that publication data for GI newspapers vary. This is because of the irregular nature of the sources. In general, I have listed only as much or as little information as the particular publication chose to include.

SOURCES

Chapter 1

Janowitz quote: Morris Janowitz, "Volunteer Armed Forces and Military Purpose," *Foreign Affairs*, April 1972, p. 428.
second Heinl quote: Col. R. D. Heinl, "Are Z-Grams Backfiring?" *Armed Forces Journal*, December 1972, p. 29.
Fortune: Juan Cameron, "Our Gravest Military Problem Is Manpower," *Fortune*, April 1971, pp. 60–63.

SECTION I

PARAGRAPH 1
"reluctant retrenchment": Juan Cameron, "The Armed Forces' Reluctant Retrenchment," *Fortune*, November 1970, p. 68.
Kerwin: *HADS*, 92, 1, *Part 9*, p. 556.
Bagley: *HADS*, 92, 2, *Part 6*, p. 1044.
PARAGRAPH 2
C.O.: *Semiannual Report of the Director of Selective Service, January 1, 1972–June 30, 1972*, p. 52.
draft-classification appeals: *Semiannual Report of the Director of Selective Service, January 1, 1971–June 30, 1971*, p. 53.
PARAGRAPH 3
Oakland resistance: *Christian Century*, June 10, 1970, p. 719.
Chicago delinquencies: Chicago *Daily News*, January 28, 1970.
fiscal 1969 figures: *Semiannual Report of the Director of Selective Service, July 1, 1969–December 31, 1969*, p. 18.
206,000 delinquents: "Amnesty," *Hearings Before the Subcommittee on Courts, Civil Liberties, and the Administration of Justice of the Committee on the Judiciary, House of Representatives, 93rd Congress, 2nd Session*, pp. 36–37.
PARAGRAPH 4
September 1969 figures: *The Nation*, September 15, 1969, pp. 248–49.
Tarr report: *Semiannual Report of the Director of Selective Service, January 1, 1970–June 30, 1970*, p. 1.
figures on Jan.–Sept. 1970: *Semiannual Report of the Director of Selective Service, July 1, 1970–December 31, 1970*, p. 41.
figures on January 1971–March 1972: *HISC, Volume III*, p. 7331 and pp. 7446–65.
PARAGRAPH 5
ROTC enrollment: "Statement of Secretary of Defense, Melvin R.

Laird, Before the Senate Armed Services Committee," February 15, 1972, p. 159; *Guardian,* January 17, 1973, p. 2.

ROTC attacks: *HISC, Volume II,* pp. 7008–9; Lt. Gen. Walter Kerwin, *HADS, 92, 1, Part 3,* p. 465.

PARAGRAPH 6

working-class volunteers: Charles Moskos, *The American Enlisted Man* (New York: Russell Sage Foundation, 1970), p. 195.

Figure 1: *Armed Forces Journal,* May 1972, p. 44.

PARAGRAPH 7

Navy Times: Navy Times, May 17, 1972, p. 40.

Zumwalt remarks: *SASC, 93, 1, Part 2,* p. 693.

Laird statement: *Progress in Ending the Draft and Achieving the All-Volunteer Force,* August 1972, p. 36.

GAO data: Comptroller General, *Problems in Meeting Military Manpower Needs in the All-Volunteer Force,* May 2, 1973, p. 29 and p. 2.

PARAGRAPH 8

waiting lists: *Hearings Before the Special Subcommittee on the Volunteer Armed Force and Selective Service of the Committee on Armed Services, U. S. Senate, 92nd Congress, Second Session,* p. 196.

shortages: Comptroller General, op. cit., p. 56.

PARAGRAPH 9

1970 retention rate: Office of Assistant Secretary of Defense for Public Affairs, Magazine and Book Branch.

Army retention problems: Comptroller General, op. cit., p. 34.

Bagley quote: "Statement of Vice-Admiral David H. Bagley Before the Defense Subcommittee of the Senate Appropriations Committee on Navy Military and Reserve Personnel Appropriations," 1972, p. 11.

twenty-nine job ratings: *SASC, 92, 2, Part 1,* p. 201.

nuclear program: New York *Times,* October 9, 1972, p. 38.

over-all retention: Comptroller General, op. cit., p. 35.

PARAGRAPH 10

Fortune quote: Juan Cameron, "Our Gravest Military Problem . . . ," p. 61.

Westmoreland testimony: *HASC, 92, 2, Part 1,* p. 9905.

Jordanian crisis: New York *Times,* December 25, 1970, p. 1.

Abrams testimony: *HASC, 93, 1, Part 1,* p. 883.

Navy shortages: Bagley statement, *supra,* p. 11, and Comptroller General, op. cit., p. 35.

Zumwalt remarks: *SASC, 93, 1, Part 2,* pp. 602–3.

Warner remarks: Ibid., p. 571.

SECTION II

PARAGRAPH 1

desertion statistics and Figure 2: Office of Assistant Secretary of Defense for Public Affairs, Magazine and Book Branch.

PARAGRAPH 3

Fitt data: "The Problems of Deserters from Military Service," *Hearings Before a Subcommittee of the Committee on Armed Services, U. S. Senate, 90th Congress, Second Session,* pp. 3–4.

1969 survey in Sweden: New York *Times,* May 1, 1969, p. 6.

New York *Times* report: New York *Times,* October 5, 1969, p. 58.

PARAGRAPH 4

HumRRO study: *The Prediction of AWOL, Military Skills and Leadership Potential,* Technical Report 73-1.

Bob Musil quote: "The Truth About Deserters," *The Nation,* April 16, 1973, pp. 495–99.

PARAGRAPH 5

Pentagon fact sheet: Office of Assistant Secretary of Defense for Public Affairs, Magazine and Book Branch.

SECTION III

PARAGRAPH 2

Figure 3: Office of the Assistant Secretary of Defense for Manpower and Reserve Affairs.

PARAGRAPH 3

Oakland: *HISC, Volume I,* p. 6660. New York *Times,* June 3, 1970, p. 70.

PARAGRAPH 4

C.O.-approval figures: Office of the Assistant Secretary of Defense for Manpower and Reserve Affairs.

SECTION IV

PARAGRAPH 1

Marine Corps definitions: "Statement of Major General Edwin Wheeler before the Defense Subcommittee, Committee on Appropriations, U. S. Senate, in support of the FY 1973 Military Personnel and Marine Corps Budget Request," 1972, p. 43.

Navy quote: *SASC,* 92, 2, *Part 1,* p. 203.

Wheeler quote: Wheeler statement, *supra,* p. 39.

Figure 4: Office of the Assistant Secretary of Defense for Manpower and Reserve Affairs.

PARAGRAPH 2

recruit attrition: *HADS,* 92, 2, *Part 6,* p. 729 and p. 1035. New York *Times,* December 2, 1973, p. 55.

SECTION V

PARAGRAPH 2

HumRRO report and Figure 5: *Preliminary Findings from the 1971 Survey of Drug Use,* Technical Report 72-8.

PARAGRAPH 3

Harris poll: February 1972.

PARAGRAPH 4

drug investigations: *HADS*, 92, 1, *Part* 3, p. 252.

drug discharges: Office of the Assistant Secretary of Defense for Manpower and Reserve Affairs.

90th Replacement Battalion study: "Inquiry into Alleged Drug Abuse in the Armed Services," *Report of a Special Subcommittee of the Committee on Armed Services, House of Representatives, 92nd Congress, First Session*, April 23, 1971, p. 2203.

PARAGRAPH 5

Armed Forces Journal: *Armed Forces Journal*, December 1972, p. 22.

Murphy and Steele report: *The World Narcotics Problem*, March 21, 1973, p. 51.

Abrams quote: *SASC*, 93, 1, *Part* 2, p. 492.

SECTION VI

PARAGRAPH 1

Congressional complaints: *Hearings Before the Special Subcommittee on Recruiting and Retention of Military Personnel of the Committee on Armed Services, House of Representatives, 92nd Congress, First and Second Sessions*, p. 8117.

mutiny statistics: *HISC, Volume II*, p. 7057.

Ayers quote: New York *Times*, September 5, 1971, p. 36.

Article-15 figures: Office of the Assistant Secretary of Defense for Manpower and Reserve Affairs.

PARAGRAPH 2

law-officer quote: "Army in Anguish," Washington *Post*, September 13, 1971, p. 1.

Clark testimony: *Hearings on Recruitment and Retention*, p. 8445.

Ayers findings: New York *Times*, September 5, 1971, p. 36.

Heinl quote: *Armed Forces Journal*, June 1973, p. 42.

SECTION VII

PARAGRAPH 4

Fort Devens clerk network: *GI Press Service*, III, 3, April 1971, p. 9; "At War with the Army," *Phoenix*, March 2, 1971.

Chapter 2

PARAGRAPH 1

combat officers' letter: Congressional Record, October 28, 1971, p. H 10121–22.

PARAGRAPH 2

Gardner: New York *Times*, November 21, 1970, p. 31.

SECTION I

PARAGRAPH 1

CBS incident: *Inquiry into Alleged Drug Abuse in the Armed Services, Report of a Special Subcommittee of the Committee on Armed Services, House of Representatives, 92nd Congress, 1st Session,* April 23, 1971, p. 2205.

Figure 6: *Preliminary Findings from the 1971 DOD Survey of Drug Use,* Human Resources Research Organization, Technical Report 72-8, pp. 23 and 24, Tables 18 and 19.

PARAGRAPH 2

Figure 7: *Hearings by Special Subcommittee on Alleged Drug Abuse in the Armed Services of the Committee on Armed Services, House of Representatives, 91st Congress, 2nd Session,* p. 1832.

PARAGRAPH 3

Defense Department interview findings: *A Follow-up of Vietnam Drug Users,* Special Action Office for Drug Abuse Prevention, Executive Office of the President, April 1973, pp. 7 and 12.

Cam Ranh Bay: *Alleged Drug Abuse Report,* p. 2150.

Can Tho: Ibid., p. 2194.

PARAGRAPH 4

HumRRO figures: *Preliminary Findings,* pp. 32 and 42.

25th-Infantry study: *Alleged Drug Abuse Report,* p. 2200.

173rd-Airborne survey: New York *Times,* April 4, 1970, p. 3. *Hearings . . . on Alleged Drug Abuse,* p. 1930.

September 1971 report: "CINCPAC Study for Evaluation of PACOM Drug Abuse Treatment/Rehabilitation Programs," *Hearings on H.R. 9503 Before the Special Subcommittee on Drug Abuse in the Armed Services of the Committee on Armed Services, House of Representatives, 92nd Congress, 1st and 2nd Sessions,* p. 7679.

SECTION II

PARAGRAPH 1

Ayers quote: New York *Times,* August 4, 1969, p. 3.

PARAGRAPH 2

Wingo report: *Life,* October 24, 1969, p. 36.

Quang Tri: *Newsweek,* February 2, 1970, p. 24.

Da Nang: New York *Times,* October 16, 1969, p. 22.

Long Binh: New York *Times,* November 14, 1969. New York *Times,* November 21, 1969.

Pleiku: *Newsweek, supra. The Ally,* December 1969.

Saigon: New York *Times,* December 25, 1969. New York *Times,* December 30, 1969.

PARAGRAPH 3

Chu Lai: USSF files. interview, David Addlestone, September 6, 1973.

petition campaign: *Overseas Weekly (Pacific edition)*, October 30, 1971, p. 3. *Overseas Weekly (Pacific edition)*, November 6, 1971, p. 2. interview, David Addlestone.

SECTION III

PARAGRAPH 1

reports of minor refusals: *Newsweek*, October 25, 1971, pp. 67–68. Eugene Linden, "The Demoralization of an Army; Fragging and Other Withdrawal Symptoms," *Saturday Review*, January 8, 1972. Donald Kirk, "Who Wants to Be the Last American Killed in Vietnam?" New York *Times* Magazine, September 19, 1971.

PARAGRAPH 2

Songchang Valley: *The Nation*, September 8, 1969, p. 196. Charles Moskos, "Why Men Fight," *Transaction*, November 1969, p. 13. Larry Waterhouse and Mariann Wizard, *Turning the Guns Around*: Notes on the GI Movement (New York: Delta Books, 1971), pp. 118–20.

PARAGRAPH 3

Cu Chi: Cleveland *Press*, November 22, 1969. *GI Press Service*, Volume I, Number 14, December 15, 1969, p. 223.

CBS incident: *Newsweek*, April 20, 1970, p. 51. *Newsweek*, May 25, 1970, p. 45.

PARAGRAPH 4

Cambodian-invasion mutinies: *The Bond*, Volume IV, Number 5, May 13, 1970, p. 1. *Newsweek*, May 25, 1970, p. 45.

PARAGRAPH 5

Pitts: files of Lawyers Military Defense Committee. personal letter, David Addlestone, January 7, 1974.

PARAGRAPH 6

Lang Vei: New York *Times*, March 23, 1971, p. 1. *Facts on File*, 1971, p. 202. *Time*, April 5, 1971, p. 25.

McCloskey report: Congressional Record, October 28, 1971, p. H 10120.

PARAGRAPH 7

Fire Base Pace: Richard Boyle, *The Flower of the Dragon* (San Francisco, Calif.: Ramparts Press, 1972), pp. 219–56. Tape 71-37, available from Radio Free People, 133 Mercer Street, New York, N.Y. *Newsweek*, October 25, 1971, p. 67.

criticism of Boyle: staff of *Overseas Weekly* national office, Oakland, Calif., September 1972. David Addlestone, September 1973.

PARAGRAPH 8

Phu Bai: AP dispatch in Easton (Pa.) *Express*, April 12, 1972, p. 1. New York *Times*, April 15, 1972.

SECTION IV

PARAGRAPH 1
blacks not in combat: interview, David Addlestone, September 6, 1973. personal letter, David Addlestone, January 7, 1974.

PARAGRAPH 2
Da Nang: New York *Times*, August 19, 1968, p. 5.
Long Binh: New York *Times*, October 1, 1968, p. 3. New York *Times*, January 8, 1969, p. 12. New York *Times*, April 13, 1969, p. 2. *Report of the Special Civilian Commission for the Study of the U. S. Army Confinement System*, May 15, 1970, p. 46.

PARAGRAPH 3
Camp Evans: *Newsweek*, June 9, 1970, p. 50.
Camp Eagle: file of Lawyers Military Defense Committee.

PARAGRAPH 4
Long Binh: *Civil Liberties* (newsletter of the American Civil Liberties Union), Number 293, February 1973, p. 1. files of Lawyers Military Defense Committee.
Cam Ranh: files of Lawyers Military Defense Committee.

PARAGRAPH 5
McLemore: Ibid.
December demonstration: New York *Times*, December 13, 1970, p. 18.
Da Nang: Eugene Linden, "Demoralization . . . ," p. 14. *Civil Liberties, supra.*
Camp Baxter: Donald Kirk, ". . . Last . . . Killed . . . ," p. 68. Linden, "Demoralization . . . ," p. 14. *Civil Liberties, supra.*

SECTION V

PARAGRAPH 1
Mansfield and Mathias: Congressional Record, April 20, 1971, p. S 5116.

PARAGRAPH 2
fragging totals: New York *Times*, September 5, 1971, p. 36. New York *Times*, September 7, 1972.
Figure 8: "The Power of the Pentagon," *Congressional Quarterly*, 1972, p. 24.

PARAGRAPH 3
statistics on victims: *HADS*, 92, 1, *Part 9*, p. 585.

PARAGRAPH 4
Parkinson: New York *Times*, August 19, 1970, p. 16.
Herbert quote: *Playboy*, interview, July 1972.

PARAGRAPH 5
Da Nang: New York *Times*, February 8, 1970, p. 2. New York *Times*, February 9, 1970, p. 12.

PARAGRAPH 6
Nha Trang: *Time*, January 25, 1971, pp. 34 and 35.

Long Binh: files of the Lawyers Military Defense Committee.
Khe San: Eugene Linden, "Demoralization . . . ," p. 16.
Saar report: John Saar, "The Outpost Is a Shambles," *Life*, March 31, 1972, p. 32.

SECTION VI

PARAGRAPH 1
Fischer story: *The Guardian* (London), June 8, 1970. tape and letter, Max Watts, October 16, 1973.
Better Blacks United: *The Bond*, Volume VI, Number 1, January 27, 1972, p. 1.
other journalist comments: "Army in Anguish," Washington *Post*, September 16, 1971, p. 12. *Time*, January 25, 1971, p. 34. Eugene Linden, "Demoralization . . . ," p. 15. Fred Gardner, New York *Times*, November 21, 1970, p. 31.
PARAGRAPH 2
Hackworth quote: *Ramparts*, January 1973, pp. 28–29.
PARAGRAPH 3
Alsop: *Newsweek*, December 7, 1970, p. 104.
Westmoreland reference: *Time*, January 25, 1971, p. 34.
appeals for withdrawal: "Army in Anguish," Washington *Post*, September 15, 1971, p. 8.
Laird: San Francisco *Examiner*, January 17, 1971.

Chapter 3

SECTION I

PARAGRAPH 1
Lt. Howe: John Rechy, "Conduct Unbecoming; Lieutenant on the Peace Line," *The Nation*, February 21, 1966, pp. 204–8.
Fort Hood 3: *We Won't Go; Personal Accounts of War Objectors*, collected by Alice Lynd (Boston: Beacon Press, 1968), pp. 181–202.
Howard Levy: Ira Glasser, "Justice and Captain Levy," *Columbia Forum*, Spring 1969, pp. 46–49.
Harvey and Daniels: New York *Times*, March 7, 1969, p. 11. Adam Yarmolinsky, *The Military Establishment* (New York: Harper & Row, 1971), pp. 361–62.
PARAGRAPH 2
Gardner and Fort Jackson: *HISC, Volume III*, p. 7522.
"Summer of Support": New York *Times*, August 12, 1968, p. 1.
PARAGRAPH 3
Fort Knox: New York *Times*, November 8, 1969, p. 13. *FTA*, October 1969.
"Shelter Half": USSF files.

Fort Dix coffeehouse: New York *Times*, February 15, 1970, p. 32.
"Green Machine": *Duck Power*, May 22, 1970.

SECTION II

PARAGRAPH 1

Heinl estimate: Col. Robert D. Heinl, "The Collapse of the Armed
Forces," *Armed Forces Journal*, June 7, 1971.

Defense Department estimate: Rowland A. Morrow, *HISC*, *Volume
II*, p. 7070.

Vietnam GI: personal letter from George Schmidt, January 24, 1974;
George was active in the Chicago draft-resistance movement,
worked with *Vietnam GI*, and in 1970 helped found the Chicago
Area Military Project.

Act: Tape and letter from Max Watts, October 16, 1973; Max has
been an active supporter of GI resisters in Europe for many years.

Strikeback and *Pawn's Pawn*: *Vietnam GI*, August 1968, p. 3.

FTA and *Fatigue Press*: USSF files.

PARAGRAPH 2

early ASU: *The Bond*, Volume II, Number 2, February 18, 1968.

PARAGRAPH 3

Fort Hood activism: *HISC*, *Volume III*, pp. 7275–79 and p. 7381.

Fort Hood 43: Waterhouse and Wizard, *Turning the Guns Around*,
p. 71.

Bruce Peterson: David Zeiger, *The History of the Oleo Strut Coffeehouse, 1968–1972*, August 1972, p. 3 (hereafter cited as *Zeiger
Report*); David worked as a civilian staff assistant at the Oleo Strut
for over two years.

PARAGRAPH 4

April 27 demonstration: *The Bond*, Volume II, Number 5, May 13,
1968, p. 4.

sanctuary: New York *Times*, July 18, 1968, p. 3.

October 12 rally: Waterhouse and Wizard, *Turning the Guns Around*,
pp. 72–73. *Fact Sheet on GI Dissent* (Washington, D.C.: LINK,
n.d.), p. 3. The Servicemen's Link to Peace operated at 1029 Vermont Avenue, N.W., in Washington, D.C., during 1968 and 1969.

SECTION III

PARAGRAPH 1

Fort Lewis: *HISC*, *Volume I*, p. 6584. *The Bond*, Volume III, Number 2, February 17, 1969, p. 3.

PARAGRAPHS 2 AND 3

The Fort Jackson 8: Robert Sherrill, "Must the Citizen Give Up His
Civil Liberties When He Joins the Army?" New York *Times* Magazine, May 18, 1969.

GIs Speak Out Against the War: The Case of the Ft. Jackson 8,
interviews by Fred Halstead (New York: Pathfinder Press, 1970).

PARAGRAPH 4
Joe Miles: GI *Press Service*, Volume I, Number 1, June 26, 1969, p. 9. *HISC, Volume I*, p. 6571. *HISC, Volume III*, p. 7302.

PARAGRAPH 5
USSF: *WIN*, Volume V, Number 21, December 1, 1969, p. 21.
PCS: *HISC, Volume II*, pp. 6869–70. *HISC, Volume I*, p. 6660.

SECTION IV

PARAGRAPH 1
Fort Bragg: GI *Press Service*, Volume I, Number 10, October 30, 1969, p. 153.
Fort Sam Houston: Ibid.
Fort Carson: New York *Times*, November 7, 1969, p. 13.
Fort Lewis: Ibid., October 29, 1969, p. 5.

PARAGRAPH 2
Washington actions: GI *Press Service*, Volume I, Number 12, November 27, 1969, p. 179.
Los Angeles: *Attitude Check*, December 1969.

PARAGRAPH 3
GIs for Peace: El Paso *Times*, August 18, 1969, p. 1. John Rechy, "The Army Fights an Idea," *The Nation*, January 12, 1970, pp. 8–11. *The Gigline*, Christmas 1969, Volume I, Number 5, p. 9.

PARAGRAPH 4
Fort Bragg: *HISC, Volume I*, p. 6571.
Pendleton MDM: *Marine Corps Gazette*, January 1971, p. 46. *HISC, Volume III*, p. 7264. Waterhouse and Wizard, *Turning the Guns Around*, p. 126.

PARAGRAPH 5
Fort Dix: personal experience. personal letter from George Schmidt, January 24, 1974.
Fort Knox: *HISC, Volume I*, p. 6618. *Army Times*, May 19, 1971, p. 34.

PARAGRAPH 6
Fort Bliss: *The Gigline*, Volume II, Number 4, April 1970, p. 5.

SECTION V

PARAGRAPH 1
ASU April 15 actions: *The Bond*, Volume IV, Number 4, April 22, 1970, p. 1.
Austin: *The Bond*, Volume IV, Number 5, May 13, 1970, p. 4.
Fairbanks: GI *Press Service*, Volume II, Number 7, May 22, 1970, p. 9.

PARAGRAPH 2
Armed Forces Day: *About Face* (USSF), Volume II, Number 3, April/May 1972, p. 4.
Summary of actions: fact sheet of "GI Task Force," May 1970, pub-

lished in *The Gigline*, Volume II, Number 5, May/June 1970, pp. 6–7.

PARAGRAPH 3

GI Press Service petition: *GI Press Service*, Volume II, Number 9, September 21, 1970, p. 2.

SECTION VI

PARAGRAPH 1

Prison conditions: *Report of the Special Civilian Commission for the Study of the U. S. Army Confinement System*, Austin Mac-Cormick, Chairman, May 15, 1970.

PARAGRAPH 2

Fort Bragg: Waterhouse and Wizard, *Turning the Guns Around*, pp. 116–18.

Fort Carson: *Aboveground*, August 1969.

Fort Dix: New York *Times*, June 6, 1969, p. 33.

Fort Riley: Waterhouse and Wizard, *Turning the Guns Around*, p. 118. *The Bond*, Volume III, Number 8, August 25, 1969, p. 3.

Fort Ord: San Francisco *Examiner*, May 21, 1969.

Fort Jackson: *The Bond*, Volume III, Number 7, July 22, 1969, p. 1.

PARAGRAPH 3

Camp Pendleton: New York *Times*, September 16, 1969, p. 95. Peter Barnes, *Pawns: The Plight of the Citizen-Soldier* (New York: Alfred A. Knopf, 1972), pp. 235–37. "Inquiry into the Reported Conditions in the Brig, Marine Corps Base Camp Pendleton, California," *Report of the Special Subcommittee to Probe Disturbances on Military Bases of the Committee on Armed Services, House of Representatives, 91st Congress, Second Session*, February 25, 1970.

PARAGRAPH 4

Fort Knox: *The Bond*, Volume IV, Number 6, June 17, 1970, p. 5.

Fort Dix: *The Bond*, Volume IV, Number 8, August 26, 1970, p. 1. *Up Against the Bulkhead*, Number 5, December 1970, p. 6.

Fort Belvoir: *Open Sights*, Volume II, Number 6.

Fort Ord: *HISC, Volume I*, p. 6741.

PARAGRAPH 5

Fort Bragg: *Newsweek*, August 25, 1969, p. 20. *U.S. News and World Report*, September 1, 1969, p. 26.

Fort Hood: *FTA*, September 1970.

Fort Carson: *FTA*, September 1970.

PARAGRAPH 6

Camp Lejeune: Flora Lewis, "The Rumble at Camp Lejeune," *Atlantic*, January 1970, pp. 35–41. New York *Times*, August 10, 1969, p. 1. New York *Times*, August 15, 1969, p. 23.

PARAGRAPH 7

aftermath at Lejeune: Flora Lewis, "The Rumble . . . ," p. 37.

blacks: Ibid., p. 40. New York *Times*, December 9, 1969, p. 108.

Chapter 4

SECTION I

PARAGRAPH 1
Fort Lewis: USSF files. personal letter from George Schmidt, January 24, 1974. *The Bond*, Volume IV, Number 12, December 16, 1970, p. 5.

PARAGRAPH 2
Fort Bliss: personal experience. *Gigline*, Volume III, Number 3, May 1971, pp. 4 and 5.

PARAGRAPH 3
USSF: *HISC, Volume I*, p. 6392. USSF Conference, Williams Bay, Wisconsin, November 24, 1971.

PCS: *HISC, Volume I*, pp. 6619–21 and p. 6660.

GI Office: New York *Times*, August 9, 1970, p. 52.

LMDC: David Addlestone, interview, September 6, 1973.

National Lawyers Guild: *HISC, Volume III*, pp. 7532 and 7533. *CN*, Volume II, Number 1, February 15, 1971, p. 22.

CAMP: "A Short History and Analysis of the Chicago Area Military Project," November 22, 1972.

PARAGRAPH 4
Fred Gardner criticisms: "Case Study in Opportunism: The GI Movement," reprinted in *HISC, Volume III*, pp. 7522–25.

Fort Ord: *CN*, Volume II, Number 3, April 10, 1971, p. 13. *CN*, Volume II, Number 4, May 22, 1971, p. 18.

Fort Campbell: *HISC, Volume I*, pp. 6513–16. *CN*, Volume II, Number 4, May 22, 1971, pp. 10–11.

PARAGRAPH 5
lettuce boycott: Mankiewicz-Broden column, Chicago *Sun-Times*, January 7, 1971. *CN*, Volume II, Number 1, February 15, 1971, p. 18. *CN*, Volume II, Number 2, March 15, 1971, p. 13.

SECTION II

PARAGRAPH 1
Washington-area GIs: *GINDB*, Number 6, June 1971, pp. 8 and 12.

support of VVAW: *CN*, Volume II, Number 4, May 22, 1971, p. 3.

memorial service: *GI Press Service*, Volume III, Number 4, May 1971, p. 8.

April 24: personal experience.

PARAGRAPH 2
Mayday actions: *GINDB, supra*, p. 8. personal experience.

PARAGRAPH 3
Fort Lewis strike: *GINDB*, Number 5, May 1971, p. 2. letter to Fort Bliss GIs for Peace, July 1971.

PARAGRAPH 4
Armed Farces Day report: *CN*, Volume II, Number 4, May 22, 1971.
PARAGRAPH 5
Beaufort: *Up Against the Bulkhead*, Number 8, June 1971, p. 9.
Walter Reed: *GINDB*, Number 6, June 1971, p. 12.

SECTION III

PARAGRAPH 1
stockade incident: *The Bond*, Volume V, Number 7, July 24, 1971,
p. 2.
Harvey and Priest campaign: *GINDB*, Number 11, March 1972, p. 3.
Zeiger Report, pp. 16 and 17.
PARAGRAPH 2
Tyrrell's boycott at Fort Hood: *GINDB*, Number 7, July 1971, pp.
7–11. *CN*, Volume II, Number 6, July 15, 1971, p. 9.
PARAGRAPH 3
Tyrrell's boycott, nationally: *About Face* (*USSF*), Volume II, Number 1, February 1972, p. 2. *GINDB*, Number 7, July 1971, p. 6.
GINDB, Number 10, January 1972, p. 71.
PARAGRAPH 4
GAO Report: New York *Times*, May 18, 1972, p. 1.
Fort Bragg: *Bragg Briefs*, Volume IV, Number 1, March 1971.
Fort Campbell: *CN*, Volume II, Number 8, September 18, 1971,
p. 17.
PARAGRAPH 5
Fort Huachuca: *GI Press Service*, Volume III, Number 6, September
1971, p. 2. *CN*, Volume II, Number 7, August 15, 1971, p. 2.
CN, Volume II, Nunber 9, November 15, 1971, p. 5.
PARAGRAPH 6
GICC: *GINDB*, Number 10, January 1972, p. 14.
PARAGRAPH 7
Fort Sam Houston: *Your Military Left*, Volume I, Number 5, November 1971, p. 2.
Fort Campbell: *CN*, Volume II, Number 9, November 15, 1971, p. 1.
Fort McClellan: Ibid.
Fort Hood: *HISC*, *Volume III*, p. 7283. *GINDB*, Number 11, March
1972, p. 5.

SECTION IV

PARAGRAPH 2
Fort Hood: *Zeiger Report*, pp. 20 and 21. *CN*, Volume II, Number
10, December 15, 1971, p. 15. *CN*, Volume III, Number 1, February 15, 1972, p. 5.
PARAGRAPH 3
Fort Gordon: New York *Times*, October 28, 1971. New York *Times*,
February 19, 1972.
Fort McClellan: *Time*, November 29, 1971, p. 24.

PARAGRAPH 5
Fort Sam Houston: *About Face (USSF)*, Volume III, Number 3, April–May 1972, p. 3. *CN*, Volume II, Number 5, May 15, 1972, p. 8.
Fort Hood: *GINDB*, Number 12, April–June 1972, p. 19.
PARAGRAPH 6
Ad Hoc Committee: New York *Times*, April 24, 1972. Washington *Post*, April 19, 1972, p. B1. Committee report, dated April 21, 1972.

Chapter 5

SECTION I

PARAGRAPH 1
desertion movement: tape and letter from Max Watts, October 1973.
PARAGRAPH 2
Kaiserslautern: *Overseas Weekly*, June 1, 1969. (All issues cited are European edition.) Max Watts, op. cit.
GI papers: *Overseas Weekly*, February 15, 1970, p. 18.
Grafenwöhr: *Overseas Weekly*, September 21, 1969. *GI Press Service*, Volume I, Number 9, October 16, 1969, p. 133.
Augsburg: *We've Got the brASS*, Number 3, p. 8.
coffeehouse: *Overseas Weekly*, February 15, 1970, p. 17.
PARAGRAPH 3
black groups: *Time*, September 21, 1970, p. 36. *The Bond*, Volume IV, Number 10, October 21, 1970, pp. 1 and 3. *GI Press Service*, Volume III, Number 2, March 1971, p. 13. Max Watts, op. cit.
PARAGRAPH 4
Heidelberg gathering: Max Watts, op. cit. *The Next Step*, Volume I, Number 2, July 19, 1970, p. 1.
PARAGRAPH 5
Mannheim: *We've Got the brASS*, Number 4, March 1970. Max Watts, op. cit.
Hohenfels: *Overseas Weekly*, November 15, 1970, p. 3.
Schweinfurt: *Overseas Weekly*, May 31, 1970, p. 2.
McNair: Washington *Post*, February 10, 1971, p. B5. *CN*, Volume I, Number 7, January 5, 1971, p. 24.
Render report: New York *Times*, December 12, 1970, p. 13.
PARAGRAPH 6
Nellingen events: *Overseas Weekly*, September 6, 1970, and October 4, 1970.
PARAGRAPH 7
Neu Ulm: *Overseas Weekly*, September 13, 1970.
Bad Hersfeld: *CN*, Volume I, Number 7, January 15, 1971, p. 23.
Aschaffenburg: Ibid.
Mannheim: *The Next Step*, October 28, 1970.
Ayers Kaserne: *The Next Step*, Volume II, Number 2, January 28, 1971, p. 3.

SECTION II

PARAGRAPH 1

Symington: *Supplemental Manpower Hearing Before the Committee on Armed Services, U. S. Senate, 92nd Congress, 1st Session, on H.R. 6531,* p. 107.

Daniel: *Hearings Before the Special Subcommittee on Recruiting and Retention of Military Personnel of the Committee on Armed Services, House of Representatives, 92nd Congress, 1st and 2nd Sessions,* p. 8352.

Nuremberg quote: "Army in Anguish," Washington *Post,* September 12, 1971, p. 16.

PARAGRAPH 2

Fifty-four incidents: *CN,* Volume II, Number 10, December 15, 1971, p. 6. Max Watts, op. cit.

hashish use: New York *Times,* July 7, 1972, p. 6.

PARAGRAPH 3

Karlsruhe and Nuremberg: *Overseas Weekly,* April 11, 1971, pp. 2 and 3.

Camp Pieri: Ibid. Max Watts, op. cit.

PARAGRAPH 4

Darmstadt 53: *Hearings Before the Special Subcommittee on Recruiting and Retention of Military Personnel of the Committee on Armed Services, House of Representatives, 92nd Congress, 1st and 2nd Sessions,* pp. 8739–49. *HADS,* 92, 2, *Part 6,* p. 198. Max Watts, op. cit.

PARAGRAPH 5

Fulda and Augsburg: *SOS News,* Volume II, Number 3, March 1972, p. 4. (SOS operated in Los Angeles during part of 1971 and 1972 as a fund-raising and support organization for GI projects.) *Forward,* Number 6, December 1971, p. 25. *CN,* Volume III, Number 9, September 15, 1972, p. 6.

PARAGRAPH 6

sabotage at Wiley Barracks: Max Watts, op. cit.

Stuttgart: New York *Times,* August 15, 1972, p. 5.

Schweinfurt: *CN,* Volume III, Number 6, June 15, 1972, p. 1.

Frankfurt: *CN,* Volume III, Number 11, November 15, 1972, p. 7.

SECTION III

PARAGRAPH 2

sanctuary: *Christian Century,* November 26, 1969, pp. 1526–28. New York *Times,* August 24, 1969, p. 9.

Kaneohe: New York *Times,* August 12, 1969, p. 23. *Newsweek,* August 25, 1969, p. 20.

PARAGRAPH 3

Koza: *Newsweek,* December 12, 1969, p. 49. *GI Press Service,* Volume I, Number 10, October 30, 1969, p. 156.

Po'ch'ŏn: *The Bond*, Volume IV, Number 8, August 26, 1970, p. 8.

2nd Infantry Division: from the Japanese newspaper *Asahi Shimbun*, reported in *CN*, Volume II, Number 5, June 15, 1971, p. 30.

Seoul: Richard DeCamp, "The GI Movement in Asia," *Bulletin of Concerned Asian Scholars*, Winter 1972, p. 114.

Camp Humphreys: Chicago *Daily News*, May 25, 1971, p. 13. *CN*, Volume II, Number 5, June 15, 1971, p. 31.

Render visit: *Newsletter on Military Law and Counseling* (CCCO-West, 140 Leavenworth St., San Francisco), August–September 1971.

PARAGRAPH 4

Semper Fi: Clark Smith, "Marine Doves and the Baffled Brass," *The Nation*, September 1970, pp. 199–202. DeCamp, "The GI Movement in Asia," p. 110.

PARAGRAPH 5

July 4 rebellion: Smith, "Marine Doves . . . ," p. 201.

1971 uprising: *CN*, Volume III, Number 1, February 15, 1972, p. 14. *CN*, Volume III, Number 6, June 15, 1972, p. 5.

PARAGRAPH 6

Camp Drake: *GI Press Service*, Volume II, Number 1, January 21, 1970, p. 14.

Korea Free Press: *GINDB*, Number 10, January 1972, p. 37.

Fort Buckner: *GI Press Service*, Volume II, Number 4, March 13, 1970, p. 4.

Chapter 6

Orwell: George Orwell, *Nineteen Eighty-four* (New York: Harcourt, Brace & Company, 1949), pp. 186–87.

Branfman: Fred Branfman, "The New Totalitarianism," *Liberation*, February-March-April 1971.

1. SEASICK SAILORS

SECTION I

PARAGRAPH 1

Intrepid: New York *Times*, January 3, 1968, p. 3.

Ciesielski: *The Bond*, Volume III, Number 2, February 17, 1969, pp. 1 and 4.

Roger Priest: *Time*, May 11, 1970, p. 82. Waterhouse and Wizard, *Turning the Guns Around*, p. 85.

PARAGRAPH 2

San Diego MDM: Los Angeles *Free Press*, February 13, 1970. Waterhouse and Wizard, *Turning the Guns Around*, p. 80.

Long Beach and Alameda: *HISC*, *Volume III*, p. 7299. *Up Against the Bulkhead*, Number 4, p. 4. *CN*, Volume I, Number 4, October 8, 1970, p. 15.

PARAGRAPH 3
Great Lakes: personal letter, George Schmidt, January 24, 1974.
PARAGRAPH 4
COM: New York *Times*, June 3, 1970, p. 11. New York *Times*, June 7, 1970, p. 8. interview, Lt. Delbert Terrill, September 6, 1973.
PARAGRAPH 5
San Diego: "Why Wait?" Concerned Military, July 1972. *COMmon Sense*, Volume II, Number 1, p. 9.
Norfolk: Ibid., p. 10.
Iceland: Ibid., p. 8.
PARAGRAPH 6
Citizens Commission: Washington *Post*, November 24, 1970, p. A9.
Washington press conference: *Facts on File*, 1971, p. 34.
Los Angeles press conference: Ibid., p. 92.

SECTION II

PARAGRAPH 1
Portsmouth: CN, Volume II, Number 4, May 22, 1971, p. 6.
Philadelphia and Newport: Ibid., pp. 6 and 7.
Great Lakes: Ibid., p. 13.
San Diego: Ibid., p. 17. *Fatigue Press*, Number 6, June 1971, p. 9.
PARAGRAPH 2
San Diego: "Why Wait?" *Liberty Call*, Volume I, Number 2, June 14, 1971. CN, Volume II, Number 9, November 15, 1971, p. 3.
PARAGRAPH 3
Coral Sea: *Up Against the Bulkhead*, Number 10, November 1971, p. 7. CN, *supra*, p. 3. *The Ally*, November 1971, p. 8. SOS *News*, March 1972, p. 3.
PARAGRAPH 4
Coral Sea in Hawaii: SOS *News*, op. cit. *Village Voice*, March 30, 1972, p. 38.
newspaper: *About Face* (USSF), Volume II, Number 2, March 1972, p. 1.
Peterson story: New York *Times*, January 9, 1972, p. 2.
Chaffee: *About Face* (USSF), *supra*.
PARAGRAPH 5
Kitty Hawk: "Why Wait?" SOS *News*, *supra*.

SECTION III

PARAGRAPH 1
Combat work schedule: *Hearings Before a Subcommittee of the Committee on Appropriations, House of Representatives, 92nd Congress, 1st Session*, Part 3, p. 748.
PARAGRAPH 2
Midway: CN, Volume III, Number 4, April 15, 1972, p. 17.
Ticonderoga: SOS *News*, June 1972, p. 5.

America: Up Against the Bulkhead, Number 12, September 1972, p. 3. New York *Times,* June 6, 1972, p. 11.

Oriskany: CN, Volume III, Number 8, August 15, 1972, p. 4. *SOS Newsletter,* Number 3, August 1, 1972, p. 2.

PARAGRAPH 3

Enterprise: CN, Volume III, Number 10, October 15, 1972, p. 3. *SOS Newsletter,* Number 6, September 1972, pp. 1–4.

PARAGRAPH 4

Seasick: HISC, Volume III, pp. 7533–35. *CN,* Volume III, Number 4, April 15, 1972, p. 6.

"Center": "Report on West Coast GI Project," August 1972, by Paul Lauter, Executive Director, USSF.

PARAGRAPH 5

demonstration: *CN,* Volume III, Number 6, June 15, 1972, p. 8.

speed-up: *CN,* Volume III, Number 7, July 15, 1972, p. 7.

SECTION IV

PARAGRAPH 1

William Rush: Col. Robert Heinl, "Are Z-Grams Backfiring?" *Armed Forces Journal,* December 1972, p. 29. *CN,* Volume III, Number 4, April 15, 1972, p. 17. *GINDB,* Number 12, April–June 1972, pp. 3–5.

PARAGRAPH 2

Glennon: CN, Volume III, Number 5, May 15, 1972, p. 1.

PARAGRAPH 3

Nitro: New York *Times,* April 25, 1972, p. 1.

quote: *SOS News,* June 1972, p. 2.

PARAGRAPH 4

Hunley: CN, Volume III, Number 8, August 15, 1972, p. 2.

Yokosuka: *SOS News,* August 1972, pp. 4 and 5.

PARAGRAPH 5

Subic protesters: *Up from the Bottom,* Volume II, Number 6, December 15, 1972, p. 8. *SOS Newsletter,* Number 8, n.d., p. 3.

SECTION V

PARAGRAPH 1

total black percentage: *Congressional Quarterly,* "The Power of the Pentagon," 1972, p. 34.

1972 black percentage: New York *Times,* November 12, 1972, p. 4-E.

quote: *Report by the Special Subcommittee on Disciplinary Problems in the U. S. Navy of the Committee on Armed Services, House of Representatives, 92nd Congress, 2nd Session,* p. 17686.

PARAGRAPH 2

Kitty Hawk: Ibid., pp. 17674–76. New York *Times,* November 29, 1972, p. 24. New York *Times,* December 26, 1972, p. 1.

PARAGRAPH 3
Hassayampa: Time, November 27, 1972, p. 20.
Sumter: New York *Times,* January 11, 1973, p. 25.
Midway and Norfolk: New York *Times,* November 28, 1972, p. 17.
Intrepid: CBS Evening News, January 26, 1973.
PARAGRAPH 4
Constellation quote and description: Henry P. Leifermann, "A Sort
    of Mutiny; The Constellation Incident," New York *Times* Maga-
    zine, February 18, 1973, p. 17. *Report on Disciplinary Problems,*
    pp. 17677–79. New York *Times,* November 25, 1972, p. 20.
PARAGRAPH 5
Zumwalt meeting: New York *Times,* November 11, 1972, p. 1.

SECTION VI

PARAGRAPH 2
Anderson: Up Against the Bulkhead, Number 5, 1970, p. 2.
Chilton: CN, Volume IV, Number 1, January 15, 1973, p. 4.
PARAGRAPH 3
Forrestal: New York *Times,* November 28, 1972, p. 18. New York
    Times, December 8, 1972, p. 18.
Ranger: Village Voice, February 1, 1973, p. 16. New York *Times,*
    June 13, 1973, p. 5.
other *Ranger* sabotage: John Jekabson, "The Demoralization of the
    U. S. Navy," *Alternate Features Service,* Number 76, January 5,
    1973.
PARAGRAPH 4
FY 1971 figures: *HISC, Volume II,* p. 7051.
Constellation: New York *Times,* November 15, 1972.
Duncan: *CN,* Volume III, Number 11, November 15, 1972, p. 4.
House report: *Report on Disciplinary Problems,* pp. 17670 and 17684.
PARAGRAPH 5
"rescheduling" quote: Ibid., p. 17674.
"discipline" quote: Ibid., p. 17691.
PARAGRAPH 6
discharges: New York *Times,* February 2, 1973, p. 1.

2.   "AIRMANCIPATION"

SECTION I

PARAGRAPH 1
Wright-Patterson: *GI Press Service,* Volume I, Number 2, July 10,
    1969, p. 26.
Grissom: *GI Press Service,* Volume II, Number 5, March 27, 1970,
    p. 9.
Chanute: *The Bond,* Volume IV, Number 6, June 17, 1970, p. 1.

Barksdale and Grand Forks: A *Four Year Bummer*, Volume II, Number 4, June 1970, p. 6.
PARAGRAPH 2
P.E.A.C.E.: tape and letter, Max Watts, October 16, 1973. *Facts on File*, 1971, p. 590.
PARAGRAPH 3
Misawa: DeCamp, "The GI Movement in Asia," p. 114.
Yokota: Ibid., pp. 115–16. CN, Volume II, Number 7, August 15, 1971, p. 12.
Clark: HISC, *Volume III*, pp. 7532–33. *The Bond*, Volume IV, Number 8, August 26, 1970, p. 6. *SOS News*, June 1972, p. 3.
Kadena: DeCamp, "The GI Movement in Asia," op. cit., p. 113. CN, Volume II, Number 1, February 15, 1971, pp. 5–7.

SECTION II

PARAGRAPH 1
Twenty-five black groups: *Air Force Times*, December 16, 1970, p. 9.
Plattsburgh: *The Bond*, Volume V, Number 9, September 25, 1971, pp. 1 and 5.
Chanute: *The Bond*, Volume V, Number 6, June 30, 1971, p. 2. *The Bond*, Volume V, Number 8, August 27, 1971, p. 8. CN, Volume II, Number 7, August 15, 1971, p. 30.
PARAGRAPH 2
Travis: Chicago *Daily News*, May 25, 1971, p. 13. *The Bond*, Volume V, Number 6, June 30, 1971, pp. 1 and 8.
PARAGRAPH 3
McChord: CN, Volume II, Number 8, September 15, 1971, p. 16.

SECTION III

PARAGRAPH 1
1972 analysis: "Staff Analysis of Recent Trends in GI Movement Organizing Activities, December, 1971–April, 1972," in House Internal Security Committee files.
PARAGRAPH 2
Travis: CN, Volume II, Number 4, May 22, 1971, p. 19.
Mountain Home: HISC, *Volume III*, p. 7326.
arson attack: *About Face* (USSF), Volume II, Number 1, February 1972, p. 2.
PARAGRAPH 3
Mountain Home: *Helping Hand*, Volume I, Number 5, October 1971, p. 4.
Lackland: *Your Military Left*, Volume I, Number 5, November 1971, p. 4.
Minot: CN, Volume II, Number 9, November 15, 1971, p. 6.
Westover: CN, Volume II, Number 10, December 15, 1971, p. 14.
Lowry: CN, Volume II, Number 9, November 15, 1971, p. 1.
Davis-Monthan: Ibid.

PARAGRAPH 4
January 8 demonstrations: *About Face* (*USSF*), Volume II, Number 1, February 1972, p. 1.
PARAGRAPH 5
early-April demonstrations: *About Face* (*USSF*), Volume II, Number 3, April–May 1972, p. 3.
Offutt: *CN*, Volume III, Number 5, May 15, 1972, p. 5.
Mountain Home: Ibid., p. 6.
PARAGRAPH 6
Tokyo press conference: *The First Amendment*, Volume II, Number 6, May 1, 1972, pp. 4 and 5.
Philippines: *American Report*, June 23, 1972, p. 8.
PARAGRAPH 7
Offutt: *CN*, Volume IV, Number 1, January 15, 1973, p. 1.
PARAGRAPH 8
Evans: Washington *Post*, January 20, 1973, p. 4.
Heck: Ibid. Steven Roberts, "Two Pilots, Two Wars," New York *Times* Magazine, June 10, 1973, p. 14.
PARAGRAPH 9
heroin use: Congressional Record, October 17, 1972, p. 6.
fodding: *CN*, Volume III, Number 10, October 15, 1972, p. 6.
PARAGRAPH 10
letters and quotes: *CN*, Volume IV, Number 6, June 15, 1973, p. 3.
Holtzman suit: New York *Times*, June 6, 1973, p. 10. New York *Times*, July 26, 1973, p. 5.
Dawson: New York *Times*, July 28, 1973, p. 3.
PARAGRAPH 11
B-52 cuts: Washington *Post*, May 31, 1973, pp. 1 and 9.

Chapter 7

SECTION I

PARAGRAPH 1
GI Alliance: *GINDB*, Number 12, April–June 1972, p. 9. *CN*, Volume III, Number 3, March 15, 1972, p. 5.
Fort Bragg: *Bragg Briefs*, Volume VI, Number 2, p. 9. *GINDB*, Number 13, January 1973, pp. 2–6.
Fort Hood: *Zeiger Report*, p. 22.
PARAGRAPH 2
Ogden: New York *Times*, May 6, 1973, p. 11. Ibid., June 9, 1973, p. 12.
Duluth: About Face (*USSF*), Volume VII, Number 5, June 1973, p. 6. *Up Against the Bulkhead*, Number 15, June–July 1973, p. 8.
PARAGRAPH 3
Long Beach: CN, Volume IV, Number 3, March 15, 1973, p. 15. CN, Volume IV, Number 4, April 15, 1973, p. 13.
Portsmouth: *Grapes of Wrath*, July 1973, p. 5. *CN*, Volume IV, Number 6, June 15, 1973, p. 7.

SECTION II

PARAGRAPH 1
Inchon: San Francisco *Examiner*, February 1, 1973, p. 11.
Franklin D. Roosevelt: CN, Volume IV, Number 8, August 15, 1973, p. 14.
Coral Sea: Ibid., p. 9.
PARAGRAPH 2
Black Servicemen's Caucus: USSF files. *GINDB*, Number 19, March 1974, p. 18.
Camp Lejeune: *CN*, Volume IV, Number 5, May 15, 1973, p. 3.
Walter Reed: *Highway 13*, Volume I, Number 6, July–August 1973, p. 1. *CN*, Volume IV, Number 4, April 15, 1973, p. 1.
PARAGRAPH 3
Lowry AFB: *CN*, Volume IV, Number 6, June 15, 1973, p. 8.
PARAGRAPH 4
Fort Lewis: *Fed Up*, March 1973, p. 1. HASC, 93, 1, *Part 1*, p. 863.
Camp Allen 13: *Grapes of Wrath*, June 1973, p. 1.

SECTION III

PARAGRAPH 1
Norfolk Defense Committee: *Grapes of Wrath*, October 1973, p. 1.
circulation estimate: personal letter from George Schmidt, March 30, 1974.
PARAGRAPH 2
anti-dissent and drug programs: Washington *Post*, January 20, 1973, p. 5. New York *Times*, August 7, 1973, p. 1. *GINDB*, Number 14, March 1973, p. 20. UPI release, Allentown (Pa.) *Sunday Call-Chronicle*, February 17, 1974, p. 2.
PARAGRAPH 3
Committee for GI Rights: *FighT bAck*, March 1973, p. 7. *Newsletter on Military Law and Counseling*, Volume IV, Number 8, February–March 1973, pp. 10 and 11.
Gesell decision: Federal District Court for the District of Columbia, Civil Action No. 835-73, February 8, 1974.
McNair barracks demonstration: *CN*, Volume IV, Number 2, February 15, 1973, p. 8.
Council on Rights and Equality: *Write On*, Number 1, September 1973, p. 1. tape and letter from Max Watts, October 16, 1973.
arson incidents: *CN*, Volume IV, Number 2, Februay 15, 1973, p. 8.
Schwabach: *FTA with Pride*, Number 8, p. 12.
Neu Ulm: tape and letter from Max Watts, October 16, 1973.
PARAGRAPH 4
Article 15 at Fort Hood: *CN*, Volume III, Number 7, July 15, 1972, p. 11. *Zeiger Report*, p. 24.
petition to Dellums: Congressional Record, December 14, 1973, p. E 8065.

SECTION IV

PARAGRAPH 1

Okinawa events: USSF files. CN, Volume IV, Number 4, April 15, 1973, p. 10. About Face (USSF), Volume III, Number 5, June 1973, p. 2. CN, Volume IV, Number 7, July 15, 1973, p. 5.

PARAGRAPH 2

Nam Phong: GINDB, Number 14, March 1973, p. 1.

July 4 arrest: New York Times, July 8, 1973, p. 9.

Yokosuka: Winter Soldier, November, 1973, p. 4.

PARAGRAPH 3

Middle East petition: Winter Soldier, November 1973, p. 5. Wildcat, Number 1, p. 3.

SECTION V

PARAGRAPH 2

Houston and Spartanburg: John Hope Franklin, From Slavery to Freedom, 3rd edition (New York: Alfred A. Knopf, 1967), pp. 460–61. Department of Defense, Report of the Task Force on the Administration of Military Justice in the Armed Forces, November 30, 1972, Volume II, p. 97.

World War II and Gurdon, Arkansas: Ibid., pp. 99–101.

uprisings and mutinies: Franklin, From Slavery to Freedom, p. 590.

Korean mutiny: Chicago Area Military Project, "Enlisted People in the Army 1756–1973," 1972, p. 11. The "Enlisted People in the Army" report, primarily the work of Emily Friedman, was serialized in the February through December 1972 issues of Camp News and later reprinted as a sixteen-page pamphlet.

PARAGRAPHS 3, 4, AND 5

Bring Em Home movement: "Enlisted People in the Army," p. 10. Mary Alice Waters, "GIs and the Fight Against the War," published by the Young Socialist Alliance, New York, New York, June 1967. R. Alton Lee, "The Army Mutiny of 1946," Journal of American History, LII, 3 (December 1966), 555–71.

PARAGRAPH 6

desertion statistics: Office of the Assistant Secretary of Defense for Public Affairs, Magazine and Book Branch.

POW actions: "Enlisted People in the Army," p. 11. Victor Hicken, The American Fighting Man (New York: The Macmillan Co., 1969), pp. 321–25.

Chapter 8

SECTION I

PARAGRAPH 1

Taylor remarks: quoted in Juan Cameron, "The Armed Forces' Reluctant Retrenchment," *Fortune*, November 1970.

Bradford: Zeb B. Bradford, "American Ground Power After Vietnam," *Military Review*, April 1972.

PARAGRAPH 2

Williamson: *Investigation into the Electronic Battlefield Program,* Hearings Before a Subcommittee of the Committee on Armed Services, U. S. Senate, 91st Congress, 2nd Session, p. 67.

Westmoreland speech: Congressional Record, October 16, 1969, pp. S 12728–29.

new weapons systems: see Michael Klare, "The Army Under Siege," *NACLA's Latin America and Empire Report*, Volume VII, Number 6, July/August 1973, pp. 9–13.

PARAGRAPH 3

"bare base" concept: Michael Klare, *War Without End* (New York: Vintage Books, 1972), pp. 160–64.

Zumwalt quote: "The Navy Tomorrow," *Ordnance*, January–February 1972, p. 285.

PARAGRAPH 4

Nixon: quoted in Michael Klare, *War Without End*, p. 323.

Iran: Senator James Abourezk, "New War in the Offing," *The Nation*, February 16, 1974.

PARAGRAPH 5

Janowitz estimate: "Volunteer Armed Forces and Military Purpose," *Foreign Affairs*, April 1972, p. 434.

Klare: *War Without End*, p. 352.

SECTION II

PARAGRAPH 1

Laird: "Statement of Secretary of Defense, Melvin R. Laird, Before the Senate Armed Services Committee," February 15, 1972, p. 160.

Greenbook: *Army*, October 1971, p. 82.

PARAGRAPH 2

budget figures: Secretary of Defense James R. Schlesinger, *Annual Defense Department Report*, FY 1975, p. 195. Martin Binkin, *U. S. Reserve Forces: The Problem of the Weekend Warrior* (Washington, D.C.: The Brookings Institution, 1974), pp. 12–14.

equipment transfers: Martin Binkin, . . . *Weekend Warrior, supra.*

PARAGRAPH 3

civil call-ups: Martin Binkin, . . . *Weekend Warrior*, p. 21.

combat readiness: Laird statement, *supra*, p. 11.

Fort Hood: Ibid.

"Alkali Canyon": Reservists Committee to Stop War, "Organizing National Guardsmen at Summer Camp; A Report on the Reservists Committee's Summer Camp Project," Boston, October 1973, p. 1.

Naval Reserve carriers: New York *Times*, October 12, 1971, p. 60.

Brehm proposal: News Release 449-74, Office of the Assistant Secretary of Defense for Public Affairs.

PARAGRAPH 4

manpower reduction and quote: *House of Representatives Report 93-383*, 93rd Congress, 1st Session, p. 74.

Brookings determination: Martin Binkin, . . . *Weekend Warrior*, pp. 62–63.

Schlesinger: *Defense Department Report FY 1975*, pp. 194 and 196.

PARAGRAPH 6

Reservists Committee: interview, Ernie Thurston, Reservists Committee to Stop War, Boston, Massachusetts. files of the Reservists Committee to Stop War.

RAW: Boston *Globe*, August 30, 1970.

PARAGRAPH 7

Madison: *Redline*, Number 18, February–March 1973, p. 6.

BALD: files of Reservists Committee to Stop War.

Reserve and National Guard Organizing Committee: Ibid.

SECTION III

PARAGRAPH 1

Figure 9: "Now Military Is Putting Women into 'Men Only' Jobs," *U.S. News and World Report*, December 10, 1973, p. 83.

75 per cent of jobs: *SASC*, 93, 1, *Part 8*, p. 5383.

Laird 1972 prognosis: Melvin Laird, *Progress in Ending the Draft and Achieving the All-Volunteer Force*, August 1972, pp. 31–33.

PARAGRAPH 2

"tokenism": *Report by the Subcommittee on the Utilization of Manpower in the Military of the Committee on Armed Services, House of Representatives, 92nd Congress, 2nd Session*, June 28, 1972, p. 14631.

Army enlisted statistics: *Hearings Before the Special Subcommittee on the Utilization of Manpower in the Military of the Committee on Armed Services, House of Representatives, 92nd Congress, 1st and 2nd Sessions*, p. 12443 and Appendix 1, p. VII.

Air Force enlisted statistics: Ibid., p. 12453 and Appendix 1, p. VIII.

Navy enlisted statistics: Ibid., p. 12455 and Appendix 1, p. VII.

Army and Air Force officers: calculated from above data.

women's job assignments: Ibid., p. 12441.

PARAGRAPH 4

Andrea Sternberg: *Up Against the Bulkhead*, Number 17, February 1974, p. 5.

Chapter 9

SECTION I

PARAGRAPH 1

Army haircut regulation: New York *Times*, June 1, 1970, p. 3.

Zumwalt: NBC-TV Special Report on *CVN-70*, February 20, 1973. New York *Times*, November 13, 1970, p. 1.

Westmoreland: New York *Times*, December 9, 1970, p. 1.

Nixon proposals: *Congressional Digest*, May 1971, pp. 141 and 160.

PARAGRAPH 2

VOLAR experiment: New York *Times*, July 1, 1972, p. 5.

Fort Benning: *Hearings Before the Special Subcommittee on Recruiting and Retention of Military Personnel of the Committee on Armed Services, House of Representatives, 92nd Congress, First and Second Sessions*, pp. 8458–71.

Fort Ord: New York *Times*, August 29, 1971, p. 1.

PARAGRAPH 3

racial policies: *Army*, October 1971, pp. 20 and 51. "Statement of Secretary of Defense, Melvin R. Laird, Before the Senate Armed Services Committee," February 15, 1972, pp. 173–74. "Statement of Vice-Admiral David H. Bagley Before the Defense Subcommittee of the Senate Appropriations Committee on Navy Military and Reserve Personnel Appropriations," 1972, p. 7.

PARAGRAPH 5

drug policies: New York *Times*, December 19, 1971, p. 2. *Marine Corps Gazette*, December 1971, p. 6.

criticisms: *Report of the Subcommittee on Drug Abuse of the Committee on Armed Services, U. S. Senate, 92nd Congress, First Session*, 1971, pp. 16 and 46.

PARAGRAPH 6

Fort Carson experiments: New York *Times*, November 2, 1970, p. 51. *Life*, February 5, 1971, p. 22. *Hearings Before the Recruiting and Retention Subcommittee*, pp. 8532–8698.

SECTION II

PARAGRAPH 1

113 per cent increase: Martin Binkin and John D. Johnston, *All-Volunteer Armed Forces: Progress, Problems, and Prospects* (Washington, D.C.: The Brookings Institution, 1973)—Senate Armed Services Committee printing, June 1, 1973, p. 24.

November 1971 increase: *House of Representatives Report 92-433, 92nd Congress, First Session*, p. 23.

fiscal 1974 cost: reported in Binkin and Johnston, *All-Volunteer Armed Forces*, p. 24.

PARAGRAPH 2
Figure 10: "The All-Volunteer Force and the End of the Draft,"
Special Report of Secretary of Defense Elliot L. Richardson, March
1973, p. 10. *Army,* October 1971.
PARAGRAPH 3
April 1973 figures: *SASC, 93, 1, Part 2,* p. 1215.
bonus extension: *Armed Forces Journal,* December 1972, p. 10.
fiscal 1974 cost: Binkin and Johnston, *All-Volunteer Armed Forces,*
p. 24.
Callaway report: New York *Times,* February 21, 1974, p. 12.
PARAGRAPH 4
Kennedy quote: "The Power of the Pentagon," *Congressional Quar-
terly,* 1972, p. 55.
Special Pay Act: *Special Report of Secretary Richardson,* pp. 25–26.
cost by fiscal 76: Binkin and Johnston, *All-Volunteer Armed Forces,*
p. 2.
PARAGRAPH 5
manpower budget figures: Secretary of Defense James R. Schlesinger,
Annual Defense Department Report FY 1975, p. 21.
Stennis remarks: *SASC, 92, 2, Part 1,* p. 142.
Soviet percentage: "Statement of Secretary of Defense, Melvin R.
Laird, Before the Senate Armed Services Committee," February 15,
1972, p. 32.
Senate warning: *Senate Report* 92-359, p. 16.
PARAGRAPH 6
Pentagon fiscal 1974 statistics: Binkin and Johnston, *All-Volunteer
Armed Forces,* p. 24.
GAO estimates: The Comptroller General, *Problems in Meeting
Military Manpower Needs in the All-Volunteer Force,* May 2, 1973,
p. 5.
Califano estimate: *New Republic,* April 21, 1973, p. 31. for full ex-
change, see: Washington *Post,* March 22 and 31, 1973, and *New
Republic,* March 3, March 24, and April 21, 1973.
PARAGRAPH 7
1967 panel report: *Report to the Committee on Armed Services,
House of Representatives, 90th Congress, First Session,* February 28,
1967, p. 18.

SECTION III

PARAGRAPH 1
Froehlke: *HASC, 93, 1, Part 1,* p. 847.
Gates analysis: *The Report of the President's Commission on an All-
Volunteer Armed Force* (London: Collier-Macmillan, Ltd., 1970)
pp. 27 and 32.
PARAGRAPH 2
Ayers: New York *Times,* September 5, 1971, p. 36.
Gates analysis: *Report of the President's Commission,* p. 33.

SECTION IV

PARAGRAPH 1
"Army in Anguish" quotes: Washington *Post*, September 20, 1971, p. 12.
Hebert quote: *HASC*, 92, 2, *Part* 1, p. 9480.
PARAGRAPH 2
Army recruitment results: New York *Times*, December 9, 1973, p. 9. New York *Times*, July 29, 1973, p. 39. New York *Times*, February 21, 1974, p. 12.
Figure 11: Schlesinger, *1975 Report*, p. 176.
PARAGRAPH 3
Kelley: Washington *Post*, June 4, 1973.
PARAGRAPH 4
Westmoreland to Franklin: New York *Times*, July 1, 1973, p. 20.
Laird quote: *Final Report to the Congress of Secretary of Defense Melvin R. Laird*, January 8, 1973, p. 9.

Chapter 10

SECTION I

PARAGRAPH 1
number of recruiters: *Christian Science Monitor*, March 24, 1973, p. 7. *HASD*, 92, 2, *Part* 6, p. 96.
1975 cost: *House Report* 93-1255, p. 16.
Figure 12: Martin Binkin and John D. Johnston, *All-Volunteer Armed Forces: Progress, Problems and Prospects* (Washington, D.C.: The Brookings Institution, 1973)—Senate Armed Services Committee printing, June 1, 1973, p. 23. 1974 figures from *House Report* 93-662, p. 30.
PARAGRAPH 2
Rooney complaint: Washington *Post*, February 28, 1972, p. 1.
Plymouth incident: *Newsletter on Military Law and Counseling* (CCCO-West, 140 Leavenworth St., San Francisco, Calif.), Volume IV, Number 3, June–July 1972, p. 9.
PARAGRAPH 3
Dorchester incident: *Newsletter on Military Law and Counseling* Volume IV, Number 8, February–March 1973, p. 10.
Navy report: *Report of the Special Subcommittee on Disciplinary Problems in the U. S. Navy of the Committee on Armed Services, House of Representatives*, 92nd Congress, 2nd Session, p. 17671.
PARAGRAPH 4
CID investigation: reported in New York *Times*, June 15, 1973, p. 9.
Army Audit report: *Report of Audit: Recruiting the All-Volunteer Army*, U. S. Army Audit Agency, Audit Report: SO 73-49, April 13, 1973.

PARAGRAPH 5

Rogers report: NBC Television News Special, Sunday, November 11, 1973.

PARAGRAPH 6

Committee on Military Justice quote: "The Enlistment Contract— How 'Contractual'?" by John Hanley and Tom Johnson, Committee for Legal Research on the Draft and Military, November 28, 1972, p. 54.

PARAGRAPH 7

Figure 13: Boston *Globe*, March 25, 1973. Office of the Assistant Secretary of Defense for Public Affairs, Magazine and Book Branch.

public service: *HASD*, 92, 2, *Part* 3, p. 136.

SECTION II

PARAGRAPH 1

Kelley testimony: *Hearings Before the Special Subcommittee on Recruiting and Retention of Military Personnel of the Committee on Armed Sevices, House of Representatives, 92nd Congress*, p. 8089.

Youth in Transition study: Jerome Johnston and Jerald Bachman, *Young Men Look at Military Service: A Preliminary Report* (Institute for Social Research, April 1971), pp. 60–61.

1964 survey: Harold Wool, *The Military Specialist* (Baltimore: The Johns Hopkins Press, 1968), pp. 111–12.

1955 survey: Ibid., pp. 107–8.

PARAGRAPH 2

unemployment quotes: Wool, *The Military Specialist*, pp. 99–100.

Brookings Institution study: Binkin and Johnston, *All-Volunteer Armed Forces*, p. 44.

University of Michigan study: Jerome Johnston and Jerald Bachman, *Young Men and Military Service* (Ann Arbor: Institute for Social Research, 1972), pp. 134–35.

Kelley statement: *Hearings Before the Subcommittee on the Volunteer Armed Force and Selective Service of the Committee on Armed Services, U. S. Senate, 92nd Congress, 2nd Session*, p. 193.

PARAGRAPH 4

high school graduates: *Special Report of Secretary of Defense Elliot Richardson on the All-Volunteer Force and the End of the Draft*, March 1973, p. 14.

Navy mental-category scores: "Organizational Adaption to an All-Volunteer Military: Assessment of Basic Indicators," by Morris Janowitz and Sam Sarkesian, prepared for the International Sociological Association, March 1973, p. 25.

Schlesinger quote: Secretary of Defense James R. Schlesinger, *Annual Defense Department Report FY 1975*, p. 177.

SECTION III

PARAGRAPH 1

quote and occupational data: Wool, *The Military Specialist*, pp. 54–56.

PARAGRAPH 2

occupation figures: Ibid.

PARAGRAPH 3

NORC data on combat: Charles Moskos, *The American Enlisted Man* (New York: Russell Sage Foundation, 1970), p. 203.

Wool findings: Wool, *The Military Specialist*, p. 79.

PARAGRAPH 4

McNamara on Project 100,000: quoted in Wool, *The Military Specialist*, pp. 181–82.

Kerwin report: *Hearings Before a Subcommittee of the Committee on Appropriations, House of Representatives, 92nd Congress, 1st Session, Part 3*, p. 525.

Wool quote: Wool, *The Military Specialist*, p. 183.

PARAGRAPH 5

NORC veterans survey: Moskos, *The American Enlisted Man*, p. 205. Wool, *The Military Specialist*, p. 184.

1955 survey: Wool, op. cit., pp. 147–48.

PARAGRAPH 6

Biderman study: A. D. Biderman and L. M. Sharp, "The Convergence of Military and Civilian Occupational Structures; Evidence from Studies of Military Retired Employment," *American Journal of Sociology*, 73 (January 1968), pp. 381–99.

PARAGRAPH 7

Modern Volunteer Army report: *The Volunteer Soldier; His Needs, Attitudes and Expectations*, by Dr. Scott M. Cunningham, Report Number 72-2, October 21, 1972, pp. 18 and 36.

PARAGRAPH 8

misutilization: The Comptroller General of the United States, *Improper Use of Enlisted Personnel*, May 6, 1971, pp. 1 and 21.

non-occupational duties: Wool, *The Military Specialist*, p. 60.

SECTION IV

PARAGRAPH 2

paid-schooling study: Johnston and Bachman, *Young Men and Military Service*, pp. 180–86.

"Four for Four" plan: Ibid., pp. 227–29.

PARAGRAPH 4

Fort Jackson orientation experiment: HASD, 92, 2, *Part 6*, p. 101.

Chapter 11

PARAGRAPH 2

figures for first 11 months: Stuart Loory, "Our Volunteer Army: Some Second Thoughts," New York *Times*, January 29, 1974.

Gates estimate: *The Report of the President's Commission on an All-Volunteer Armed Force* (London: Collier-Macmillan, Ltd., 1970), p. 140.

82nd Airborne: Schlesinger, *Defense Department Report FY 1975,* p. 184.

PARAGRAPH 3

Figure 14: Secretary of Defense James R. Schlesinger, *Annual Defense Department Report FY 1975,* p. 186.

SECTION I

PARAGRAPH 2

occupation percentages: Congressional Black Caucus, *Racism in the Military: A New System for Rewards and Punishment,* May 15, 1972, reprinted in the Congressional Record, October 14, 1972, pp. E 8674–88 (hereafter cited as *Racism in the Military*), p. 2.

blacks in combat: Adam Yarmolinsky, *The Military Establishment* (New York: Harper & Row, 1971), p. 342.

critique of AFQT: Department of Defense, *Report of the Task Force on the Administration of Military Justice in the Armed Forces,* November 30, 1972, Volume I, pp. 45–50.

Moskos finding: Charles Moskos, *The American Enlisted Man* (New York: Russell Sage Foundation, 1970), p. 217.

PARAGRAPH 3

grade distribution: DOD, *Task Force on Military Justice,* Volume IV, p. 305.

NAACP findings: The National Association for the Advancement of Colored People, *The Search for Military Justice,* April 22, 1971, p. 3.

black officers: Office of the Assistant Secretary of Defense for Public Affairs, Magazine and Book Branch.

PARAGRAPH 4

NAACP quote: *The Search for Military Justice,* p. 16.

Heidelberg: Ibid., p. 17.

Black Caucus assessment: *Racism in the Military,* p. 2.

PARAGRAPH 5

dapping: DOD, *Task Force on Military Justice,* Volume I, pp. 60–61.

Black Muslims: Ibid., p. 99.

PARAGRAPH 6

quote on anti-Spanish regulations: Ibid., p. 61.

PARAGRAPH 7

Article-15 percentage: Ibid., pp. 27–28.

quote on military justice: *Racism in the Military*, p. 2.

black legal officers: *The Search for Military Justice*, p. 13.

court-martial percentages: DOD, *Task Force on Military Justice*, Volume I, pp. 30–31.

PARAGRAPH 8

50 per cent in pretrial: *Racism in the Military*, p. 3. *The Search for Military Justice*, p. 9.

more severe punishment: DOD, *Task Force on Military Justice*, Volume I, pp. 28–29.

PARAGRAPH 9

1971 inmate statistics: New York *Times*, November 4, 1971.

percentages at Fort Leavenworth and Lowry AFB: DOD, *Task Force on Military Justice*, Volume I, pp. 32–33.

length of confinement: Ibid., p. 32.

PARAGRAPH 10

NAACP claim: *The Search for Military Justice*, p. 15.

Air Force statistics: *Racism in the Military*, p. 3.

quote: DOD, *Task Force on Military Justice*, Volume I, p. 33.

PARAGRAPH 11

"systemic" and quote: Ibid., p. 19 and p. 22.

PARAGRAPH 12

percentage of officers from South: Charles Coates and Roland Pellegrin, *Military Sociology: A Study of American Military Institutions and Military Life* (University Park, Md.: Social Science Press, 1965), p. 89.

Janowitz quote: Morris Janowitz, *The Professional Soldier: A Social and Political Portrait* (New York: The Free Press, 1960), p. 88.

PARAGRAPH 13

Camp Lejeune study quote: New York *Times*, August 10, 1969, p. 67.

Task Force quote: DOD, *Task Force on Military Justice*, Volume I, p. 40.

SECTION II

PARAGRAPHS 2 THROUGH 6

Korean incident: documents and correspondence in Washington office of Lawyers Military Defense Committee. New York *Times*, December 4, 1973.

PARAGRAPHS 7 THROUGH 10

Little Rock incident: documents and correspondence in Washington office of Lawyers Military Defense Committee. *Wall Street Journal*, February 14, 1974, p. 1.

SECTION III

PARAGRAPH 2

NAACP quote: *The Search for Military Justice*, p. 3.

Task Force position: *Task Force on Military Justice*, Volume I, p. 49.

recommendations: These and the following suggestions draw heavily
on reform proposals of the Congressional Black Caucus, the DOD
Task Force, and the NAACP.

PARAGRAPH 3
Task Force quote: *Task Force on Military Justice*, Volume I, p. 51.
PARAGRAPH 5
Black Caucus quote: *Racism in the Military*, p. 3.

Chapter 12

SECTION I

PARAGRAPH 1
Marshall Commission quote: Harry A. Marmion, *The Case Against
a Volunteer Army* (Chicago: Quadrangle Books, 1971), Appendix
III, p. 102.
Westmoreland quotes: New York *Times*, August 17, 1973.
PARAGRAPH 3
Reeves survey: Thomas Reeves and Karl Hess, *The End of the Draft*
(New York: Vintage Books, 1970), p. 175.
USSF conference: *GINDB*, Number 10, January 1972, pp. 44 and 72.
Veteran survey: Hamid Mowlana and Paul H. Geffert, "Vietnam
Veterans Against the War: A Profile Study of Dissenters," appendix
to *The New Soldier*, edited by David Thorne and George Butler
(New York: Collier Books, 1971), pp. 172–74.
Goodman quote: included in personal letter from Max Watts, April
12, 1973.

SECTION II

PARAGRAPH 2
Heinl quote: Col. Robert D. Heinl, "Military Justice Under Attack,"
Armed Forces Journal, June 1973, p. 42.
Howze quote: Hamilton Howze, "Military Discipline and National
Security," *Army*, January 1971, p. 12.
Westmoreland quote: General William C. Westmoreland, "Military
Justice—A Commander's Viewpoint," *The American Criminal Law
Review*, X, 1 (July 1971), 5.
PARAGRAPH 3
Stouffer findings: Samuel A. Stouffer et al., *The American Soldier*,
Volume II: *Combat and Its Aftermath* (Princeton, N.J.: Princeton
University Press, 1949), pp. 107–18.
Korean study: Roger Little, "Buddy Relations and Combat Perform-
ance," *The New Military*, edited by Morris Janowitz (New York:
W. W. Norton & Company, 1964), pp. 195–223.
Vietnam: Charles Moskos, "Why Men Fight," *Transaction*, Novem-
ber 1969, pp. 13–23.

SECTION III

PARAGRAPH 3

soldier-superior: Eric Waldman, *The Goose Step Is Verboten; The German Army Today* (New York: The Free Press of Glencoe, 1964), pp. 79 and 80.

Complaint Order: Ibid., p. 83. Col. T. N. Dupuy, *The Almanac of World Military Power* (Dunn Loring, Va.: T. N. Dupuy Associates, 1970), p. 87.

penal code: Waldman, *The Goose Step . . .* , pp. 84 and 85.

Vertrauensmann: Ibid., pp. 86–88. Peter Barnes, *Pawns: The Plight of the Citizen Soldier* (New York: Alfred A. Knopf, 1972), p. 252.

PARAGRAPH 4 AND 5

additional *Bundeswehr* reforms: Waldman, op. cit.

PARAGRAPH 6

Sweden: Reeves and Hess, *The End of the Draft*, p. 182.

Canada: *Army Times*, January 13, 1971.

Great Britain, etc.: Barnes, *Pawns*, p. 202.

China: John Gittings, *The Role of the Chinese Army* (London: Oxford University Press, 1967), pp. 193–97 and p. 251.

SECTION IV

PARAGRAPH 2

French Military Code: quoted in *HISC, Volume I,* p. 6644.

SECTION V

PARAGRAPH 2

Amick and Stolte: John Schulz, "The Civilianization of Military Law," a lecture presented at the Institute for Policy Studies, Washington, D.C., July 11, 1973.

Avrech: Ibid. CN, Volume IV, Number 4, April 15, 1973, p. 15.

Levy: Schulz, "Civilianization. . . ." *CN,* Volume IV, Number 5, May 15, 1973, p. 15.

PARAGRAPH 3

West Point case: *Military Law Digest* (a project of the Public Law Education Institute, Washington, D.C., John Schulz, editor), Number 1, November 1972, p. 13.

Flower: Schulz, "Civilianization. . . ."

Jenness and Spock: *Military Law Digest*, Number 2, December 1972, pp. 26 and 27.

PARAGRAPH 4

Hawaii decision: *Military Law Digest*, Number 1, p. 12.

Williams decision: Schulz, "Civilianization. . . ." CN, Volume IV, Number 6, June 15, 1973, p. 15.

SECTION VI

PARAGRAPH 4
Schmidt quote: personal letter from George Schmidt, March 30, 1974.
PARAGRAPH 6
GI-movement prescription: *GINDB*, Number 14, March 1973, p. 11.

RESEARCH GUIDE

To encourage further study, I shall outline the procedures for investigating GI resistance and armed-forces policy. GI newspapers are the fundamental reference material for servicemen's dissent. Because of the spontaneous and extensive nature of the movement, however, these periodicals were never collected in a systematic way. As a consequence, no comprehensive file of GI newspapers exists, so the researcher is forced to search through a number of incomplete collections maintained by widely separated individuals and organizations. One of the most important files is in the home of attorney Ken Cloke in Santa Monica, California. An early supporter of MDM, Ken several years ago assembled over seven hundred copies of GI newspapers in preparation for a planned study of GI resistance. The work was never produced, but Ken's records remain an invaluable guide to the GI movement—particularly its otherwise inaccessible early years. The largest, most inclusive inventory is contained in the files of the United States Servicemen's Fund, currently under the trusteeship of former USSF treasurer Robert Zevin, Cambridge, Massachusetts. The USSF files contain a huge number of GI papers—probably the largest collection in existence—dating from the earliest days of the movement to the present. Many major papers such as *Fatigue Press* are included in nearly full volume. Records for the period from 1971 to the present are particularly thorough. In addition to newspapers, the USSF files contain large volumes of vital correspondence, internal reports, memoranda, funding requests, etc.—an invaluable guide to the inner workings of the GI movement. The records of the Chicago Area Military Project—now at the VVAW national office in Chicago—are another essential source of information. In addition to numerous GI papers and news clippings, the collection contains a complete volume of *Camp News*, the best single reference on the history of resistance.

Other important documents include the following: the complete volume of the *GI Press Service*, available from former editor Bob Wilkinson, c/o the Socialist Workers Party, Washington, D.C.; the files of the American Sevicemen's Union and *The Bond*, in New York City; the records of *Up Against the Bulkhead*, at 98 Chenery Street in San Francisco; and my own personal collection of GI papers and documents.

In preparing this book, I have consulted or worked with the following people, all of whom have extensive personal involvement in anti-draft and GI-movement activity: Max Watts, Heidelberg, Germany; George Schmidt (former activist with CAMP), Chicago; David Addlestone (director of the Lawyers Military Defense Committee), Washington, D.C.; Paul Lauter (former Executive Director of USSF), Manhasset, New York; Dave Zeiger (former civilian assistant at the Oleo Strut), Los Angeles; Tom Culver (veteran Air Force organizer), Cambridge, England; George Bacon (a founder of *Semper Fi*), Hotchkiss, Colorado; Phil Willayto (civilian assistant to *Grapes of Wrath*), Norfolk, Virginia; John Schulz (editor of the *Military Law Digest*), Washington, D.C.; Jane Fonda, Santa Monica, California; and Kathy Gilberd (staff member of the GI Project Alliance), San Diego, California. Two others with broad experience in the GI movement, particularly its early phases, are Sid Peterman of the Pacific Counseling Service, and Fred Gardner of San Francisco.

The task of obtaining manpower statistics and information on personnel affairs from the military establishment is quite difficult. Perhaps the best source is the annual series of hearings held before Congressional committees considering the Defense Budget. Published in multiple volumes each summer and fall, the hearings normally include a major section devoted to "manpower," as well as numerous, often fleeting references to disciplinary problems, racial unrest, the all-volunteer force, etc. They are available from the Congressional committees themselves or from the Government Printing Office; they are also stored in Government Depository Libraries. The four sets of hearings are: Senate Armed Services Committee, *Authorization for Military Procurement*; Senate Appropriations Defense Subcommittee, *Department of Defense Appropriations*; House Armed Services Committee, *Hearings on Military Posture*; House Appropriations Defense Subcommittee, *Department of Defense Appropriations*. One of the frankest discussions of unrest in the Army in these volumes is contained in *Hearings Before a Subcommittee of the Committee on Appropriations, House of Representatives, 92nd Congress, 1st Session, Part 9*, pp. 548–619.

In addition, the two Armed Services Committees, especially the House Committee, appoint subcommittees to investigate special issues and problems of military manpower. The schedule of subcommittee assignments changes often and should be checked each year with the main Committee office. The following subcommittees were particularly valuable in this work; their hearings and/or reports contain a great deal of useful information:

❖ Subcommittee on Treatment of Deserters from Military Service, Senate Armed Services Committee, 90th Congress, 2nd Session, Senator Daniel Inouye, chairman.

❖ Special Subcommittee to Probe Disturbances on Military Bases, House Armed Services Committee, 91st Congress, 2nd Session, Rep. William Randall (D-Mo.), chairman.

❖ Special Subcommittee to Investigate Alleged Drug Abuse in the Armed Services, House Armed Services Committee, 91st Congress, 2nd Session, Rep. G. Elliot Hagan (D-Ga.), chairman.

❖ Subcommittee on Drug Abuse in the Military, Senate Armed Services Committee, 92nd Congress, 1st Session, Senator Harold Hughes, chairman.

❖ Special Subcommittee on the Utilization of Manpower in the Military, House Armed Services Committee, 92nd Congress, 2nd Session, Rep. Otis Pike (D-N.Y.), chairman.

❖ Subcommittee on the Volunteer Armed Force and Selective Service, Senate Armed Services Committee, 92nd Congress, 2nd Session, Senator Lloyd Bentsen, chairman.

❖ Special Subcommittee on Recruitment and Retention of Military Personnel, House Armed Services Committee, 92nd Congress, 2nd Session, Rep. W. C. Daniel (D-Va.), chairman.

❖ Special Subcommittee on Disciplinary Problems in the U. S. Navy, House Armed Services Committee, 92nd Congress, 2nd Session, Rep. Floyd Hicks (D-Wash.), chairman.

The most comprehensive Congressional study of GI resistance is the House Internal Security Committee's three-volume report *Investigation of Attempts to Subvert the U.S. Armed Services*, published in 1972 during the 92nd Congress. Although extremely biased and childishly preoccupied with mythical Communist conspiracies, the Committee managed to assemble an enormous amount of documentary material in over eleven hundred pages of testimony.

Data on personnel statistics and new manpower programs are best obtained from the Department of Defense itself. The best guide to Pentagon policies is the Secretary of Defense's annual posture statement, currently published by Secretary Schlesinger as the *Annual Defense Department Report*. The annual report is available from the Armed Services Committees during February or March, or at other times from the Government Printing Office. Important analytical material can also be obtained from the Pentagon's frequently used behavioral-study "think tank," the Human Resources Research Organization, in Alexandria, Virginia. The General Accounting Office in Washington also publishes occasional studies of volunteer-force and manpower-utilization topics, as does The Brookings Institution. Statistics can be obtained through the Office of the Assistant Secretary of Defense, Manpower and Reserve Affairs, The Pentagon, Washington, D.C., or can be routed through a sympathetic congressman. The best and most convenient source for authors, however, is the Office of the Assistant Secretary of Defense, Public Affairs, Magazine and Book Branch, The Pentagon, Washington, D.C.

THE GI PRESS

Frequently the only written record of GI resistance, servicemen's newspapers are essential to an understanding of the crisis in the ranks. Unfortunately our knowledge of these vital documents is incomplete and fragmentary, reflecting the precarious and often transitory nature of GI organizations. In March of 1972, the Defense Department reported that some 245 separate GI newspapers had been published up to that date. Adding the approximately twenty new journals founded since then and assuming that some isolated and short-lived papers have been overlooked, I estimate the total number at near three hundred.

Figure 15 attempts to illustrate the pattern of development of these newspapers. It is based on charts of the GI papers listed below, arranged longitudinally according to time (the original charts were exhibited during my seminar "GI Resistance and the Decline of the Armed Forces," presented at the Institute for Policy Studies on January 25, 1974; they are available in my files). The graph includes only the 259 periodicals that I have been able to identify and is often based on uncertain guesses about the duration of some titles. It probably underestimates the total number of active papers, therefore, and should be used with caution. Nonetheless, it offers a heretofore unavailable view of the broad outlines of the changing nature of dissent.

The graph clearly shows that the GI movement was at its height from mid-1969 to mid-1972, reaching a peak in 1970 following the invasion of Cambodia. It also strikingly illustrates the sharp impact of the air-war strategy on the movement in the Air Force and the Navy, with dissent in the technological services rising steadily throughout the period of escalated bombing—during the aerial blitz of early 1972, nearly equaling the level of protest in the two ground services. Finally, it indicates that while withdrawals from Indochina have reduced GI resistance, the movement remains active today and, given sufficient support, is likely to continue into the future.

Below is a comprehensive list of all the past and present GI newspapers I have been able to locate. This compilation of 259 papers omits several dozen journals written by GI exiles in Canada and Sweden. The dates of operation of many have been left purposely vague because of the difficulty in determining exactly when they began or stopped. Except where an exact month is given, the reader should regard times as only estimates. Papers marked with an asterisk (*) and followed by an address are those still being published as of the fall of 1974.

total number
of papers

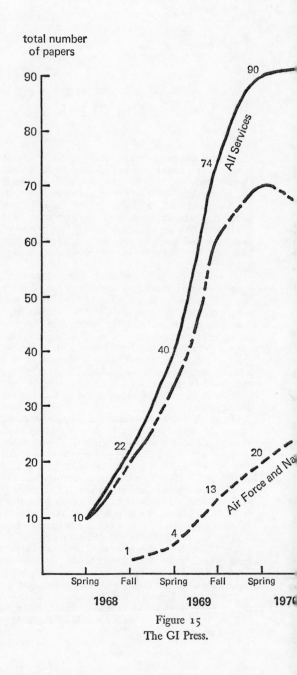

Figure 15
The GI Press.

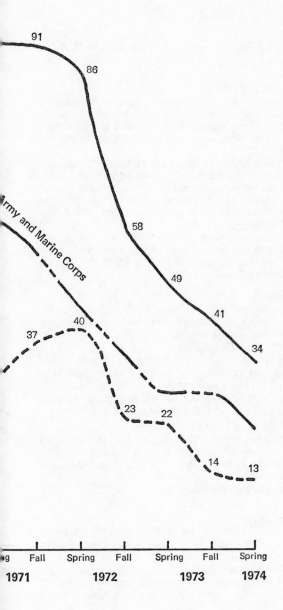

91

86

Army and Marine Corps

58

49

41

37   40

34

23   22

14   13

Fall   Spring   Fall   Spring   Fall   Spring
1971   **1972**   **1973**   **1974**

1. *Army and Marine Corps Papers in the United States*

*THE BOND (New York City)
the voice of the American Servicemen's Union . . . founded in
June 1967, in Berkeley . . . moved to New York in early 1968 . . .
during the height of the Vietnam War distributed to tens of thousands of GIs world wide . . . 58 West 25th Street, New York,
New York, 10010

VETERANS STARS AND STRIPES FOR PEACE (Chicago, Ill.)
the first paper aimed at servicemen . . . founded by "Veterans for
Peace in Vietnam" in September 1967 . . . circulation of approximately sixty thousand . . . distributed to GIs by Vets for Peace
chapters throughout the country . . . active until 1972

VIETNAM GI (Chicago, Ill.)
the most influential early paper . . . surfaced at the end of 1967
. . . distributed to tens of thousands of GIs, many in Vietnam
. . . closed down after the death of founder Jeff Sharlet in June
1969 . . . revived briefly in May 1970

THE ALLY (Berkeley, Calif.)
founded in the spring of 1968 . . . edited by Clark Smith . . . influential in the early development of resistance . . . approximately
forty issues published through early 1972

AS YOU WERE (Fort Ord, Calif.)
the first paper at Fort Ord . . . founded in late 1968 . . . aided
by PCS founder Sid Peterman . . . thirteen issues to April 1970

COUNTERPOINT (Fort Lewis, Wash.)
published by the "GI-Civilian Alliance for Peace" . . . surfaced
near the end of 1968 . . . published until the end of 1969

FATIGUE PRESS (Fort Hood, Tex.)
one of the most active papers of the entire movement . . . founded
in mid-1968 . . . published regularly from the "Oleo Strut" coffeehouse until the second half of 1972 . . . circulation at times exceeded five thousand

FLAG-IN-ACTION (Fort Campbell, Tenn.)
founded in December 1968 . . . active only briefly

FTA (Fort Knox, Ky.)
the most famous GI paper . . . one of the first edited entirely by
GIs . . . appeared initially in June 1968 and lasted until the fall
of 1972 . . . a lone thirty-third issue surfaced in April of 1973

HEAD ON (Camp Lejeune, N.C.)
one of the first Marine papers . . . founded in 1968 by Bob Kukiel,
an active-duty Vietnam veteran . . . later merged with *Wish* at
nearby Cherry Point MCAS

LAST HARASS (Fort Gordon, Ga.)
published initially from late 1968 until the latter part of 1970 . . .
revived in the spring of 1971 . . . last appeared in late 1971

LOGISTIC (Fort Sheridan, Ill.)
active briefly in late 1968 and early 1969 . . . suppressed after
only a few issues when the GI editors were punitively transferred

PAWN'S PAWN (Fort Leonard Wood, Mo.)
a short-lived effort first appearing in mid-1968 . . . associated with
"Mad Anthony Wayne's" coffeehouse . . . disappeared after its
closing in early 1969

SHORT TIMES (Fort Jackson, S.C.)
one of the most successful early papers . . . founded during 1968
. . . published regularly until the spring of 1972

STRIKEBACK (Fort Bragg, N.C.)
one of the first all-GI papers . . . lasted only a few issues . . .
started in June 1968

TASK FORCE (San Francisco, Calif.)
published by GIs and civilians . . . founded in August 1968 . . .
aided by the Student Mobilization Committee . . . disappeared in
1970

ULTIMATE WEAPON (Fort Dix, N.J.)
started in December 1968 . . . edited by Sp/4 Allen Myers, a
member of the Young Socialist Alliance . . . active into 1970

ABOUT FACE (Los Angeles, Calif.)
founded in 1969 by "GIs and Vietnam Veterans Against the War"
. . . distributed at various Southern California bases until mid-1972

ABOVEGROUND (Fort Carson, Colo.)
an effective early paper, founded in August of 1969 . . . replaced
in mid-1970 with the more militant MDM paper *Counterattack*

ATTITUDE CHECK (Camp Pendleton, Calif.)
started in the fall of 1969 . . . associated with the "Green Machine" coffeehouse . . . ended by a split between blacks and whites
in the summer of 1970

AWOL Press (Fort Riley, Kans.)
several issues published from late 1969 to mid-1970

BAYONET (Presidio, Calif.)
short-lived . . . late 1969 through mid-1970

*BRAGG BRIEFS (Fort Bragg, N.C.)
one of the most successful papers . . . founded in the spring of
1969 . . . published regularly through 1971 and irregularly to the
present . . . circulation has at times exceeded five thousand . . .
G.I. Union, P.O. Box 437, Spring Lake, N.C., 28390

THE CHESSMAN (Beaufort MCAS, S.C.)
started in mid-1969 . . . lasted only about one year

DO IT LOUD (Fort Bragg, N.C.)
published by the "Black Brigade" . . . active from late 1969 into
1970

DULL BRASS (Fort Sheridan, Ill.)
founded after the demise of *Logistic* . . . lasted about one year

*FED UP (Fort Lewis, Wash.)
founded in late 1969 . . . associated with the "Shelter Half" coffeehouse . . . after a dormant period, revived by a chapter of Vietnam Veterans Against the War (VVAW) . . . P.O. Box 9098, Tacoma, Wash. 98409

GIGLINE (Fort Bliss, Tex.)
first published by "GIs for Peace" in the summer of 1969 . . . printed regularly until mid-1972 . . . circulation in 1971 averaged around twenty-five hundred

GI ORGANIZER (Fort Hood, Tex.)
less influential than *Fatigue Press* . . . founded in early 1969 . . . short-lived

GI PRESS SERVICE (New York City and Washington, D.C.)
founded, in June 1969, by the Student Mobilization Committee . . . a central news agency on GI organizing . . . ceased publication in the fall of 1971

GREEN MACHINE (Fort Greely, Alaska)
active for about a year from late 1969 into 1970

HARD TIMES (Fort Huachuca, Ariz.)
active from mid-1969 to early 1970

HEAD ON WISH (Cherry Point and Camp Lejeune, N.C.)
the result of a merger of *Head On* and *Wish* . . . lasted only a few months during the summer and fall of 1969

HERESY II (Fort Leonard Wood, Mo.)
existed briefly in late 1969

LEFT FACE (Fort McClellan, Ala.)
founded in the latter part of 1969 . . . published for a time by "GIs and WACs Against the War" . . . appeared regularly until the summer of 1972

THE LOOPER (San Francisco, Calif.)
published by California National Guardsmen in late 1969 and early 1970

MARINE BLUES (San Francisco, Calif.)
published regularly by Marine Corps reservists from the spring of 1969 to mid-1970

NAPALM (Fort Campbell, Tenn.)
founded in 1969 . . . published irregularly until 1971

THE NEW SALUTE (Baltimore, Md.)
published briefly by Baltimore-area GIs in 1969 . . . merged with *Open Ranks*

OBLIGORE (New York City)
published by Marine Corps reservists from September 1969 through most of 1970

OPEN RANKS (Baltimore, Md.)
founded in the latter part of 1969 . . . produced by "Baltimore

GIs United," originally centered at Fort Holabird . . . in September 1970 and for a short while afterward published by soldiers at Edgewood Arsenal

OPEN SIGHTS (Washington, D.C.)
first published by Washington-area GIs from the spring of 1969 until mid-1971 . . . associated during 1970 and 1971 with the "DMZ" coffeehouse . . . revived by local servicemen in the first half of 1972, but ceased operation at the end of that year

THE PAWN (Fort Detrick, Md.)
the work of "Frederick GIs United" . . . published from November 1969 through 1970

POLYLOGUE (Fort Gordon, Ga.)
published by GIs and civilians in Augusta . . . founded in November 1969

RAP (Fort Benning, Ga.)
founded during 1969 by Fort Benning soldiers . . . later a community paper for Columbus . . . active into 1971

ROUGH DRAFT (Fort Eustis, Va.)
the first known paper in the Tidewater area . . . in operation from March 1969 through 1970

SHAKEDOWN (Fort Dix, N.J.)
founded in March 1969 . . . aided by SDS activists with the Fort Dix coffeehouse . . . ceased operation during 1970

SPARTACUS (Fort Lee, Va.)
existed briefly in late 1969 and part of 1970

SPD NEWS (Fort Dix, N.J.)
written by soldiers in the Special Processing Detachment . . . aided by the ASU office in New York . . . active from the spring of 1969 into 1970

TOP SECRET (Fort Devens, Mass.)
founded during 1969 . . . active for approximately one year

UP FRONT (Los Angeles, Calif.)
founded by a group of Camp Pendleton Marines, and airmen from various Southern California bases . . . published from the spring of 1969 to the end of that year

WISH (Cherry Point MCAS, N.C.)
existed briefly in early 1969 before merging with *Head On*

YOUR MILITARY LEFT (Fort Sam Houston, Tex.)
first published from early 1969 until the second half of 1970 . . . revived, in July 1971, by the "GI Co-ordinating Committee" . . . continued until the latter part of 1973

ALL READY ON THE LEFT (Camp Pendleton, Calif.)
successor to *Attitude Check* . . . published by the white faction of Pendleton MDM, from August of 1970 until the first part of 1971

ANCHORAGE TROOP (Fort Richardson, Alaska)
published for approximately a year, from early 1970 until early 1971

BLACK UNITY (Camp Pendleton, Calif.)
an MDM paper published by blacks as a successor to *Attitude Check* . . . founded in the second half of 1970 . . . in operation for less than a year

B-TROOP NEWS (Fort Lewis, Wash.)
a "unit newsletter" circulated with the 1st/3rd Cavalry during the first half of 1970

CAMP NEWS (Chicago, Ill.)
journal of the "Chicago Area Military Project" . . . a few mimeographed issues in early 1970 . . . then published on a regular, monthly basis from September 1970 through August 1973

CONFINEE SAYS (Camp Pendleton, Calif.)
written by inmates of the Camp Pendleton brig . . . smuggled out and printed by MDM during 1970

COUNTERATTACK (Fort Carson, Colo.)
published by MDM from July 1970 until the second half of 1971

EM 16 (Fort Knox, Ky.)
appeared briefly during mid-1970

FIRST OF THE WORST (Fort Lewis, Wash.)
another "unit newsletter," published in the second half of 1970

IN FORMATION (Fort Knox, Ky.)
founded in early 1970 . . . in operation for less than a year

LEWIS-McCHORD FREE PRESS (Fort Lewis, Wash.)
established by the "GI Alliance" in August 1970 . . . active until 1974 . . . replaced by *GI Voice*

MORNING REPORT (Fort Devens, Mass.)
first appeared in the spring of 1970 . . . continued until mid-1972

ON KORPS (Camp Lejeune, N.C.)
edited by a group of Marines, including at least one officer, during 1970 . . . sometimes referred to as *Encore* . . . suppressed by transfers and arrests

OUR THING (Redstone Arsenal, Ala.)
published briefly during 1970

PAYBACK (El Toro MCAS, Calif.)
published, at times irregularly, from July 1970 until mid-1972 . . . the voice of Orange County MDM

RAW TRUTH (Boston, Mass.)
written by "Reservists Against the War" . . . started in October 1970 . . . ceased publication in the fall of 1971

*REDLINE (Berkeley, Calif. and Boston, Mass.)
the voice of "Reservists Committee to Stop War" . . . mailed nationally to over two thousand reservists . . . published in Berkeley from early 1970 to the spring of 1972 and in Boston from May 1972, to the present . . . 355 Boylston Street, Boston, Mass. 02116

RIGHT ON POST (Fort Ord, Calif.)
published by MDM from the spring of 1970 until the end of that year

SHRAPNEL (Fort Ord, Calif.)
founded in March 1970 . . . short-lived

SPREAD EAGLE (Fort Campbell, Tenn.)
a short-lived effort of early 1970

UNDERWOOD (Fort Leonard Wood, Mo.)
published sporadically during 1970 and 1971 . . . successor to
Heresy II . . . mainly the work of civilian activists in St. Louis

UNITY NOW (Fort Ord, Calif.)
edited by soldiers of the Special Processing Detachment from the
second half of 1970 into early 1971

YAH-HOH (Fort Lewis, Wash.)
published briefly during the summer of 1970 by "Hew-Kacaw-
Na-Ya," an organization of American Indian servicemen and
-women

ABOUT FACE (New York City)
the newsletter of the United States Servicemen's Fund . . . active
from May 1971 to the fall of 1973

THE ALTERNATIVE (Fort Meade, Md.)
short-lived . . . early 1971

ARCTIC ARSENAL (Fort Greely, Alaska)
edited by Young Socialist Alliance member Ed Jurenas . . . active
from the spring of 1971 through the end of the year

BARRAGE (Fort Sill, Okla.)
founded in October 1971 . . . written by the "Ft. Sill Area United
Front" . . . active until mid-1972

BLACK VOICE (Fort McClellan, Ala.)
listed by the House Internal Security Committee as active in the
period December 1971 to March 1972

BRASS NEEDLE (Fort Lee, Va.)
appeared briefly in the second half of 1971

CHESSMAN II (Beaufort MCAS, S.C.)
published from mid-1971 to the summer of 1972

FORUM (Fort Sill, Okla.)
apparently only one issue, in August 1971

FRAGGING ACTION (Fort Dix, N.J.)
affiliated with the National Lawyers Guild counseling project . . .
active from the spring of 1971 to mid-1972

FORT POLK PUKE (Fort Polk, La.)
apparently also known for a time as *Different Drummer* . . . short-
lived . . . spring and summer of 1971

*GI NEWS AND DISCUSSION BULLETIN (New York City
and San Diego, Calif.)
political-analysis journal circulated among a select group of several
hundred GI organizers and counselors . . . started by USSF in
New York in January 1971 . . . since late 1973, published by the
GI Project Alliance . . . P.O. Box 8056, San Diego, Calif., 92102

LAST INCURSION (Fort Bragg, N.C.)
published by soldiers of Fayetteville VVAW . . . active briefly in the first half of 1971

LIBERATED CASTLE (Fort Belvoir, Va.)
published from the spring of 1971 until late 1971 . . . founded by a group calling itself the "Servicemen's Liberation Front"

THE OPPRESSED (Walter Reed Medical Center, Washington, D.C.)
active during the summer and fall of 1971

THE PAPER (Cherry Point MCAS, N.C.)
founded in August of 1971 . . . active until the fall of 1972

PEOPLE'S PRESS (Fort Campbell, Tenn.)
first appeared in early 1971 . . . affiliated with the "People's House". . . ceased operation in the fall of 1972

POW (Fort Ord, Calif.)
active from March 1971 until the summer of 1972

*RAGE (Camp Lejeune and New River MCAS, N.C.)
first appeared in the fall of 1971 . . . still published by the Jacksonville Defense Committee . . . P.O. Box 301, Jacksonville, N.C., 28542

ROSE GARDEN (Twentynine Palms Marine Base, Calif.)
apparently only one issue . . . spring 1971 . . . produced by activists at Riverside

SQUARE WHEEL (Fort Eustis, Va.)
active from the fall of 1971 through the first half of 1972

WHACK! (Fort McClellan, Ala.)
the only known women's paper . . . published by members of the Women's Army Corps School from the spring of 1971 to the end of that year

WHERE ARE WE? (Fort Huachuca, Ariz.)
founded in the spring of 1971 . . . later produced in co-operation with airmen of Davis-Monthan AFB . . . disappeared in mid-1972

CALL UP (Milwaukee, Wisc.)
published in the first half of 1972 by Milwaukee-area reservists

CUSTER'S LAST STAND (Fort Riley, Kans.)
founded in early 1972 . . . published irregularly until early 1973

FIRST CASUALTY (Fort Benning, Ga.)
active briefly in early 1972

*HIGHWAY 13 (Fort Meade, Md.)
founded by VVAW in the fall of 1972 . . . published continuously to the present . . . now written by soldiers at Fort Meade and aided by the American Friends Service Committee of Baltimore . . . 319 E. 25th St., Baltimore, Md. 21218

THE RAG (Chicago, Ill.)
the voice of the "Reservist and National Guard Organizing Committee" . . . active from late 1972 to the end of 1973 . . . in January 1974, merged with *Wildcat* (see below)

SOS NEWS (Los Angeles, Calif.)
a civilian-written fund-raising newsletter . . . the successor of previous West Coast SOS groups . . . active throughout 1972

WOODPECKER (Fort Leonard Wood, Mo.)
active briefly in mid-1972

*GI NEWS (Chicago, Ill.)
newsletter of the VVAW National GI Project . . . founded after the collapse of *Camp News* in the fall of 1973 . . . 827 W. Newport Avenue, Chicago, Ill. 60657

*WILDCAT (Chicago, Ill.)
founded in the summer of 1973 by more than a dozen activists in Baltimore and Chicago, including several former members of CAMP . . . an attempt to combine GI organizing and the new labor insurgency . . . seven thousand copies distributed monthly at five separate bases . . . P.O. Box 1381, Evanston, Ill. 60204

2. Overseas Papers, All Services

*RITA NOTES (Heidelberg, Germany)
the very first GI publications . . . mass-distribution pamphlets circulated in Germany as early as 1966 . . . *RITA Act* an outgrowth of these notes . . . over four hundred and fifty issues to the present . . . Marstallstrasse 11a, 69 Heidelberg, W. Germany

*ACT (Heidelberg, Germany)
one of the first GI papers . . . founded, in January 1968, by deserters with RITA, "Resisters Inside the Army" . . . sometimes known as *RITA Act* . . . Marstallstrasse 11a, 69 Heidelberg, W. Germany

SECOND FRONT (Paris, France)
an early effort of 1968 . . . editors later started *We've Got the brASS* during 1969

WHERE IT'S AT (Berlin, Germany)
founded in April 1968 with the aid of civilian activists in the German SDS . . . active until 1970

THE ASH (Kaiserslautern, Germany)
two issues published in late 1969 by soldiers of Daenner Kaserne

BAUMHOLDER GIG SHEET (Baumholder, Germany)
written by soldiers affiliated with the American Servicemen's Union . . . active during 1969 and part of 1970

GRAFFITTI (Heidelberg, Germany)
active during parts of 1969 and 1970 . . . edited for a time by Sp/4 Bruce Scott

HAIR (Misawa AFB, Japan)
founded, in July 1969, by blacks . . . suppressed after three issues . . . revived in 1970 with the aid of Beheiren . . . published in association with the "Owl" coffeehouse until late 1971

KILL FOR PEACE (Camp Drake, Japan)
active during 1969 and 1970

KOREA FREE PRESS (South Korea)
founded in the fall of 1969 near the Korean DMZ by men of the
2nd Infantry Division . . . only a few issues . . . later published
within the United States and mailed to Korea

SPEAK OUT (Hanau, Germany)
published briefly in the spring of 1969

SYDNEY FTA (Sydney, Australia)
one, perhaps two, issues distributed to GIs on furlough in Australia
. . . 1969 or 1970

VENCEREMOS (Frankfurt, Germany)
founded by soldiers of the 97th General Hospital . . . published
in 1969 and early in 1970

WE'VE GOT THE brASS (Frankfurt, Germany)
active during 1969 and 1970 . . . associated with the "First
Amendment" coffeehouse

WE'VE GOT THE brASS (Tokyo, Japan)
the Asian edition . . . patterned after its European counterpart
. . . published during 1969 and the first half of 1970 . . . name
then changed to *Fall In At Ease*

THE WITNESS (Schwäbisch Gmünd, Germany)
published in 1969 and part of 1970 by soldiers stationed in the 4th
Battalion/41st Artillery

ABOUT FACE (Heidelberg, Germany)
the voice of "Unsatisfied Black Soldiers" . . . associated with the
July 4, 1970, Call for Justice . . . active to the fall of 1972

CALL UP (Heidelberg, Germany)
first published in September 1970 by "Soldiers for Democratic Action," at Patton Barracks

CAN YOU BEAR McNAIR (Berlin, Germany)
published during 1970 and part of 1971 by troops of McNair Barracks

DEMAND FOR FREEDOM (Kadena AFB, Okinawa)
founded by black airmen in the fall of 1970 . . . ceased operation
in 1971

EXPOSURE (Stuttgart, Germany)
published by blacks during 1970

FALL IN AT EASE (Tokyo, Japan)
started in the second half of 1970 . . . aided by activists with the
Pacific Counseling Service . . . active throughout 1971 and part
of 1972

FREEDOM RINGS (Tokyo, Japan)
a little-known paper circulated in the Tokyo area in late 1970 and
part of 1971

FTA WITH PRIDE (Heidelberg, Germany)
founded after the demise of *Graffitti* in mid-1970 . . . aided by

American students at the University of Heidelberg . . . seven issues through the fall of 1971 . . . succeeded by *FighT bAck* (see below)

THE GIESSEN EAGLE (Giessen, Germany)
published briefly during 1970

THE NEXT STEP (Heidelberg, Germany)
aided by civilians . . . active from July 1970 through 1971 . . . contained news and political analysis of resistance in Europe

THE O. D. (Hawaii)
in existence briefly during 1970

P.E.A.C.E.—PEOPLE EMERGING AGAINST CORRUPT ES-TABLISHMENTS (England)
one of the most successful Air Force papers . . . founded in the summer of 1970 . . . fourteen issues through the fall of 1971

PROPERGANDER (Kaiserslautern, Germany)
published by soldiers of the 440th Signal Battalion . . . spring 1970 into 1971

RIGHT ON (Camp Drake, Japan)
published briefly during 1970

*SEMPER FI (Iwakuni, Japan)
founded in January 1970 . . . published continuously to the present . . . affiliated with the "Hobbit" coffeehouse . . . P.O. Box 49, Iwakuni-shi, Yamaguchi-ken, Japan

STARS N BARS (Iwakuni, Japan)
published briefly during 1970 by men in the Iwakuni brig

STUFFED PUFFIN (Keflavik, Iceland)
edited by naval officers of the Concerned Officers Movement in September 1970 . . . suppressed by local commanders after only one issue

UP AGAINST THE WALL (Berlin, Germany)
aided by civilians . . . successor to *Where It's At* . . . active from mid-1970 into 1971

VOICE OF THE LUMPEN (Frankfurt, Germany)
affiliated with the Black Panther Party . . . founded in December 1970 . . . active during 1971

THE WHIG (Clark AFB, the Philippines)
published from mid-1970 to the latter part of 1971 . . . the voice of "Airmen for a Democratic Air Force"

YAND (Itazuke AFB, Japan)
published, by "Young Americans for a New Direction," during 1970

YOKOSUKA DAVID (Yokosuka, Japan)
founded in early 1970 by sailors associated with the American Servicemen's Union . . . re-established in the fall of 1971 with the aid of PCS . . . active until the fall of 1972

THE ABOLITIONIST (Okinawa)
active briefly in the early part of 1971

BLACK TRIBUNAL FOR AWARENESS (Karlsruhe, Germany)
published briefly in the fall of 1971

DIG IT (Baumholder, Germany)
a short-lived successor to Baumholder *Gig Sheet* . . . 1971

FIRST AMENDMENT (Yokota AFB, Japan)
published from mid-1971 into 1972

*FORWARD (Berlin, Germany)
aided by civilians . . . founded in April 1971 . . . still active . . .
1, West Berlin 45, Postfach 163, Germany

LEFT FLANK (Camp Hansen, Okinawa)
published briefly in mid-1971

*LIBERATED BARRACKS (Hawaii)
founded in September 1971 . . . published with the aid of civilians
to the present . . . 525 Kalaheo, Kailua, Hawaii

*OMEGA PRESS (Koza, Okinawa)
founded in 1971 . . . later affiliated with the "People's House"
. . . distributed in Koza and Kin . . . P.O. Box 447, Koza, Okinawa, Japan

THE MAN CAN'T WIN IF YOU GRIN (Okinawa)
active briefly in early 1971

THE ROAD (Bad Kreuznach, Germany)
a short-lived effort of early 1971

WE ARE SOMEBODY TOO (Karlsruhe, Germany)
published by blacks during 1971

WHY (Okinawa)
a little-known paper active in late 1971

*THE BRIDGE (Butzbach, Germany)
published by "The American Group," mostly servicemen, held in
a German prison . . . founded in 1972 . . . fifteen issues through
early 1974 . . . P.O. Box 320, Butzbach, W. Germany

CRY OUT (Clark AFB, the Philippines)
successor to *The Whig* . . . published during 1972 until suppressed
by the Marcos government in October 1972

*FighT bAck (Heidelberg, Germany)
founded in the summer of 1972 . . . the largest GI paper in Europe
. . . eighteen issues through April 1974 . . . 69 Heidelberg, Marstallstrasse 11a, Germany

FTA WITH PRIDE (Wiesbaden, Germany)
founded at Camp Pieri in the summer of 1972 by Sgt. Terry Bott
. . . one of the most successful all-GI papers in Germany . . . active until late 1973

HANSEN FREE PRESS (Camp Hansen, Okinawa)
published during 1972 and part of 1973 . . . affiliated with the
"United Front" . . . supplanted by *Omega Press*

THE NEW TESTAMENT (Schweinfurt, Germany)
founded in the spring of 1972 . . . active into 1973

1776—RIGHT TO REVOLUTION (Japan)
a little-known paper published in early 1972

SEASICK (Subic Bay, the Philippines)
   short-lived, but one of the most important papers in the Navy . . .
   active from early 1972 until October of that year

SEIZE THE TIME (Heidelberg, Germany)
   brief successor to *About Face* . . . published by blacks in late 1972

THE WILEY WORD (Neu Ulm, Germany)
   published by soldiers of Wiley Barracks during 1972 and part of
   1973 . . . also called *The Word*

*FREEDOM OF THE PRESS (Yokosuka, Japan)
   written by sailors with the "New People's Center" . . . Yokosuka-
   shi, Kanagawa-ken, Japan

OFF THE BRIDGE (Yokosuka, Japan)
   monthly newsletter of the VVAW chapter at the "New People's
   Center" . . . active during 1973 . . . replaced by *Freedom of the
   Press*

STRIPES AND STARS (England)
   published from January 1973 to June 1973 by airmen at U.S. bases
   in England

THE TRUTH (Butzbach, Germany)
   published briefly during 1973 by the "Committee for GI Rights"

UNITED FRONT (Yokosuka, Japan)
   an anti-homeporting newsletter distributed to men of the U.S.S.
   Midway in mid-1973

WRITE ON (Bitburg AFB, Germany)
   affiliated with the "Council on Rights and Equality" . . . founded
   in September 1973 . . . now dormant

*ZERO (Paris, France)
   the work of GIs and resister/exiles . . . founded in 1973 . . . c/o
   Quaker Center, 114 rue Vaugirard, Paris, 6, France

*SEPARATED FROM LIFE (England)
   founded in January 1974 at Alconbury Air Base . . . evolved out
   of the haircut defiance case of Sgt. Dan Pruitt . . . 2 Turquand St.,
   London, SE 17, 1 LT, United Kingdom

3. *Air Force and Navy Papers in the United States*

THE UNDERGROUND OAK (Oakland Naval Hospital, Calif.)
   perhaps the first paper in the Navy . . . founded in November 1968
   . . . later known as *The Oak* . . . published through 1969

AEROSPACED (Grissom AFB, Ind.)
   published by a "GIs Against the War" chapter . . . active from
   late 1969 to the fall of 1970

BROKEN ARROW (Selfridge AFB, Mich.)
   founded in mid-1969 . . . very successful . . . twenty issues published until 1971

DUCK POWER (San Diego, Calif.)
the voice of San Diego MDM . . . one of the first Navy papers . . .
active during 1969 and part of 1970

EYES LEFT (Travis AFB, Calif.)
active briefly during 1969

FINAL FLIGHT (Hamilton AFB, Calif.)
in operation from the second half of 1969 into 1971

FORWARD MARCH (N. Severn, Md.)
active during the latter part of 1969 and early 1970

A FOUR YEAR BUMMER (Chanute AFB, Ill.)
affiliated with the "Red Herring" coffeehouse . . . successor to
Harass the Brass . . . active from late 1969 to the fall of 1970 . . .
ceased operation in early 1971

G.A.F. (Barksdale AFB, La.)
a little-known paper active from late 1969 into 1971

HARASS THE BRASS (Chanute AFB, Ill.)
one of the first Air Force papers . . . founded with the aid of
students at the University of Illinois, in May 1969

OM (Washington, D.C.)
a very famous early paper . . . edited by Roger Priest . . . active
from April 1969 to 1970

TRUTH INSTEAD (Treasure Island, Calif.)
short-lived . . . founded in November 1969

U.S.A.F. (Wright-Patterson AFB, Ohio)
edited by "United Servicemen's Action for Freedom" . . . active
only briefly in mid-1969

ALL HANDS ABANDON SHIP (Newport, R.I.)
affiliated with the "Potemkin" bookshop . . . founded with the aid
of draft resisters in mid-1970 . . . edited by members of the sailor
organization BuRevPers, "Bureau of Revolutionary Personnel,"
. . . ceased operation in the second half of 1972

CATHARSIS (Quonset Point NAS, R.I.)
appeared for a short time during mid-1970

COMmon SENSE (Washington, D.C.)
newsletter of the Concerned Officers Movement . . . distributed
to some three thousand junior officers throughout the services . . .
active from the spring of 1970 to early 1972

CRACKED (MacDill AFB, Fla.)
a popular paper published from late 1970 into 1971

DARE TO STRUGGLE (San Diego, Calif.)
successor to *Duck Power* . . . published by MDM from mid-1970
into 1971

GREAT LAKES TORPEDO (Great Lakes NTC, Ill.)
a weekly mimeographed newsletter published by MDM from January 1970 through April 1971

NAVY TIMES ARE CHANGIN (Great Lakes NTC, Ill.)
the main newspaper of Great Lakes MDM . . . one of the most

successful sailor newspapers . . . founded in February 1970 . . .
active until 1973

NOW HEAR THIS (Long Beach, Calif.)
published briefly in late 1970, temporarily replacing the MDM
paper *Out Now* (see below)

ON THE BEACH (Norfolk, Va.)
active from mid-1970 into 1971

OUT NOW (Long Beach, Calif.)
the voice of Long Beach MDM . . . published erratically from
the first half of 1970 into 1972

POTEMKIN (U.S.S. *Forrestal*)
published briefly in early 1970 aboard the *Forrestal* . . . edited by
American Servicemen's Union member Al Rita

SNORTON BIRD (Norton AFB, Calif.)
initially active during 1970 . . . revived in mid-1971 and published
into 1972

STAR SPANGLED BUMMER (Wright-Patterson AFB, Ohio)
founded during 1970 by "GIs United" . . . edited by Vietnam
veteran Sgt. Gary Staiger . . . revived after a dormant period in
the latter part of 1971 . . . active until 1973

*UP AGAINST THE BULKHEAD (San Francisco, Calif.)
originally founded by Alameda MDM in early 1970 . . . published
since as a multiservice newspaper . . . distributed at Bay Area airports and elsewhere to tens of thousands of servicemen . . . 98
Chenery Street, San Francisco, Calif. 94131

AIR FOWL (Vandenberg AFB, Calif.)
listed by the House Internal Security Committee as active in the
period December 1971 to March 1972

BERGSTROM BENNIES (Bergstrom AFB, Tex.)
listed by the House Internal Security Committee as active in the
period December 1971 to March 1972

THE BOLLING OTHER (Bolling AFB, Washington, D.C.)
published briefly in late 1971 and early 1972 by Sgt. Gordon Youngs

CO-AMBULATION (Fairchild AFB, Wash.)
listed by the House Internal Security Committee as active in the
period December 1971 to March 1972

COCKROACH (Minot AFB, N.D.)
active briefly in early 1971

DESTROYER (Philadelphia, Pa.)
affiliated with the "Liberty Hall" coffeehouse . . . active from the
spring of 1971 to the end of that year

F.I.D. (Kodiak Naval Station, Alaska)
published by junior officers and enlisted men with the "Concerned
Servicemen's Movement" . . . active from early 1971 to the spring
of 1972

FREE FIRE ZONE (Hanscom Field, Mass.)
published from early 1971 to early 1972

GETTING TOGETHER (Lowry AFB, Colo.)
published regularly from September 1971 until mid-1972

*HELPING HAND (Mountain Home AFB, Ida.)
founded in the spring of 1971 . . . affiliated with the "Covered
Wagon" coffeehouse . . . P.O. Box 729, Mountain Home, Ida.
83647

KITTY LITTER (U.S.S. *Kitty Hawk*)
circulated aboard the *Kitty Hawk* in late 1971 and early 1972 . . .
printed with the aid of the Center for Servicemen's Rights and
Concerned Military in San Diego

THE KNOT (Minot AFB, N.D.)
published by airmen and officers from the fall of 1971 into 1972
. . . name later changed to *My Knot*

LIBERTY CALL (Portsmouth, N.H.)
founded in the spring of 1971 . . . shortly afterward merged into
Off the Brass at nearby Pease AFB (see below)

LIBERTY CALL (San Diego, Calif.)
the voice of "Concerned Military" . . . founded in the spring of
1971

LUKEWARM (Luke AFB, Ariz.)
published by servicemen associated with the Concerned Officers
Movement during 1971

MAC DILL FREEK PRESS (MacDill AFB, Fla.)
published during 1971 and the first part of 1972 . . . successor to
Cracked

99th BUMMER (Westover AFB, Mass.)
affiliated with the "Off the Runway" coffeehouse . . . founded in
July 1971 . . . ceased operation in mid-1972

OFF THE BRASS (Pease AFB, N.H.)
the voice of "Servicepeople for Peace and Justice" . . . active from
early 1971 to mid-1972

OLIVE BRANCH (Jacksonville, Fla.)
active during 1971 and part of 1972

SACSTRATED (Fairchild AFB, Wash.)
active during the early part of 1971

SCAPED SENTINAL (Beale AFB, Calif.)
active during early and mid-1971

SOUND OFF (Bremerton, Wash.)
the voice of "Bremerton Area Concerned Military" . . . distributed
at the Puget Sound Naval Complex from early 1971 into 1972

*SPECIAL WEAPONS (Kirtland AFB, N.M.)
founded in the latter part of 1971 and published until mid-1972
. . . revived in early 1973 . . . aided by the Albuquerque War
Resisters League . . . P.O. Box 25363, Albuquerque, N.M. 87425

TAILFEATHER (Lackland AFB, Tex.)
published from the fall of 1971 into 1972

TRAVISTY (Travis AFB, Calif.)
founded in the summer of 1971 . . . active until the second half
of 1973

*UP FROM THE BOTTOM (San Diego, Calif.)
   founded in September of 1971 . . . a joint effort of Concerned
   Military and the Center for Servicemen's Rights . . . 820 Fifth
   Avenue, San Diego, Calif. 92101

WE ARE EVERYWHERE (U.S.S. *Coral Sea*)
   distributed aboard the *Coral Sea* by SOS activists from the fall of
   1971 to early 1972

WRITE ON (Norton AFB, Calif.)
   published briefly in the summer of 1971

THE BACON (March AFB, Calif.)
   active from mid-1972 until the spring of 1973

THE COALITION (Mather AFB, Calif.)
   short-lived . . . early 1972

FAT ALBERT'S DEATH SHIP TIMES (Charleston, S.C.)
   founded in the summer of 1972 . . . published by the Charleston
   Defense Committee under the title *Death Ship Times*

*GRAPES OF WRATH (Norfolk, Va.)
   published by the Norfolk Defense Committee . . . founded in
   November 1972 . . . still active, with a circulation of nine thousand
   . . . distributed at Charleston as well as Norfolk . . . P.O. Box
   1492, Norfolk, Va. 23501

HOLLOW MAN (Holloman AFB, N.M.)
   in existence briefly in early 1972

HUNLEY HEMORRHOID (U.S.S. *Hunley*)
   circulated aboard the *Hunley* during the first half of 1972

LONGBITCH (U.S.S. *Long Beach*)
   distributed on the *Long Beach* in early 1972

OFFUL TIMES (Offutt AFB, Neb.)
   affiliated with the Omaha Military Project . . . active from April
   of 1972 until early 1973

THE OTHER HALF (Glenview NAS, Ill.)
   founded by sailors and Marines in the first half of 1972 . . . active
   to the latter part of 1973

THE OTHER VOICE (Richards-Gebaur AFB, Mo.)
   active briefly in mid-1972

RECONNAISSANCE (Forbes AFB, Kans.)
   short-lived . . . mid-1972

SKY DOVE (Lockbourne AFB, O.)
   founded in April 1972 . . . active for less than a year

SOS ENTERPRISES LEDGER (U.S.S. *Enterprise*)
   distributed aboard the *Enterprise* in the summer of 1972

SOS NEWSLETTER (San Francisco, Calif.)
   published by a civilian SOS group from early 1972 into 1973 . . .
   contained valuable, often firsthand accounts of resistance in the
   Seventh Fleet

STRAIGHT SHEET (Duluth AFB, Minn.)
   published by "Concerned Military" in the first half of 1972

THIS IS LIFE? (U.S.S. *Gridley*)
distributed aboard the *Gridley* while at San Diego in the summer of 1972

TOGETHER (MacDill AFB, Fla.)
short-lived . . . early 1972

UNDERTOW (Boston, Mass.)
published briefly by sailors in the Boston area . . . founded in August 1972

BLOWS AGAINST THE EMPIRE (Kirtland AFB, N.M.)
written by airmen at the Kirtland military hospital . . . spring 1973

BLUE SCREW (Lowry AFB, Colo.)
founded in May of 1973 . . . active until the spring of 1974 . . . replaced by *UCMJ*

*FIGHT BACK (Long Beach, Calif.)
published by sailors and civilian activists at the "Drydock" organizing center . . . successor to *Payback* . . . 701 W. Broadway, Long Beach, Calif. 90812

*FREE DULUTH (U.S.S. *Duluth*)
written by sailors of the *Duluth* . . . founded during the first half of 1973 . . . aided by the Center for Servicemen's Rights . . . 820 Fifth Avenue, San Diego, Calif. 92101

I WILL FEAR NO EVIL (Kirtland AFB, N.M.)
an offshoot of Special Weapons . . . written by GIs at the Kirtland hospital in the first half of 1973

MOTHBALL BLUES (Philadelphia, Pa.)
one issue only . . . written by sailors of the Philadelphia Naval Shipyard in November 1973

*GI VOICE
founded by the GI Alliance in 1974 to replace the *Lewis-McChord Free Press* . . . Box 411, Tillicum, Wash. 98492

PIG BOAT BLUES (U.S.S. *Chicago*)
founded in early 1974 . . . written by crew members of the *Chicago* . . . aided by the Center for Servicemen's Rights in San Diego . . . four or five issues through mid-1974

*SCAGGIE AGGIE REVIEW
written by sailors aboard the U.S.S. *Agerholm* . . . several issues through mid-1974 . . . supported by the Center for Servicemen's Rights . . . 820 Fifth Avenue, San Diego, Calif. 92101

*UCMJ
founded in June 1974 by "United Colorado Military for Justice" to replace *Blue Screw* . . . distributed at Lowry AFB and Fort Carson . . . c/o VVAW, P.O. Box 18591, Denver, Colo. 80218

INDEX

About Face, 94
Aboveground, 62
Abrams, General Creighton, 10
Act, 55, 93
Action for Boston Community Development, 188–89
Active-duty enlistments (1971–72), 7–8
Addlestone, David, 34, 39, 44, 144
Ad Hoc Committee on Equal Treatment and Opportunity, 74
Ad Hoc Military Buildup Committee, 90–91
Administrative-discharge system, 232–33
Aerospaced, 127
Afro haircuts, 174
Air Force: air war resistance, 126–37; AWOL rate, 12; "bare base" concept, 161; black demonstrations, 129–31; black servicemen (all-volunteer), 201; conscientious objection (in-service applications), 16; desertion rate, 13; drug abuse, 20; enlistments (1973), 184; first mass political organizing, 127; future active force of, 162; human-relations program, 130; manpower crisis, 7; number of black officers, 205; punitive discharges, 18; Vietnam bombings and, 131–37
Air Force Times, 129
Air-war resistance, 106–37; Air

Force, 126–37; naval, 107–26
Alameda Naval Station, 112
All Hands Abandon Ship, 110–11
Allison, Jeffrey, 124, 143
All Ready on the Left, 64
All-volunteer force, 172–243; advertising operation, 189–90; apprehensions about, 182–85; black servicemen and, 201–19; changes accompanying, 172–76; cost of, 176–80; enlistments, 177; failure of, 185–86; human-relations councils, 174; job-training appeals, 194–97; military democracy and, 220–27; proposals for reform, 197–200; proposed trial introduction, 199; reason for, 180–82; reasons for enlistment, 191–94; recruitment efforts, 187–200
Ally, The, 57, 58
Alsop, Stewart, 48–49
Altman, S. H., 192
America (ship), 115–16
American Articles of War of 1775, xiv
American Civil Liberties Union, 78, 230, 240
American Friends Service Committee (AFSC), 237
American Indian servicemen, 77
American Servicemen's Union (ASU), 55–56, 61, 62, 66, 71, 76, 93, 104, 105, 129
American Soldier, The, 224–25
Amick, Don, 233

Desertion, 10–15, 50, 93, 107, 133, 152, 182; motivations for, 14–15; Senate hearings on (1968), 14

Destroyer, 110

Dewey (ship), 107

Dixon, 100

DMZ (coffeehouse), 80, 81–82

Draft, the: classification appeals, 5; opposition to, 4–6, 7

Drug use, 19–23, 72, 97, 98; amnesty program, 174–75; HumRRO survey on, 29–32; by service location (Army, 1971), 29–30; in West Germany, 99, 144

Duck Power, 107

Duluth (ship), 140

Duncan, Admiral Charles K., 125

Duncan, Sergeant Don, 78

"Early out" program, 101

Eighth Army headquarters (Seoul), black resistance at, 103

Electronic sensing devices, use of, 160–61

El Paso anti-war protests, 52, 63–64

El Paso GIs for Peace Demonstration (1970), 65–66

Emerson, Major General Henry, 213

EM-16 (newspaper), 65

Enlisted Man's Magna Carta, 151

Enlisted Men's Rights and Grievances Committee, 140

Enterprise (carrier), 115

Enterprise Ledger (newspaper), 115

Equal Opportunity programs, 217

Evans, Captain Dwight, 135

Evans, Sergeant Wayne, 134

Fairchild AFB, 133

Fatigue Press, 55, 56, 57, 83, 90

Fayetteville *Observer*, 83

Fechter, A. E., 192

Fed Up, 76

Federal Trade Commission, 188

Fellowship for Reconciliation in New York, 237

Field, James, 123

FighT bAck, 102, 143, 238

Filipinos, naval use of, 119

First Amendment, 59, 86, 94, 153, 235

First Amendment (newspaper), 128

First of the Worst, 77

Fischer, William, 47

Fitt, Manpower Assistant Secretary, 14

Flexible response, strategy of, 159

Flower, Tom, 234

Flower of the Dragon (Boyle), 38

Flugger, Captain Michael, 137

Fonda, Jane, 66, 67, 78, 87, 111

Food service, 140

Forbes AFB, 133

Foreign Affairs (journal), 3

Forrestal (ship), 123–24, 125, 143

Fort Belvoir, 72–73, 81

Fort Benning, 24, 56, 67, 173

Fort Bliss, 26, 52, 65, 67, 69, 77, 82, 83, 89, 152, 222

Fort Bliss GIs for Peace, 63

Fort Bragg, 55, 59, 60, 67, 82, 83, 85, 86, 139, 147, 152, 162, 222; black uprising at (World War II), 149; enlisted men's club brawl, 73; Moratorium demonstration (1968), 62; stockade uprising (1968), 70–71

Fort Buckner, 105

Fort Campbell, 79, 86, 162

Fort Carson, 24, 62, 64, 66, 67, 175–76; stockade uprising (1969), 71

Fort Devens, 27, 67

Fort Dix, 38, 65, 66, 71, 234; black uprising at (World War II), 149; SPD incident